GYMNASTICS GUIDE

GYMNASTICS GUIDE

edited by Hal Straus

World Publications
Mountain View, California

Library of Congress Cataloging in Publication Data

Gymnastics guide.

    Includes index.
    1. Gymnastics—Addresses, essays, lectures.
2. Gymnasts—Biography—Addresses, essays, lectures.
I. Straus, Hal.
GV461.G9   796.4'1'0922 [B]   78-55790
ISBN 0-89037-139-3

Acknowledgments

To Glenn Sundby, Lyn Moran, Tom Sauters, and the rest of the *International Gymnast* staff, deep gratitude for their advice and contributions. Thanks also to Dr. Frank Bare and the U.S. Gymnastics Federation for their support of this project; to Dr. Harold Frey for his expert advice and suggestions; and to Sylvia Kingsbook for her hard work.

The following articles were reprinted by special permission of *International Gymnast* magazine and the authors: "Motivation, Dedication, and Determination," by Linda Metheny, April 1977; "Interview: Peter Kormann," by Dick Criley, October 1977; "Olga!" by Lyn Moran, April 1978; "Olympic and International Problems That Need to Be Met before 1980," by Gene Wettstone, January 1977.

"Specificity of Stress and Training," by James R. Brown, reprinted by permission of *Olympische Turnkunst* magazine; "Dance and Gymnastics: Notes from an Official," by Noreen Connell, reprinted by permission of *Dance* magazine; "Gymnastics Fever," by Anita Verscoth, reprinted with special permission of *Horizon* magazine and the author.

Contents

Foreword

Gymnastics has been with us for hundreds of years, but only recently has it gained the attention of the American public and found a welcome reception. As this book mentions frequently, it was only a few years ago that the sport attracted few participants and many times even fewer spectators. Fortunately for our gymnasts of today that situation has changed dramatically.

The *Gymnastics Guide* is virtually all-encompassing in its approach to the sport. A bit of history, and a number of comments from many who have either watched it change or made it change over the years. Techniques are described, and some inside looks into some of the world's greatest gymnasts are provided.

The sport has become a form of sport-art during the past several years. Performances with special lighting and music, and without the use of judges and scoring have presented a unique side of this beautiful sport. Some of the largest crowds have come to see these performances with no concern about "winning." Few sports can make such a claim.

Internationally, the sport has grown, especially in the USA, Great Britain, Canada, Australia, and New Zealand. Perenially strong nations with large numbers of participants remain powers to be reckoned with on the floor of competition. A 1978 International Gymnastics Federation (F.I.G.) survey of its 620 member nations showed some 15,000,000 gymnasts worldwide. The largest gymnastics nation in the world is the Soviet Union and the USSR's enviable record in world and Olympic competitions speaks well for the quality of their training program.

In reading this very complete guide I am impressed with the names of contributors. So many of them have been great gymnasts, highly regarded writers, and gymnastics coaches for a number of years. I compliment the editor and contributors for their efforts and feel the *Gymnastics Guide* will be a worthwhile addition to any sports or gymnastics library.

Frank L. Bare
Executive Director U.S.G.F.
Vice-President, F.I.G.

Introduction

first became fascinated with gymnastics in 1972 when I fell madly in love with a Russian named Ludmilla Tourischeva. She was only a girl of twenty then, but on television she was a vision of womanly grace. She whirled, she leapt; her dance across the floor vibrated with strength and sexuality—yet she did it all with a serenity and poise I had rarely seen in a dancer. It was not until her routine was half-completed that I realized it was not a dance exhibition at all, but coverage of the 1972 Olympic Games.

For me, then, appreciation began with the artistic side of gymnastics. When I realized that the art was also a sport, that I would be able to enjoy the drama of competition along with the beauty of ballet and modern dance—I was hooked forever.

In compiling this book, I have tried to remain loyal to this unique dual nature of gymnastics. On the "art of the sport" you will be enthralled by Dan Millman's lyrical "Gymnastics and the Art of Living." The chapters on dance training and rhythmic gymnastics further emphasize the important role of ballet and modern dance education. Part III includes extensive physical conditioning programs, including: flexibility exercises, weight training exercises, and yoga and diet programs for the gymnast.

In gymnastics performances, the influence of the mind may be as important as the functioning of the body—particularly for the dangerous and concentration-demanding maneuvers. Dr. Massimo's essays on conquering fear of the apparatus merit special attention here.

No "guide" to gymnastics would be deserving of the title without material on safety. So, there are chapters on apparatus safety, personal protective equipment, first aid, and injury care and prevention, presented primarily for the coach and trainer. And while the coach is glancing at these instructional aids, he or she will also enjoy the perceptive tips on coaching by such people as Linda Metheny and Don Tonry.

Like other arts and sports, gymnastics lives and dies by its champions—and the world of gymnastics truly has international champions. There are sketches of the great Russians (Andrianov, Tourischeva, Korbut); the Romanian whiz-kid, Nadia Comaneci; and from the United States, a star of the past, Cathy Rigby, and one of the future, Kurt Thomas.

Just as a good tour guide will give the traveler a taste of what it's like to live in a different land, a gymnastics guide should give a taste of the life of a gymnast. The 1976 Olympian Leslie Wolfsberger has written beautifully on this subject. Her article on the physical, emotional, and economic demands of women's gymnastics in America should be read by all aspiring gymnasts.

Even if you are not an active gymnast, but only a fan like myself, don't feel left out. Dick Criley writes on how to be an "active spectator," which means understanding the complexities of the separate events in a gymnastics competition. International judges William Roetzheim and Jackie Fie simplify the judging and scoring rules to a point where even the judges themselves will understand them.

Gymnastics is not a fantasy Never-Neverland of grace and enchantment. Like any other sport, it has its problems. The major problems explored by several authors in this book emerge in the areas of safety and insurance, economics, popular acceptance, and that old bugaboo, subjective judging. The problems will hopefully be solved in time. As the contributors to "The Future" (Part X) suggest, gymnastics will become the popular cultural link between art and athletics, the first true "artisport."

The list of contributors in the *Gymnastics Guide* reads like a "Who's Who" (which is understandable being that I contacted many of them through the USGF's *Who's Who in Gymnastics 1977*). Eight contributors have participated in the Olympic Games as either gymnast, coach, or judge; many more have experience at the national and international level. The idea was to compile a book international in scope (there are contributions from West German, Hungarian, Canadian, and Japanese writers, as well as Americans from Massachusetts, Oregon, Illinois, and California), and a book that would have wide appeal—to men and women, novice and advanced gymnasts, coaches, trainers, judges, and fans. This was probably an impossible task. If the book succeeds even partially, it is because of the generous time, support, and enthusiasm of the gymnastics community; so it is to them this book is dedicated.

Hal Straus

Part 1 will take you on a trip back through time, from the present to other eras when gymnastics was something different than it is now. Gymnastics Fever *examines the present proliferation of gymnastics programs in American schools and clubs. The Olympic history of men's and women's gymnastics is spotlighted in the next two chapters, and the sport is traced all the way back to its ancient beginnings in the next.*

Modern rhythmic gymnastics, a branch of the sport relatively new in the United States, is also explored in this part, and finally an artful connection is forged between creating gymnastics art and creating an artful life.

1

GYMNASTICS PANORAMA

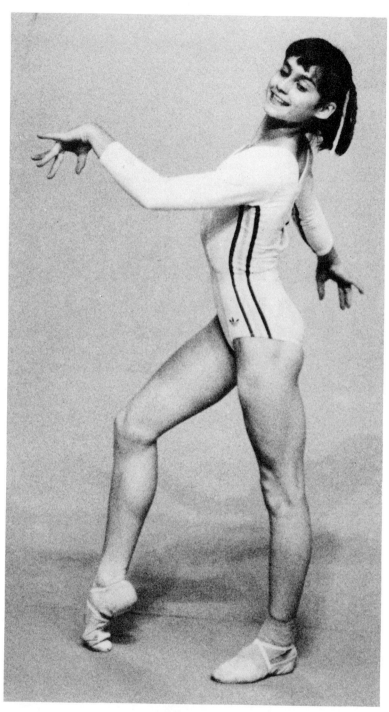

Nadia Comaneci (*International Gymnast* photo)

1

Gymnastics Fever

Anita Verschoth

My dream and greatest hope is to be a gymnast. I watched Nadia, Olga, and many, many others, but Nadia is the one I always think of. I find myself to be very much like Nadia. Nadia was recognized and maybe I will be too. All I have to do is work at it . . . I am longing desperately for a vault, a balance beam, uneven parallel bars, a coach, and competition. I signed up at the YWCA, but they said there were too many kids and I'm on a waiting list. I got very depressed. Could you send me a manual or something?

—Anne Cataffo
New York

Anne Cataffo's letter is just one of many such pleas received lately by the United States Gymnastics Federation in Tucson, Arizona, by former Olympic gymnasts Cathy Rigby Mason and Kim Chace, and by gymnastic coaches, sportswriters, and television commentators. American girls even write for advice to Olga Korbut in Russia and Nadia Comaneci in Romania.

They say they want to be daring and dazzling like Olga, flawless and fearless like Nadia. And they are willing to work hard. The gymnastics fever has gripped the country, infecting not only youngsters but a number of adults, too. For every new performer there are dozens of converted spectators. Gymnastics has become a spectacular and highly popular show.

At the Montreal Olympics last summer Nadia Comaneci's room looked like a flower shop. "You have put joy into our lives," read one card sent by a couple from Chicago. It is the sort of accolade that is usually reserved for an opera star or a prima ballerina.

Unsmiling, her pale porcelain face somber with concentration, fourteen-year-old Nadia, five feet tall and with a wispy eighty-six-pound body, performed flawlessly and collected seven perfect scores of 10. No gymnast had ever before earned a single 10 in Olympic competition. And she won three gold medals, a silver, and a bronze.

No matter that Nikolai Andrianov of Russia topped the world in the men's competition, that he won one more gold medal and one more silver than Comaneci, and that his performance was considered by experts to be the most athletic one at the games. There were no flowers for Andrianov. "Women are always more interesting to watch than men," he explained modestly. Comaneci was the one the 86,000 people came to see, some of them paying two hundred dollars for a sixteen-dollar ticket. And millions more watched on television screens around the world.

Frank Bare, executive director of the U.S. Gymnastics Federation, does not understand how "little girls like Rigby, Korbut, and now Comaneci could cause this phenomenal boom in gymnastics, in *women's* gymnastics, in recent years. Maybe the explanation is that girls can see themselves engaging in an athletic activity that is both feminine and glamorous." But plenty of grown men and women, too, thrill to Comaneci doing her three back handsprings on the narrow balance beam. Abie' Grossfeld, the men's gymnastics coach at Southern Connecticut State College in New Haven (his student Peter Kormann won the first Olympic medal, a bronze, for the United States in forty-four years at Montreal), thinks that Nadia's appeal might be related to the old pastime of girl-watching: "Most announcers are men. They play up body looks and beauty a lot. The men do more spectacular stunts, but the women are prettier to watch."

Another coach, Bud Marquette, of the Long Beach (California) Turners, who developed Rigby in the sixties and early seventies, sees a change in the audience for gymnastics. "The public is better educated now. People realize that the girls are superb athletes, too. They see that gymnastics is as appealing and demanding as figure skating."

So girls who once would have trained at an ice rink and others who would have taken ballet lessons are now enrolling in gymnastics classes. Older women, too, have begun to work out in gyms to improve their bodies. Rhythmic gymnastics, a more balletic form of the sport that does not require apparatus, is even catching on in this country. Clubs have sprung up everywhere in recent years, and their members are mostly female and mostly young. As for the boys, some of them still think that gymnastics is a sport for sissies—an old and absurd stigma.

When blond and diminutive Cathy Rigby made the 1968 Olympic team at the age of fifteen, the first flush of gymnastics fever became apparent. Her teammate, twenty-one-year-old Linda Metheny, was just as accomplished an athlete, but it was Cathy whom sportswriters singled out as "Pixie," "Kewpie doll," and "Barbie doll." Then, at the 1970 World Championships in Yugoslavia she won a silver medal on the balance beam—a first for an American girl. She cried when the medal was hung around her neck.

Two years later, at the Munich Olympics, Korbut, the birdlike Russian sprite, wept bitterly when she fell off the uneven bars, and her audience cried with her. She also performed the first back flip on the beam and started the trend toward more athletic and acrobatic routines for girls. The drama Korbut acted out, deep despair in failure and boundless happiness when she triumphed the following day (she won three golds and a silver), started her romance with the public, which lasted four years. Then Comaneci took center stage, and if she is not loved quite as dearly as Korbut, she is revered for her perfection.

Gymnastics first came to the United States in the late nineteenth century, when immigrants from Germany and Czechoslovakia formed their Turner and Sokol clubs. (A German,

Friedrich Ludwig Jahn, called the Old Man of gymnastics, had founded the first gymnastics club in Berlin in 1811.) But for decades the sport was thought to be something that people with heavy European accents did in the spirit of togetherness. Until 1962 it was only one of many sports governed by the Amateur Athletic Union, but the AAU did little for it. Gymnastics meets were badly organized; they often dragged on from 2:00 P.M. until 2:00 A.M., and two thousand spectators were considered a huge crowd. In 1960 there were about five thousand gymnasts in the whole country, a third of them girls, and only a few among them were active competitors. For the boys, the sport was part of the regular program in certain schools and colleges, but the girls had no other place to go but the few old Turner clubs.

Back in 1956, when Muriel Davis Grossfeld, now a successful coach in Milford, Connecticut (she is divorced from Abie Grossfeld), made the Olympic team at the age of fifteen, there were no more than two dozen serious women competitors to choose from. "We were just a handful," says Grossfeld, "but an amazing handful. We had no coaches, and we worked out on equipment that can best be described as bizarre." By contrast, last year American girls had to pass through a seeding system of competitions on local, regional, and national levels before they could reach the Olympic trials, where twenty-six were chosen to compete for the team of seven that went to Montreal.

Frank Bare, an NCAA champion in the fifties, recalls those early days: "A typical championship meet would have forty-two men and eleven women, and we had a hard time putting together an Olympic team, which calls for six men and six women and two alternates. We took seven men to Tokyo in 1964, and though the seventh man was injured and couldn't work, we still needed him as an alternate, because he was literally all we had."

In 1962 the top gymnastics coaches got together and decided to separate from the AAU and form the USGF. (A member of the International Gymnastics Federation sets the rules for international competitions.) Men's gymnastics was a part of the first Olympics of 1896—with individual competitions in the vault, the pommel horse, the horizontal bar, the parallel bar, and the rings (floor exercise for men was added in 1956). But women were included for the first time in 1928, and then only in team exhibitions. In 1952 they were finally allowed to compete in four events—the vault, the balance beam, the uneven parallel bars, and floor exercise.

The USGF enlivened the sport considerably. Many former competitors turned to coaching and opened private clubs. In Long Beach, Marquette started the Southern California Acro Team (SCATS) and was one of the first coaches to accept girls, Rigby among them, for exhibitions in Europe. Now there were rewards for the hard work of training—travel, meeting people, and the large and enthusiastic European audiences.

By 1970 there were about fifty thousand gymnasts in the United States, 75 percent of them boys. Since then the USGF has had trouble keeping track of the numbers. "We figure there are now over half a million *competing* gymnasts in the country," says Bare, "and about eighty percent of them are women."

A big club in the United States has four hundred students, most of them beginners, intermediates, or plain lovers of the sport. Only a dozen members are likely to get as far as one of the eight regional meets. From there, those who post an average score of 9.0 compete in an elite qualifying meet, and the top fifteen there go on to the national championship.

Elite students work out at their clubs six hours a day, six days a week, and usually pay a fee of $100 to $150 a month. In Connecticut, Muriel Grossfeld employs a staff of eight for her four hundred students (forty-five of them boys). She has recently opened a new $86,000 gym, and a second building is under construction.

According to Ed Knepper, the director of the U.S. Independent Club Association in Wilmington, Delaware, the number of clubs has risen to three thousand, many of them with three hundred to four hundred students and a half-dozen coaches. Spectator figures have increased, too: crowds of fourteen thousand to eighteen thousand have become quite common for such drawing cards as the visiting teams from Russia or Romania, especially when Korbut or Comaneci is along. Even the very first Russian tour of the United States in 1973, with Korbut and company (underwritten by Faberge, the cosmetics company), drew huge crowds in eight cities and eventually earned its own way at the box office.

"Before Munich," says Marlene Bene, Bare's assistant, "you could not sell a gymnastics event to a big arena. Competitions were held at university gyms. Now we can get any big arena in the country. Madison Square Garden is always sold out. An exhibition by the Russians in Cleveland in 1975 attracted 20,202 people, our biggest crowd ever."

Television stations are clamoring not only for such exhibitions and competitions, but also for prime-time specials like the CBS documentary "Nadia—From Romania with Love." Indeed, the money earned from television is filling the coffers of the USGF. According to Rick Appleman, who handles promotion for the USGF, "Our 1976/77 contract with ABC provides us with ten times the revenue we received from TV in 1973." The federation's total budget has gone from $37,000 in 1963 to $560,000 in 1976.

Still, in international competitions U.S. gymnasts have been badly lagging behind the Eastern Europeans. At the Munich Olympics, Rigby finished tenth overall, and in Montreal Kim Chace was the top American girl, in fourteenth place. "We need to start girls at an earlier age on the difficult tricks," says Chace, who is now twenty-two and coaches at her father's school in Revere Beach, Florida. "I learned to do one twist. Now they are doing double twists in floor exercise. It takes years to build up enough strength and muscles so that you don't get hurt when you try these things."

Although American girls are going into gymnastics at an earlier age—Muriel Grossfeld takes them at three and a half— many clubs are so concerned about the possibility of lawsuit if a student is injured that they are cautious about what they teach. "Instructors are leery of teaching difficult tricks," says Ed Knepper. "One gymnast gets hurt and the coach can have his entire livelihood wiped out. In Russia they don't sue."

"It's a problem," says Muriel Grossfeld, "but I have never been able to find a direct relationship between the level of gymnastics and the degree of injury. I have four girls doing back somersaults, but they don't get injured. It's the kids who come once a week we have to watch out for especially."

Will a little American girl now ten years old be the Nadia of 1980 in Moscow? Not likely, as long as such countries as East Germany, Romania, and Russia, which have always been strong in gymnastics, enjoy the advantage of well-organized, efficient, and long-range government-subsidized programs. Comaneci was picked out by her coach, Bela Karolyi, from a kindergarten class when she was six. (In the past American girls did not even start gymnastics until they were thirteen.) She worked out at his government-sponsored school for seven years. Then, at the 1975 European championships in Norway, in her first senior competition, she was the surprise winner. Karolyi, who has been combing kindergartens since 1962, believes that a girl's career lasts from the age of eight until twenty. "During those years there is no fear," he says. "No problems. Women gymnasts have done so many more difficult feats in recent years because they are younger now."

Knepper thinks there is one more big difference between our girls and the East Europeans. He insists that their chances of succeeding are enhanced by a greater desire to find a way out of a drab life. "Sports is all they have," he says. "Our country offers too many distractions." However, Rod Hill, who runs the Denver School of Gymnastics, points out that "some of our coaches push their kids too hard. If you do that, a kid will say, 'The heck with it,' and drop out."

Muriel Grossfeld thinks we have adequate facilities, "but we need better direction," she says. Sometimes described as a tough coach determined to produce Olympians, Grossfeld says that she hates "this violent push that everybody has to become an Olympian. I just want to turn out the best gymnasts I can." But if one of her students shows up overweight, Grossfeld is liable to ban her from the gym "until that situation has been corrected."

Former Olympian Linda Metheny, who runs a gymnastics academy at Eugene, Oregon, with her husband, Dick Mulvihill, says, "We have a few girls who are as dedicated as a Comaneci. We have enough clubs and a lot of coaches, but we need more knowledgeable coaches. We lack in the area of research—the mechanical analysis of all the movements—and in the psychological aspects of the sport. The Romanians do training in areas of mental discipline and concentration. We coaches have got to get together. We have to start a national program to find out where the new talent is."

Thanks to the USGF's lucrative television deals, such a

program is now getting under way. Last January, Bare asked coaches around the country to send their top juniors, girls aged ten to fourteen, to a special testing session at Springfield, Missouri, specifying certain requirements pertaining to body type, athletic style, commitment, and courage. Thirty-three girls showed up, and they were put through a series of difficult compulsory moves—"the kind of moves," said Dick Mulvihill, "that we felt would be required in 1980." The girls were also tested on their optional routines and were given a dance test, in which they could demonstrate flexibility, strength, balance, their ability to jump, and their creativity in harmony with the music. Finally, they were examined to see whether they were overweight or had a tendency to become overweight.

The ten best performers at Springfield now make up a new Junior National Team Program, which will hold at least four training sessions a year, all expenses, including air fare, to be paid by the USGF. . . The athletes will be introduced to the caliber of competition required at the Olympic level, and then they will be expected to work on the new skills back at home. Famous coaches, such as Bela Karolyi, will be invited to these sessions to help train the team. The USGF is planning a similar program for boys.

"At least," says Bare, "we are no longer assembling the team at the airport before we go to an important international competition. We've got a year and a half to get these youngsters ready." Vannie Edwards, a Belcher, Louisiana, coach who was appointed the program's national director, thinks that the choice made at Springfield was a good one: "These kids are exceptional; they need special treatment. If we want to hang in there with the rest of the world, we've got to motivate that exceptional child."

One of the exceptional ten is fourteen-year-old Leslie Pyfer, whose most difficult trick at Springfield was a back flip on the beam with her legs held straight (which is quite a bit harder to do than the original Korbut flip). "I think this program is really neat," she said, flushed with enthusiasm. "I'll train real hard so I can make the team for the 1980 Olympics, and then I'll try to get a medal."

"Will you try to become as good as Nadia Comaneci?" she was asked.

"Better," she said, without batting an eyelash.

2

Highlights of Fifty Years of Men's Olympic Gymnastics

Dr. Josef Goehler

1896-1930

The first Olympic Games in Athens in 1896 drew gymnasts from only five countries. The German team was most successful—though it competed against the orders of the official German gymnastic organization. Individual competitions were held for three events—in horizontal bar, rings, and vaulting—and in some of the team competitions the German team was unopposed.

The gymnastics competition in the second Olympics need hardly be studied at all. The games were held in Paris, and the French gymnasts were virtually unopposed. They took the first six places in individual competition. In one all-around competition it was the same story even though 136 gymnasts from six countries had entered.

The 1904 Olympics in St. Louis had much greater significance. While Austrian and Swiss teams controlled the games overall, the American team, composed mainly of a German-immigrant gymnastics club from Philadelphia, took first place in gymnastics. (This was not at all surprising, since only American club teams participated in the competition.)

Meanwhile, an international gymnastics association, whose

11

members at first included only Western European countries, made efforts to launch an International Tournament. The meet finally took place in Antwerp, Belgium, during the Belgian gymnastics festival. It was here that international gymnastics really started. Only teams were evaluated, and France was victorious over Belgium, Luxembourg, and the Netherlands. Calisthenics, which bears little resemblance to modern-day floor exercises, were part of the program, but the focal point was the apparatus events: "longhorse" (vaulting), horizontal bar, parallel bars, and pommelhorse.

The second international competition in 1905 in Bordeaux, France, saw little progress in the area of drawing gymnasts from a wider range of countries. Western Europe was once again alone; the Eastern European strongholds were missing as was the United States.

For the tenth birthday of the Olympic Games, Alberto Braglia, possibly the greatest pre-World War I gymnast, distinguished himself. Not only did he win in Athens in 1906 and in 1908 and again in 1912 (London and Stockholm), he innovated sensational new movements, including the "cross" on the rings, which he was able to hold for three seconds. Later on, Braglia became a rich man in America. When he was forty-five, he wanted to train for the 1928 Olympics but was not allowed. The "artistic exhibition" that had made him rich also changed his status to professional. In 1932, however, as a trainer he contributed to the Italian gymnastics triumph in Los Angeles.

Before the outbreak of World War I, the art of gymnastics had reached a high point in Europe. Of course, even the best routines of the day would bring a smile from today's gymnast. But, it should not be forgotten that the quality of the apparatus was not very good. The horizontal bar had little spring; the parallel bars were stiff.

The Italian, Zampori, won at the 1920 Olympic Games in Antwerp, but the French took second and third place. And this time it was solely artistic gymnastics—no athletics and no formal calisthenics.

The development of gymnastics after 1920 was turbulent. Although the International Gymnastics Association insisted on including calisthenics and athletics with the apparatus exercises, a special all-around competition was initiated for purely artistic gymnastics. Six years later, in Paris, the eighth international tournament took place. It had been decided to hold the tournament every four years between Olympic games—a feature still adhered to today for the World Cup.

The year 1928 marked the first time the artistic gymnastics competition was well represented. Eleven nations entered gymnastics teams in the Olympics in Amsterdam.

At the ninth International Tournament in 1930, the first fatal fall from an apparatus occurred. Anton Malej of Yugoslavia fell from the rings and broke a neckbone.

1932-1976

In 1932, the world economic crisis prevented all but five nations from entering gymnastics teams in the Olympics at Los Angeles—and as a result, the U.S. did quite well.

In 1934, the first World Championships were held in Budapest—and that name replaced "International Tournament" from then on.

Although the 1936 games in Berlin were under the dark cloud of international politics, the stage was set for the biggest advance in gymnastics until that time. The competitions were viewed by 25,000 spectators daily! The Germans used their "home court" advantage and beat (barely) the fine Swiss team. And the Japanese previewed their future dominance of the sport. Fourteen countries entered the team competition, which assumed the form it still has today: compulsories and optionals in the six events. Frank Cumiskey, the best American gymnast of this era, placed forty-eighth.

World War II slowed the rise of artistic gymnastics. The Finns, even with heavy war casualties, were the celebrated winners of the 1948 Olympic Games in London.

At the 1952 Olympics in Helsinki, there was a record twenty-nine nations at the games. For the first time, the Russians competed with the gymnasts of the West. As the saying goes, "They came, they saw, they conquered." Viktor Tschukaren, Schagenjan, Muratow, and Koropkov all showed that gymnasts could perform the most difficult routines with dreamlike confidence.

The Russians continued their superiority at the 1954 World Championships in Rome, but the Japanese made their first sustained challenge and placed second. The Americans were not among the sixteen nations that participated. At the 1956 Olympics in faraway Melbourne, Russia won the gold, only two points ahead of Japan. The big surprise was the American team, which placed sixth. Armando Vega, Abe Grossfeld, and John Bechner, all presently active as coaches, were on that team.

In 1960, in Rome, the Japanese took firm control of the competition, beating the Russians 575.20 to 572.70. The U.S. ranked fifth.

It was not difficult for the Japanese to keep their grip on first place in the 1964 games in Tokyo. Yukio Endo became recognized as the best gymnast in the world. Eighteen nations competed, with South Korea, Taiwan, Australia, and India all performing for the first time. The Japanese team continued its mastery in 1968, scoring a 575.90 to 571.10 victory over the USSR. Five Japanese gymnasts were among the top eight competitors, including Sawao Kato, first; Nakayama, second; and Kenmotsu, fourth. Nakayama, winning the parallel bars and floor exercises, was touted as the most elegant gymnast in history; Kato was the most technically perfect.

At the 1970 World Championships, Japan again emerged victorious—even without Sawao Kato. Kenmotsu, Tsukahara, and Nakayama were standouts. Tsukahara created a sensation in vaulting with his backward somersault with a 180-degree turn. The vault was to be named after him—despite the fact that the move had been shown before by American specialists in the event.

Japan was still unreachable in the 1972 Munich Olympics: (1) Kato, (2) Kenmotsu, (3) Nakayama. The winners on the parallel bars were: Kato, Kasamatsu, Kenmotsu; at the horizontal bar: Tsukahara, Kato, Kasamatsu, Kenmotsu. A performance like this will never be repeated. (It will be virtually impossible as long as the rule prohibiting more than two gymnasts from one country to enter the individual finals is in effect.)

The exciting duel in Montreal in 1976 was won by Japan, even without the injured Fujismoto. Yet the strongest gymnast proved to be Nikolai Andrianov, who defeated Sawao Kato.

What will happen at the 1978 World Championships and beyond? A young Russian team, technically outstanding, surpassing all others in difficulty, wants to regain their gymnastics supremacy, which they lost to Japan in 1960. And for the first time in history, an American, Kurt Thomas, will lead a U.S. team into the Olympics Games with a good chance of winning a medal.

3

Highlights of Fifty Years of Women's Olympic Gymnastics

Dr. Josef Goehler

1928-1960

Perhaps 1928 may be thought of as the birthdate of wo-men's artistic gymnastics. That year, the International Gymnastics League and the organizers of the Olympics in Amsterdam dared for the first time to hold a team competition for women gymnasts. (To feature an individual competition would have been *too* daring for the time.) Five nations entered: Holland, Italy, Great Britain, Hungary, and France. There were no compulsory apparatus. Though the structure of the tournament was more or less open, the teams had to include calisthenics in its routines, as well as the apparatus.

Even by 1932, prejudice was still widespread against public exhibitions of women's gymnastics in America. The organizers of the Olympic games in Los Angeles did not include women's participation at all.

The Hungarians, on the other hand, were very much in favor

of women's gymnastics; they included the competition in the first World Championships in Budapest in 1934. They announced a versatile team competition, which included athletic exercises, horizontal bar, parallel bars, and horse vaulting. They also included group exercises using hand "tools" and dance, which later became the sport of rhythmic gymnastics.

The form of competition was still the same in the 1936 Olympics—team but no individual evaluation. The uneven bars were used for the first time in Berlin. Except for the floor exercises, the present-day Olympic program was initiated.

Understandably, World War II did less to retard the women's side of the sport than it did the men's. So the 1948 Olympics in London received a great deal of enthusiasm. Unfortunately, medals for individual competition were still denied women; if they had been awarded, Czech Zdenka Honsova would have taken home the gold.

With the appearance of the Russian gymnasts at Helsinki in 1952, the women's gymnastics scene suddenly changed drastically. The four event program (consisting of floor exercises, parallel bars, vaulting, and balance beam) was presented for the first time, and the Russian women proved superior in every one. They took the first six places in vaulting; Maria Gorokowskaya won the all-around competition and four silver medals.

Only nine teams entered the 1956 Olympics in Melbourne. Five communist countries, led by the USSR, took the top five ranks overall. Agnes Keleti of Hungary was victorious in three events. (Keleti never did return home because of the Hungarian Revolution; she is now a coach in Israel.) Larisa Latynina, however, placing second in the all-around competition, started an amazing career here that would continue for many years. In Moscow at the World Championships two years later, she won three gold medals, leading the USSR to victory over Czechoslavakia, Romania, and Japan.

That same order of finish was repeated in the 1960 Rome Olympics. Again Latynina was brilliant, winning all-around and the floor exercises. Seventeen nations had women's teams this time—all of them European, except for the U.S. (ninth) and Japan (fourth).

1962-1978

The 1962 World Championships in Prague marked the debut of rising young star, Vera Caslavska, who was just barely beaten by Latynina (78.030 to 77.932).

Caslavska would have her moment at the 1964 Tokyo Olympics. In a dramatic head-to-head duel with Latynina, she was finally able to gain the upper hand, squeezing out victory by a 77.564 to 76.998 score, and bringing Czechoslavakia to within tenths of the USSR team, 380.890 to 379.989. And the rising American interest in gymnastics showed too; Linda Metheny came in thirty-sixth with a score of 73.998.

There were more Caslavska heroics at the 1968 Games in Mexico City, as she won three more gold medals. The Russians just managed to hold on 382.85 to 382.20. The U.S. women's team was becoming stronger and stronger, as they placed sixth out of fourteen teams. Cathy Rigby took sixteenth place (74.95) and Linda Metheny twenty-eighth (74.00).

International women's gymnastics now began to skyrocket in popularity. Twenty-one nations were drawn to the 1970 World Championships at Ljubljana, Yugoslavia. A new queen stepped to the throne vacated by Caslavska: Ludmilla Tourischeva. Her grace, expressive strength, and technical ability enraptured everyone; only her earthly demeanor prevented her from becoming as popular as Caslavska. The Championships also elicited a strong showing from Cathy Rigby, who proved at Ljubljana (where she placed fifteenth) that an American could compete seriously in international competition.

Attention at the Olympics in 1972 was on the USSR-East German team duel, which was won by the USSR 380.50 to 376.55. In the individual finals, Karin Janz of East Germany twice won the gold (vaulting and uneven bars), Olga Korbut did the same (balance beam and floor exercise). Olga's extremes in moods fascinated the thousands of spectators and the millions watching on satellite television around the world. Her daring performances were given such concentration by the media, it is almost forgotten that the all-around competition was won by her compatriot Ludmilla Tourischeva. Although Cathy Rigby placed tenth, it was commonly acknowledged by the experts and the audience that most of the American gymnasts were scored too low. But even with underevaluation, the Americans placed fourth.

With the international media coverage, women's gymnastics reached a new plateau of popularity. Individual gymnasts received acclaim as never before, and the problems of international judging were spotlighted as well. Women gymnasts from twenty-two countries were represented at the World Championships in Varna, Bulgaria, in 1974. But time had changed: the 1950 World Champion Swedes could do no better than last place. As usual, the winner was the Soviet Union, which bested the East German team, competing without Janz and Zuchold. The Eastern European bloc showed overwhelming superiority—Hungary, Romania, and Czechoslavakia placed third through fifth, respectively. Once again Tourischeva emerged victorious, ahead of Korbut and the graceful Angelika Hellman. When Ann Carr's Tsukahara optional vault received only a 9.4, the audience raged for over fifteen minutes; but the judges were unshakable and would not change the score.

Only twelve teams were allowed into the competition 1 level at the 1976 Olympics in Montreal. In team competition, the ever-present Soviet team was victorious, edging out Romania, East Germany, Hungary, and Czechoslavakia—a complete Eastern bloc sweep. The biggest attraction of the competition— and perhaps of the entire Games—was the Romania team, led by the fourteen-year-old prodigy, Nadia Comaneci. She received the highest score in women's gymnastics history (an incredible 79.275), including eight perfect scores of 10, a score that had never been previously awarded at any Olympics. Olga Korbut, on the other hand, perhaps psychologically overwhelmed by the Romanian's scores, seemed unsure of herself, and placed fifth. The four individual finals ended with two gold medals each for Comaneci and Nelli Kim, the latter deemed Tourischeva's successor as Russia's queen of the art.

By 1976, the most difficult movements in women's gymnastics seemed commonplace. Double somersaults and double twists in floor exercises were no longer a sensation in Montreal. Only time will tell whether women gymnasts travel the road of dance-oriented art or the road of acrobatics.

4
The Ancient Beginnings
Sho Fukishima

EARLY HISTORY

Greece and Rome

Artifacts from ancient cultures suggest that people practiced gymnasticlike activities in early civilizations. However, most of these were thought to be types of entertainment rather than exercises or competitive forms.

The term *gymnastic* was already employed in Greek society before the fifth century B.C. Greek gymnastics was not like the modern form of exercise, but was used for training athletes for athletic competitions when athletics was already becoming a profession. From that developed the science of medical gymnastics, and at later period, educational gymnastics.

Plato describes Herodicus's gymnastics in the *Republic*. Herodicus (fourth century B.C.), who was a gymnastics teacher and a chronic invalid, had learned from his own personal experience what dieting, massage, and the like could do for one's well-being. The principles of Herodicus's system were, shortly afterward, applied to the training of athletes, and the era of medical gymnastics was soon in full swing.

A discussion of gymnastic exercises is also found in Galen's work on "Health." Some of these exercises were the same ones used informally by athletes like Milo in the sixth century B.C. During the first two centuries after Christ, Philostratus recorded "gymnastics" in his Handbook for the Athletics Coach.

To purify the humors, to get rid of excessive secretions, to soften the rigid type, and to fatten or to alter in some particular, or to warm up some portion of a person's frame, this all belongs to the science of gymnastes [coach] . . . If anyone suffers a fracture, a wound, a dimming of the eyesight, or a dislocation of some joint, he should refer it to physician. Gymnastics is not concerned with this sort of disability.

The Middle Ages

Neither the Dark nor Middle Ages presented us with such lofty ideals as the Greek "harmony of mind and body," or with such noble aspirations as those of the Olympic Games. Not until GutsMuths wrote the first manual for gymnastics were these objectives reintroduced into the world.

Medieval man was more concerned with spiritual than with physical well-being. Medieval people looked on their bodies as instruments of sin, and hence impediments to the attainment of eternal salvation. Most church fathers opposed sports and dances because of the debased character of Roman sports, as well as the close association of these activities with pagan religious ceremonies and emperor worship. Education, except for chivalric training, was under church control until the twelfth century. The sports and games of the later Middle Ages were an aspect of community life, rather than part of the formal educational curriculum. The demands of military service entailed some physical education, which in peacetime was pursued largely through rugged sports.

RENAISSANCE

The Renaissance in Europe (14th-16th century) was a period of the revival of learning. People turned to an appreciative study of the Greek and Latin classics, the long-neglected records of ancient civilization that supplied the Western nations with a new ideal of life and culture.

Gymnastics exercise was not an exception to the revival in the period. The revival of learning led to renewed interest in the original Greek and Roman sources of medical theory and practice, particularly the works of Galen.

Two Italian medical doctors who published books on medical gymnastics were undoubtedly greatly influenced by Galen's work. Girolamo Cardano (1501-76) wrote the book, *De Sanitae Tuenda* (the same title as the translation of Galen's work). The other doctor was Hieronymus Mercurialis whose book, *De Arte Gymnastica,* was known throughout Europe as an authority on medicine. Editions of his work on gymnastics, first published in 1569, continued to appear at intervals during the next hundred years.

Enlightenment in science, especially the medical theories and experiments during this period in Europe, contributed to the revival of medical gymnastics. Physicians and concerned experts wrote works that used various forms of exercise for maintaining and restoring an individual's health and hygiene. Interest in the child and the child's well-being also became increasingly evident in the growing number of pedagogical treatises. Two educationists, John Locke (1632-1704) and Jean Jacques Rousseau (1712-78) published such books. Locke authored *Some Thoughts on Education* in 1693 and Rousseau published *Emile* in 1762. Both authors expressed a strong need for exercise in the growth and development of children. At the same time, these writers influenced the way future leaders in the field of gymnastics would view gymnastic exercise.

PIONEERS FROM GERMANY AND SCANDINAVIA

In the latter part of the eighteenth century, several individuals from Germany, Denmark, and Sweden initiated strong efforts to organize gymnastic exercises into a rational system as a means of education. They valued gymnastics as a tool for human development and adapted it to a curriculum or to their own programs. Ling (1776-1839) initiated the Swedish system of gymnastics. He systematized exercises employing anatomical, physiological, and medical knowledge. Later his system influenced not only Scandinavia, but also other nations of the world. Jahn (1778-1852) who was said to be the father of German gymnastics, used the term *turnen* instead of *gymnastike.* His gymnastics, besides using many forms of activity, contained exercises for apparatus that were the invention of Jahn himself.

GutsMuths

In 1786, Johann Christoph Friedrich GutsMuths (1759-1839) became the fourth teacher of gymnastics at the Schnepfenthal Educational Institute, which was founded by another early leader of modern physical training, Christian Gotthilf Salzmann (1744-1811). GutsMuths inherited the ideology of Salzmann, as well as Johann Bernhard Basedow (1723-90). Basedow, who was influenced tremendously by Rousseau, attempted to put "naturalistic education" into practice at his school, known as the Philanthropinum. Salzmann, who was also one of the Philanthropists, was inspired by Rousseau's work, *Emile*. However, the principles of the Philanthropists did not come to full flower until the time of GutsMuths.

The educational institute at Schnepfenthal was open to all classes of society. Although GutsMuths continued to employ the existing system of his predecessors, he modified it and added more exercises as he gained experience. His daily exercises were usually practiced outdoors on a neighboring hill, where an open space under oaks had been provided with the necessary apparatus. Through his demonstrations to visitors and through his writings, GutsMuths' "natural gymnastics" were transmitted to other gymnastic leaders, not only in Germany but in many other nations, as well. One of his works, *Gymnastik fur die Jugend (Gymnastics for the Young,* 1793), was the first modern manual of gymnastics, and was translated into more than five languages.

GutsMuths advocated a hardening process for the growing child. He believed that children's regular participation in games and gymnastics developed the desirable qualities of self-reliance, courage, perseverance, judgment, observation, and presence of mind.

Nachtegall

Early in 1798 Franz Nachtegall (1777-1847), inspired by GutsMuth's *Gymnastik fur die Jugend,* organized a gymnastic club of university students and tradesmen in Copenhagen. In 1801, he introduced gymnastics into the first Folk school in Denmark, and soon many schools followed. In 1804, King Frederik VI founded the Military Gymnastic Institute, the first such gymnastic institute in the world. Nachtegall was appointed its first director. Through the institute, Nachtegall's teaching was spread throughout the entire army and navy, including the Norwegian regiment. Later civilians were also admitted to courses in the institute, which became a general teacher-training school for gymnastics.

A law passed in 1814 decreed that every school in Denmark should provide grounds and apparatus for gymnastics, and that the children should be given an hour of exercise each day, in addition to the regular schedule.

In 1828, Nachtegall published the first manual of school gymnastics to be sanctioned by the government of other European countries. He did not invent a system of his own, but borrowed his exercises from Basedow and especially from GutsMuths' *Gymnastik fur die Jugend*. Besides Nachtegall, his strong supporter, King Frederik VI played an important role in the early development of the Danish school of gymnastics. As Crown Prince, Frederik VI himself had attended Nachtegall's private gymnastics institute.

Ling

Pehr Henrik Ling (1776-1839) who was known as the founder of the Swedish system of gymnastics was also known through his literary works. In both fields, he had a vision to revive the ancient vigor of the north as described in the sagas. Although he was acquainted with Nachtegall, Ling felt that he owed little to Nachtegall's gymnastics, since he found little new in Nachtegall's work. It is likely that he was already familiar with GutsMuth's books, as well as with C.J. Tissort's book on medical gymnastics.

Ling applied himself to the study of anatomy and physiology and worked out an original system of gymnastics. Study and experiment taught him about the human body and its needs, and helped him to select and apply his exercises. About 1808, Ling added a number of free movements to the apparatus gymnastics of GutsMuths, which was the genesis of free-standing (floor) exercise. The similarity of some of Ling's exercises to those in Pestalozzi's *Elementarygymnastik* of 1807 suggests that Ling may have been influenced by the work of Pestalozzi, who was perhaps the best-known teacher in Europe at the time.

Ling was an intense patriot, eager to see his countrymen strong in body and soul and thus prepared to deal with the enemy. In 1814, he succeeded in establishing the Royal Gymnastic Central Institute, which was supported by Count Bernadotte, the Crown Prince. As in Denmark, the monarchy strongly influenced the early development of gymnastics in Sweden. Ling believed that gymnastics had a place in education, medicine, and national defense. Almost from the start, instruction was accordingly given in the three branches of educational, medical, and military gymnastics.

Ling's Swedish gymnastics could be adapted to every age-group and to different types of people, was easily practiced, and comprised a rich variety of exercise that could be done without apparatus.

Ling insisted that medicine and gymnastics must be allies, and that instructors must acquire both theoretical knowledge and practical ability.

Gymnastics should always include theory and practice. The gymnast who lacks the one or the other must always labor at a disadvantage for he does not know when or how he should use a particular movement.

At a gymnastic establishment based on true principles, wealth as well as poverty, lowliness as well as greatness, are leveled; equality for the public good ought to prevail there.

Jahn

The German system of gymnastics was founded by the intensely patriotic Friedrich Ludwig Jahn (1778-1852). He advocated nationalism, constitutional liberty, and freedom from foreign domination. In 1811, he established his *Turnplatz*, or exercise ground, at the Hasenheide. Here he laid the basis for his *Volksturnen* (people's gymnastics), which developed rapidly, and swept German youth into its movement.

He devised crude apparatus, such as jumping standards and the horizontal bar. Later, other types, such as balancing beams, vertical ropes, ladders, additional horizontal bars, pole vaulting standards, jumping ditch, running track, vaulting buck, and crude parallel bars were added. The exercises were not yet ordered or organized, but every person was an inventor and shared the result with others, learning from each in turn. It was hardly in Jahn's nature to be systematic; a formal school of gymnastics was foreign to his purpose. During the course of the movement, Jahn took notes from which he composed a book that was finally published under the title of *Die Deutsche Turnkunst*. This set forth information concerning the choice of location for a *turnplatz*, or gymnastics center, the layout, how and what kinds of apparatus to make, descriptions of many exercises, and method and rules of different kinds of games, and how to manage a *turnverein* (gymnastic society). Through this book, he more or less fixed the gymnastics terminology in Germany. The philosophy underlying the book was that gymnasts should lead active, wholesome lives in the open air. He emphasized that boys should train to work together in harmony. He also sought to kindle in them a public spirit that might one day be of service to the nation.

Turnen develops only in freedom and Turnen frees the man. It can exist only in a self-respecting society and belongs to free people. It is community living. Turnen is more than a training of the body, it stirs the individual to become a part of a group. The soul of Turnen is folk life and thrives only in the open.

Jahn's gymnastics was unlike GutsMuths's system. Exercises were heavier, girls and women were left out, and there were not enough free exercises. Most of all, Jahn's system was heavily saturated with political motives.

Spiess

Jahn's system did not greatly influence school gymnastics in Germany. The real founder of both school and girls' gymnastics was Adolph Spiess (1810-58). He was influenced by the Pestalozzi method of education, as well as by GutsMuth's gymnastics. The chief service that Spiess's main contribution to gymnastics in Germany was to make it a part of school life, rather than being confined to the *turnplatz*. Although it lasted but a decade outside the schools, Spiess's system gave Turnen a place of respect in the eyes of the public, and gave it a school procedure and purpose. From this time on, the schools fostered physical education for both boys and girls. The procedure henceforth in the schools was largely formal gymnastics, with more clearly defined objectives.

Knudsen and Bukh

K.A. Knudsen (1864-1951), who graduated from the Royal Central Gymnastic Institute in Stockholm in 1891, was a leader of school gymnastics in Denmark. Knudsen did not admit the existence of a Danish system of gymnastics, but always spoke of Lind's Swedish system. His book *Laerebog i Gymnastik* was greatly influenced by Torngrens, his teacher and Lind's student.

Nevertheless Niels Bukh (1880-1950) developed a system of physical exercise that may be said to be truly Danish. Bukh's system was based on physiological principles, as well as that of his predecessors. However, Bukh distinguished his method in two ways: first, his gymnastics had an entirely different tempo; second, the movement was, for the most part, a relief, compared to the many holding movements of the Swedish-Danish system. He stated, "It is more important to master movements than position." His system was divided into the following: (1) ordering exercises; (2) leg, arm, neck, flanks, stomach, and back exercises; and (3) walking, running, jumping, and skilled exercises. Within the different groups he divided the exercises into those that improve elasticity, those that give strength, and those that promote skill.

Summary

The trends in aims and methods of gymnastics since early Greece through the birth of modern systems differ in various cultures because of the unique cultural goals. People have developed and employed gymnastics for various reasons: to gain a healthy and strong body; to condition for an athletic contest; to become a strong soldier; to practice patriotism; or for pure recreation. Each of these was given a different term: for example, medical gymnastics, military gymnastics, school gymnastics, and recreational gymnastics.

Social, economic, and political forces gave rise to various forms of gymnastics, and these forces were different in each culture. The methods and programs of gymnastics are somewhat similar to particular ways of life, resulting from the social and cultural foundation of the nation. Gymnastics has not merely been a series of movements or a set of exercises, but a reflection of national ideals, philosophies, and traits. These pioneers developed their own systems of gymnastics within their cultural environments.

5

Modern Rhythmic Gymnastics

Helena Greathouse

Although modern rhythmic gymnastics has more than a twenty-year history in most European countries, it is relatively new in the United States. The sport draws heavily on ballet technique and uses five different kinds of hand apparatus: hoop, ball, ribbon, jumprope, and Indian Clubs. It is always performed on the floor and to the accompaniment of music.

International competition has existed on an official level for many years, and World Championships in this sport have taken place regularly every two years since 1963. The competition in modern rhythmic gymnastics (MRG) is organized in two categories—single and group performances. Routines for singles last between one and one-and-a-half minutes. During each routine, only one apparatus may be used. Group routines last between two-and-a-half and three minutes. The group consists of six members using apparatus with synchronized movements. All members of the group may use identical apparatus or, as is often the case, half may use one kind, half another.

To help distinguish MRG from artistic gymnastics, the

following elements have been officially prohibited from MRG singles and group routines:

- static elements with hold on one or both hands, legs in air
- cartwheels on one or both hands and aerial cartwheels
- all front and back walkovers
- flip-flops, roundoffs
- all saltos
- holds in split
- neck springs

However, the following preacrobatic elements are authorized:

- rolls in all directions
- passing support, on one or both arms (without any stop) with the legs not permitted to pass the vertical
- passing through a split (without any stop)
- lying on stomach: lift body to have weight on chest or shoulders, with or without using hands, legs raised behind

These elements are considered part of the exercise if they are related to the work of the apparatus and are executed by passing through the movement without stopping or interrupting the continuity of execution.

The elements or typical forms of folklore, modern dance, or classic ballet are excluded. The whole floor area must be taken into consideration when composing the routine.

All modern rhythmic gymnasts must master a number of movements to compete. The major areas of instruction are:

1. General exercises (warmup)
2. Walking, running, and dance steps
3. Ballet technique at the barre
4. Movements of arms, torso, and head
5. Body waves
6. Leaps
7. Turns
8. Balance
9. Tumbling and acrobatic elements
10. Coordination of music with movement
11. Manipulation of hand apparatus: ball, hoop, jumprope, ribbon, Indian clubs
12. Compulsory routines
13. Optional routines

COMPETITIVE: SINGLES

At every National and World Championship there are always four optional routines for singles (time limit: one to one-and-a-half minutes). Each routine should contain at least six elements of medium difficulty and at least two elements of superior difficulty. Substitution of one superior element with two medium elements is prohibited. Examples of elements of difficulty are found in *Technical Rules of Modern Rhythmic Gymnastics* (published by the USGF). Remember, these are only *examples* of such elements. Gymnasts and coaches should create *original* elements of difficulty by using listed elements of difficulty without hand apparatus, combined with difficult moves of apparatus. Originality is taken into account by judges.

Judging is based on a scale of 10 points, the same as with Artistic Gymnastics. If one element of superior difficulty is omitted from the routine, the penalty is 1 point. If one element of medium difficulty is omitted, the penalty is 0.5 point. At least 3 of the total 8 elements of difficulty must be performed with the left hand (or with the right hand if the gymnast is left-handed). If the gymnast correctly uses the opposite hand for these 3 elements of difficulty, but does not use this hand at all at any other time during the routine, the penalty is 0.5 point. If all 8 elements of difficulty are performed with the same hand, the penalty is 1.5 points.

Each hand apparatus has specific groups of movements. Elements of as many specific groups of movements as possible should be in each routine so that the routine shows a variety of the possible skills.

Routine with Indian Clubs

Indian Clubs are made of wood or plastic. The length of each is 40-50 cm (16-20 inches), and the weight is a minimum of 150 gm (5.3 ounces). The neck comprises two-thirds of the total length and the head one-third. The diameter of the small sphere at the end of the neck is not to exceed 3 cm (1¼ inches).

Large movements (Indian clubs used as extension of full arm). Examples include arcs, circles, figure-eights, swings, etc. Movements may be simultaneous or successive with both arms.

Modern Rhythmic gymnastics—Indian Clubs (Helena Greathouse photo)

Small circles. Wrist is stationary, small end of Indian club moving in palm. Each Indian club may or may not be moving simultaneously with the other.

Throwing and catching. When throwing Indian clubs, they may either circle in the air or not. Each Indian club may or may not be thrown simultaneously with the other. For example, one may be thrown while the other is given to the opposite hand or while the other is moving in another way.

Rhythmical tapping of Indian clubs. Indian clubs may tap gently against each other or on the floor in rhythm with music. (*Note:* Club(s) may never be left motionless on the floor nor may the club(s) roll on the floor.)

Routine with Ball

Balls are made of rubber with a diameter of 18-20 cm (7.2-8.0 inches). They may be any color except gold, silver, or bronze.

Rolling (free or controlled) and spinning. Either element may take place on the floor or on any part of the body. Rolls may also occur between two parts of the body (for example, circling roll alternating between palm of one hand and back of the other, spinning on palm, etc.). When rolling the ball to the floor, the ball is gently released in a roll from palm onto floor. It must not bounce. When picking ball up, the ball again rolls gently onto palm.

Bouncing. Bouncing may be either on floor or on (against) any part of the body. Ball is bounced on floor by turning palm over and giving ball a slight push downward. The entire arm moves in pushing the ball downward.

Throwing and catching. The ball is thrown by moving the entire arm. When ball is thrown, it first rolls from palm to fingertips before leaving hand. Following release of ball, the arm remains extended in the direction of ball and awaits its return. When caught, it first touches fingertips, then rolls to palm while entire arm descends.

Balancing ball. The ball is held lightly in palm with fingers slightly apart and curved around it. It is never grasped tightly. Arm(s) and body move while ball remains balanced in palm. (*Note:* Ball must be in motion at all times when on the floor. When ball is rolling or spinning on floor, it may not be left unattended but must be incorporated into the routine.)

Routine with Hoop

Hoops are made of wood or plastic. The inside diameter is 80-90 cm (32-36 inches). They may be any color except gold, silver, or bronze.

Large (swinging) movements. (Hoop is grasped tightly and extends beyond arm.) These include arcs, circles, figure-eights, etc.

Hoop movements revolving on diameter. These movements include spinning hoop on floor (on vertical diameter), slow revolving in hands (on horizontal diameter), etc.

Circling. Circling may be in hand or around any other part of the body. Proper planes must be maintained. (For example, frontal vertical, lateral vertical, horizontal, etc.) When hoop is in hand, circle between thumb and index finger.

Throwing and catching. This action may be performed in any plane. The entire arm is involved in throwing and catching movement.

Rolling. Rolling may take place on the floor or on any part of the body. On the floor the hoop movement may be in a straight line, a circle, or an arc.

Jumps and other movement through hoop. During jumps or leaps the hoop may be held with one or both hands.
(*Note:* Hoop must be in motion at all times when on floor. When hoop is rolling or spinning on floor, it may not be left unattended but must be incorporated into the routine.)

Routine with Ribbon

The stick is approximately 50 cm (20 inches) long and is made of a wood (preferably bamboo) that is somewhat elastic. It is connected to the ribbon in a swivellike arrangement. The ribbon is made of satin and is 6 meters (20 feet) long. The first meter (3 ft. 4 in.) nearest the stick is doubled. The width of the ribbon is 4-6 cm (1.7-2.4 inches). The stick is held with the end in the palm, index finger straight on the stick.

Large (swinging) movements. These are performed with the entire arm reaching as far from the body as possible. Examples include arcs, circles, figure-eights, etc., in all planes.

Small movements. These are performed with wrist only in a very precise fashion: (1) snakes (amplitude consistent) and (2) spirals.

Throwing and catching. (This group does not need to be in a routine.) Hand is in contact only with stick.

One hand on stick, one hand holding end of ribbon. (This group also does not need to be in a routine.) Various movements are possible here including figure-eights, jumps over ribbon, etc.

(*Note:* Ribbon—or any part of ribbon—may not remain motionless on floor.)

Routine with Jumprope

The proper length of the jumprope is determined by stepping in the middle of the jumprope and stretching each half so that it exactly reaches the armpits. The rope material must be hemp, and the rope is specially made so that it is thicker in the middle than at the ends.

Jumps over the rope. Jumps can be performed either over the open rope held by the two ends or over the rope folded two, three, or four times, and held by two hands. Jumps may also be performed with the rope folded in two and held by one hand.

Large (swinging) movements. If held by two hands, these swings may be performed either keeping wrists together or apart (at least shoulder-width).

Throwing and catching. These may be executed either with one hand (after rotation of folded jumprope) or with both hands (after jumping over the jumprope).

COMPETITIVE: GROUPS

The group competition consists of one optional routine only. (Time limit: 2½ to 3 minutes.) The routine is executed by six gymnasts. Typically, the routines involve participation by each gymnast in group work, in a uniform way, with a collective spirit. Besides the demands of technical difficulty concerning individual routines, the specifications of group work must be respected. These include exchanges of apparatus and movement and change of place of gymnasts to realize the different formations.

Entry. The entry does not last more than 30 seconds. This time is not counted as a part of the time allowed for the routine. Entry is measured from the time the last girl enters the competition area to when the entire group reaches a final preparatory position. (If the entry lasts more than 30 seconds, 0.3 points are deducted.) Music may or may not accompany the entry, which is complete only when all six girls have clearly reached a motionless state.

Performance. The routine must consist of at least six distinctly different forms. For example, girls may perform in a circle, a square, a line (horizontal, diagonal, vertical), in couples, in threes, etc. (Deductions: 0.3 points for each missing form.) Transitions from one form to another should be smooth and graceful and add variety to the overall impression. Each new form should have some surprise for the audience.

A portion of the group routine may be performed as a solo. However, the remaining five girls must always be in motion, i.e., they must move in a direction or while essentially in place. This idea of a solo within a group can be carried over to include two or three girls performing alone while the other girls remain in motion. After this performance (of twos or threes) within the group, the remaining girls must compensate by performing movements of equal difficulty. Another variation is for the girls to move in canon fashion (in singles, twos, or threes).

Elements of difficulty. The number of elements of difficulty for group routines is the same as for single routines. This means a minimum of 8 elements of difficulty from which at least 2 must be of superior difficulty. At least 3 of the 8 must be performed with the left hand. In addition, 4 of the 8 elements must be performed by exchanging the apparatus with a partner over a distance. (One of these 4 must be of superior difficulty and the remaining 3 of medium difficulty, except in the case of jumpropes. Jumpropes may consist of 4 elements of medium difficulty.)

The remaining 4 elements may be performed by individual members of the group. Each girl performs each element separately. Again, one of these 4 must be of superior difficulty and the remaining 3 of medium difficulty except in the case of jumpropes. If the jumprope exchange is satisfied with 4 elements of medium difficulty, the girls must have 2 elements of superior and 2 of medium difficulty in this category (individual).

	Individual		Exchanges	
	Medium	Superior	Medium	Superior
All Apparatus	3	1	3	1
Jumprope	2	2	4	0
or: Jumprope	3	1	3	1

Exchanges: ball and hoop. Medium difficulty consists of rolling and (if there is a ball bouncing it to a partner). Superior difficulty for ball, hoop, jumprope, and Indian clubs consists of throwing the apparatus a distance of over 4 meters (without bouncing). With the jumprope, no element of difficulty is counted if only one end of the jumprope is thrown. Again, 4 meters is the division between throws of superior and medium difficulty.

Until recently, ribbons were not used for the group routine at World Championships.

Judging of group routines. Judging is undertaken by two groups of judges. Each group has a total of 10 points with which to work. One group evaluates composition and the other the execution of the routine. Total score is therefore based on a scale of 20 possible points.

NONCOMPETITIVE

Rhythmic Gymnastics can also have a noncompetitive dimension. In that case, participation is just for fun, relaxation, and perhaps most importantly for the satisfaction of staying in shape. It is suitable for all women of all shapes and sizes and is not limited to any particular age-group.

There are countless programs designed to help women achieve and maintain physical fitness. Why still another program? Emphasizing rhythmic elements in exercise programs adds variety and enhances interest in fitness. Rhythmic exercises in combination with hand apparatus is something altogether different and lots of fun. Adding hand apparatus to body movement develops coordination, a fundamental factor in such feminine qualities as grace, poise, and self-confidence.

What better combination than variety, fun, and self-improvement! And if you are competitively inclined, we have seen that there are many possibilities for you in this rapidly growing women's sport.

6

Gymnastics and the Art of Living

Daniel Millman

A rt, like *love* and *beauty*, is a tricky word to define, elusive to grasp—either in the eye of the beholder or in the mind of the creator. *The American Heritage Dictionary* gives a little guidance:

Art: 2. The conscious production or arrangement of sounds, colors, forms, movements, or other elements in a manner that affects the sense of beauty; specifically, the production of the beautiful in a graphic or plastic medium.

Not a bad definition for our purposes. This definition can clearly apply to the sport of gymnastics. The primary goal of most other sports is to increase some quantity—jumping higher, running faster, or hitting harder—with the end result of winning in a competition. If the movements therein happen to be smooth, efficient, and aesthetically pleasing, that's fine, but it's not the primary goal. Only in gymnastics, and a few other sports, is there a *conscious* production or arrangement of forms, movements, or other elements in a manner that affects the sense of beauty.

37

But perhaps I am only toying with words. After all, we all love to name things. Human beings are labelers. We have names for every bug, flower, and bush . . . and every star in the heavens. The first thing we learn about another person is his or her name; when we're ill, we already begin to feel better when the doctor tells us the name of the disease. Perhaps names and labels give us a temporary sense of control and understanding in a world that seems otherwise random, unpredictable, and chaotic.

Shakespeare said it best, through the sweet lips of Juliet speaking to Romeo: "What's in a name? . . . A rose by any other name smells as sweet." What *is* in a name, anyway?

There is a tiger in the Los Angeles zoo who half-heartedly pads back and forth in his small compound. He looks a little fat and sluggish. There are other creatures by the same name in the jungles of Malaysia, Africa, and India, to which the "zoo-tiger" bears only a vague spiritual resemblance. One creature is wild, filled with power and spirit. The other is, at best, a potentially dangerous, oversized housecat, hanging onto its ultimate potential only by the thread of instinct.

Gymnasts are like those tigers. Some are like the zoo-cats, while others are spirited and truly awesome creatures. Some gymnasts are performing artists; others are not. Art is defined not by a dictionary, but by the person who creates it. Some people consciously produce art, and others produce something else. Painting, for example, is not necessarily art. There are painters who do produce art, and there are those whose canvases should be used to wrap the garbage.

The same holds true with gymnastics or any art form. Whether something is considered art or not depends on who is doing it. To create art, one must be an artist; to be an artist, however, requires not only emotional intuition, but the motivation to perfection. Maturity and responsibility for the sheer work are also required. Art is a conscious activity.

To highlight a sketch of the gymnast-artist, here is some material I wrote for *International Gymnast* magazine in which I described several classical gymnastics "types" you may recognize.

The *compulsive gymnast* uses gymnastics as yet another way to vent masochistic tendencies. He uses the apparatus to whip himself as punishment for real or imagined "sins." It is obvious to everyone that this gymnast does not enjoy training, but he sticks to it because it's the "right thing to do."

The *thrill-seeker's* primary goal is spitting in the eye of fear, by scaring the hell out of himself (and everyone else) in attempting (and usually accomplishing) moves that no sane person would dream of! He's fun to have around and keeps everyone's adrenalin flowing.

The *partial gymnast* has the potential to be an exciting performing artist—if only he liked to train. He seeks the applause of the audience. This type really turns on before a crowd, but lacks direction and motivation in practice when all eyes are not on him. His goal is the support of a faltering self-image, the creation of self-respect. Producing beauty is only secondary.

The *constructive gymnast* has healthy and stable motivation. Training is the most important time for him. His primary interest is overall fitness and self-improvement. He trains regularly and effectively, rarely too hard or too easy. As long as he gets a good workout, he's satisfied. Having nothing to prove, he isn't preoccupied with competition, so he isn't all that interested in attempting incredible moves, or in winning championships. He uses gymnastics as a means of growth. Beauty is fine if it helps him develop.

Finally, there is the realm of the *gymnast-artist*. This individual may at times possess qualities of the constructive, thrill-seeker, as well as those of the compulsive gymnast. But overall, gymnastics expresses this person's way of life. He strives for beauty. Whether making a tossed green salad, taking photographs, baking bread, arranging flowers, or sweeping the floor, his attention is on grace, ease, form, and beauty. His participation in gymnastics is only a part of a greater attitude toward life. He is not just satisfied with mere performance. For him, performing better, more beautifully, is what counts.

Only recently has gymnastics attracted the artist, promising an opportunity for creative and artistic expression. Prehistoric man likely devised the first gymnastics movements out of a need to survive, running after or from beasts during the hunt. He learned to leap over objects, and roll like a monkey (perhaps a tumbler invented the wheel by first becoming one). Gymnastics may have evolved from man's natural sense of play. We all know, after all, that swinging and flipping is fun. In Greece, home of the ancient Olympiad, gymnastic-type events such as jumping over bulls, were formalized.

Modern apparatus gymnastics was designed in Germany, where a system of exercises was used to enhance overall physical development and balance. This was a marvelous improvement over previous European approaches to physical education. However, the German invention was born from rigidity and formality—a militaristic preparation for fighting fitness, not an art form.

In fact, none of the early gymnastics forms were designed for the conscious production of beauty. Today, in the age of mass telecommunication, media presentations and television sports spectaculars captivate the imagination of millions of viewers. Gymnastics today is something new, evolving into a performance art of the highest quality, like the developed symphonic and balletic forms.

Activities like poetry, ballet, symphony and gymnastics are apt to become art forms because they require intense feeling and attention. If you want a fire, the essential elements are oxygen, fuel, and heat. In the same way, feeling and attention are essential elements of art.

Creating art is a meditative discipline, demanding involvement by the whole body, in which the heart, head, and vitality blend perfectly. This blending transforms the ordinary into the art-realm. On the other hand, it is possible to bake bread without getting emotionally involved. Only the most sophisticated artists can bring intense feeling and attention to simple, everyday activities, transmuting them to art.

Gymnastics, because of its unique demands, has the potential to become one of mankind's most inspirational performing arts—as long as it isn't limited to points, statistics, and scores. Gymnastics is a warrior's art because one's body is "on the line" during each performance. If a tennis player makes an error, a match may be at stake. A gymnast's inattention may exact a far greater price. Therefore, gymnastics has a built-in intensity.

Take away the scoring and competition from football, baseball, or other popular games. What remains is a group of players without direction, lost figures performing coordinated movements perhaps, but without a clear goal. Take away the statistics, numbers, and records from swimming or track and field, and you are left with physical fitness activities. But remove the scores and competition from gymnastics, and the essential core remains. You still see a complete performance art, independent of winning, losing, or arbitrary tabulations. There is still a clear direction, and that direction is the performance art.

With new developments in apparatus (more resilient tumbling areas, springier bars, and better landing mats), astonishing movements are possible now that would have been inconceivable a few years ago. The first four-minute mile was an unexpected feat in the world of running. But today in gymnastics, you can observe a human being spring from the floor, rise into the air, turn over three times backward, and land perfectly. This is the closest thing to magic you will see . . . and there are no mirrors!

Any good magician will tell you that it's not the trick that counts; it's the presentation. The best gymnasts are the biggest bluffers, the hams, the showmen and show women. There must be the vital element of *feeling*. The gymnast must convey that feeling through expression and dramatic flair in every movement. The gymnast-artist must recapture that magical enthusiasm of childhood, the moment of surprising accomplishment. When this happens, we all reawaken to the vitality of our own childhood, with an appreciation for the feeling of turning over in the air.

No painting, symphony, or poem becomes alive for us unless it makes us feel. Merely looking or listening or performing in some dry, theoretically appreciative way will not transport us into the realm of magic, the realm of art. We must first be able to feel inspiration, awe, humor, sadness, or wonder. Gymnastics, to be art, must evoke an emotional response.

Art and magic are not really so different. What is magic but those things that make us feel the mystery and wonder of living? In our need to make sense out of the mystery of our lives, we developed our passion for naming, for controlling. Art and magic, however, only *appear* to control. In fact, the power and beauty of art and magic is in learning to flow with and harness the natural forces. This, too, is the power of gymnastics.

Sadly, most of us have buried the capacity to feel. We've substituted hysterical emotional substitutes for anger, fear, and sorrow, thinking these contractions to be "feeling." Yet through fate, fortune, or instinct, feelings have remained burning in a few. We call such people romanticists, painters, poets, musicians, the performing artists of every age.

Feeling is not a little emotional episode, but a profound, inspiring, and deeply pleasurable radiance, expressed in every breath. For a moment, take a very slow, delicate, deep breath. Listen for the farthest sound you can hear, and feel the pleasure of the breath. Indulge this luxury of enjoying so simple a thing. Practice feeling, and you will not fail to become an artist.

Consider the humorous and miraculous fact that you are sitting here reading while the galaxies swirl into infinite space. You, a human being, are a submicroscopic speck in infinity, a passenger going nowhere through the universe. You could be a clam, sitting in its shell in a rainbow tidepool somewhere off the coast of anywhere. But instead, you are a human, living this life you know so little about. You don't really know why you're here, where you came from, or where you're ultimately going. You only know many names. Instead of trying to make sense of it all with more names and more beliefs, consider the mystery, the awe! In that moment, you cannot fail to feel.

If you gain the capacity to live in that mystery, instead of focusing on the details, the petty personal problems, your life will become spontaneous, pleasurable, and magical. This is what creates art. It is the art of feeling that is the basis for all arts. Gymnastics is one expression of that feeling. Turning a pitcher of water into a bouquet of flowers is a cheap trick in comparison! Feeling creates the magic, the art. It takes more than a few tricks to make a gymnastics artist.

Olga Korbut will be remembered for a long time. She was certainly not a typical bio-mechanical gymnastics technician. Many young gymnasts were far better technicians than she. Yet we felt her performance as she felt it. Every expression of Olga's face communicated something to us; every swing became electric. With Olga, gymnastics performances came alive for us.

Nadia Comaneci is a star who will shine in my memory long after other young superstars have outshined her. I'll remember her not only for her technical mastery—that fortunate combination of qualities that has allowed her to become the epitome of gymnastics—but rather for the quality of her performance. Her floor exercise routine made me jump out of my seat without realizing it. My breath almost stopped in attention to her magic. Not only did Nadia seem lighter-than-air, but I felt that way too.

Gymnastics can be a purely mechanical activity in which men and women are turned into machines, training the body to go through complex, precise motions, almost like a computer. This is science perhaps, but not art. I have coached gymnasts for years, and have found only a handful who truly feel their movements. For most, especially in men's gymnastics today, it is a cold, serious affair.

To once again discover art through gymnastics, men and women must be prepared from childhood to express feelings, to show unrepressed happiness, laughter, and real energy.

Now that you have an idea what gymnastics is all about, are you ready to become a gymnast? In Part 2 you will see that it requires dedication, perseverance, money, and just plain old hard work—to accompany your developing talent. This point is well illustrated by Leslie Wolfsberger, a member of the 1976 Olympic team.

If you are interested in teaching, coaching, or organizing a gymnastics program in your local area, Get That Program Going! *will be an invaluable source of ideas for funding, administration, equipment, and holding exhibitions.* The Oregon Experience *is a portrait of one of America's best gymnastics clubs, Dick Mulvihill's and Linda Metheny's Oregon Academy of Gymnastics in Eugene.*

2

STARTING OUT

Leslie Wolfsberger (Tony Duffy photo)

7

On the Way Up: Notes of an Olympian

Leslie Wolfsberger

Of the four Olympic events in gymnastics the balance beam is the most demanding for a gymnast's physical and psychological assets. The physical qualities needed to perform successfully at the highest competitive levels are: flexibility, coordination, balance, and grace, with the factors of kinesthetic awareness, strength and muscle control, and agility following closely behind. Physical endurance, speed, and timing are also important qualities but not to the same extent.

During recent years the trend in balance beam performance has been to emphasize performing tricks of great difficulty and high risk. Single elements such as walkovers, back handsprings, front or side aerials, and single tucked, piked, or twisting dismounts are tricks now considered stock elements, suitable mainly in combinations to obtain higher scores. At the highest levels of competition, gymnasts who retain balance and exhibit grace will earn maximum scores in the event. These include such difficult and high risk tricks as back handspring to immediate back tuck, or running punch front tuck or a double tucked or twisting dismount.

I believe the most important physical asset for excellence in the balance beam event is coordination. Slight errors in coordination of arms, legs, and body in performing even simple combinations of moves, place great demands on the gymnast's flexibility and balance. Under the pressures of competition only gymnasts with strong mental discipline seem able to recover from an error while relying on all of their physical assets to keep from falling off the apparatus.

PSYCHOLOGICAL DISCIPLINE

Important psychological factors and mental attitudes of the gymnast weigh heavily in training and competitions. Each individual consciously or unconsciously sets limits relating to her physical performance on the balance beam. However, even when the gymnast has great courage and attempts to work with strong coaching support, the tendency for the gymnast to hold back from making an all-out effort often results in falls and injury.

I believe that the gymnast's ability to overcome fear is most often the key to success. This, accompanied by other mental attributes, will enable the gymnast to maintain the high psychological discipline necessary to "tune out" the minor and major disturbances arising during competition. The important mental attributes in training for balance beam are self-motivation, patience, persistence, the ability to tolerate pain and discomfort, positive thinking, and concentration.

Many disturbances are encountered during the period of days, hours, and minutes preceding competition: pain from minor injuries and the mental stresses resulting from pressures placed on the gymnast by coaches, parents, and other gymnasts. I have seen gymnasts losing their confidence and composure over such minor disturbances as audience response to other gymnasts, flash bulbs, equipment arrangement, and facility lighting. The gymnast must develop the *inner discipline* to tune out these disturbances, because they will only inhibit performance.

Under the stress of competition, I have even seen gymnasts hold back or not perform their high risk tricks to the dismay of coaches and judges alike. The disappointment can be quickly measured by the look on the coach's face and the judges' unappreciative scores. The gymnast must seek to identify and reinforce the positive psychological factors necessary for successful performances under the scrutiny of the judges and audience. There is nothing like maintaining confidence in your own abilities and exhibiting the courage to retain high risk elements in your routines when the pressure is on. The audience is the most critical judge of all and their response is by far the greatest reward for your effort.

TRAINING

Gymnastics presents seemingly endless challenges to the skills of the gymnast at all levels of competition, and extensive training of mind and body is absolutely necessary. A core training program should include supplementary training to deal with special problems that occur as the body characteristics change with age and to deal with weight problems. In my own program, I utilized weight training and strict diets to meet strength and appearance requirements. My program consisted of scheduled five- and six-hour period workouts daily, except weekends. My weekends were generally utilized to catch up on my school work, religious and family activites, and relaxation. However, before any major competition these activities were sacrificed to concentrate on specific training problems and added drills in order to peak my performances.

- **Core Training** (Monday-Friday)   Hours Per Day
    - Warm-Ups (running and stretching). . . . . ½
    - Dance/Ballet. . . . . ½
    - Balance Beam 1½
    - Vault . . . . ¾
    - Uneven Bars. . . . . ¾
    - Floor and Tumbling. 1½
- **Supplementary**
    - Post-workout exercise on Universal weight machine . . . . . ½

My core training for event elements generally involved training with the team coach about 10–20% of the time with any time remaining devoted to unsupervised individual practice concentrating on areas of weakness.

Balance Beam

Balance beam practice was arranged to work my compulsory exercises two days per week and optional exercises three days. Each period on the beam included a warm-up of elementary moves, such as walking, running, leaping, and dismounting to get the feel of the apparatus. Then, under the coach's guidance, several full routines were performed with critique on each performance. Depending on the critique, the remaining time was utilized on either performing elements and portions of the routine or complete routines.

Vault

Vaulting practice was arranged to work both the compulsory and optional exercises each day. Warm-ups were conducted without spotting and crash pads utilized for practicing difficult vaults such as multiple-twisting and flipping vaults. Any spotting on vaults was limited to the learning phase of a new vault. Coaching assistance was sought after the warm-up period. Critique of each vault and demands for improvement of technique were obtained from the coach before performing the next vault.

Uneven Bars

Uneven parallel bar practice was arranged to work compulsory exercises two days a week and optional exercises three days. Warm-ups consisted of kips, stomach whips, front and back hip circles, and other swinging movements. A minimum of two full routines would be performed daily. A significant proportion of the training period was devoted to working individual elements or sequences. Great emphasis was placed on the body form and technique of each movement. Spotting was used only when learning new tricks or when safety required it.

Floor Exercise

Floor exercise was arranged to work the compulsory exercise two days a week and the optional exercises three days. Warm-ups consisted of stretching, tumbling, and dance skills, followed by a performance of a minimum of two full routines. Critique and the repetition of the problem elements was conducted after each routine. All special tumbling skills required for routines were developed on an individual basis with the coach as necessary to upgrade the optional exercises for competition.

Post-Workout Exercises

Post-workout exercises should be established to meet individual needs. In my program, a minimum weight-lifting exercise routine consisted of 50 situps, 20 leg-lifts, 20 bench presses at designated weights, 20 pull-ups, 20 leg extensions and select exercises that isolated and strengthened the muscles necessary to perform successfully elements in my routines. [*Ed. note:* See Jack Einheber's article on weight training for gymnasts in Chapter 12.]

DANCE EDUCATION

It takes years of effort and hard work to become an accomplished gymnast. A very important area of training often overlooked is dance. I believe that a youngster who learns dance *at an early age* and continues the activity as an adjunct to gymnastics has a decided advantage—especially later in the gymnastic career when called on to compose routines and select appropriate music.

Individual expression and dance skills are essential ingredients in composing interesting and artistic routines. Although a certain amount of classical ballet is absolutely necessary, the gymnast should also develop in jazz and interpretive modern dance. Many training programs do not allow sufficient time for the serious gymnast to participate in dance training. Some coaches feel that the demands of gymnastics preclude their protege from participating in outside activities. This attitude may be based on the fear of losing the athlete to another competing activity. As an alternative, more dance training should be conducted within private club training programs and allowances made in schedules to provide for more ballet and other dance training.

DIET

Gymnastics places great demands on physical fitness and energy. It is important to practice watching weight gains or losses at frequent intervals. Every pound of excess weight is an impediment to the gymnast's ability to perform with grace. It is important to maintain your center of gravity at a location as high as the body build allows.

Extra weight seems to settle on women around the thighs and hips. The result is disastrous in terms of appearance and performance. It has long been recognized that proper nutrition can be maintained without eating starchy and fatty foods such as candy, cakes, and potato chips. Crash diets sometimes sacrifice energy, stamina, and mental outlook. I found it extremely useful and enjoyable to eat the normal foods prepared for family living while monitoring my weight trends weekly. Once you are overweight it is extremely difficult to remove the excess from where it settled in an undesirable part of the body. If specific problems are encountered it is advisable to see a nutritionist for advice in dealing with the problem.

INTERNATIONAL COMPETITION

Before the 1976 Olympics, United States gymnasts were seldom entered into the big international competitions to gain the experience and reputation necessary to compete successfully in world class gymnastics. Much of the USGF effort was devoted to strengthening the sport within the United States and to raise funds essential for expanding future opportunities for women to compete at the international level. It was during this period of USGF expansion that foreign gymnasts were widely publicized throughout America to the detriment of our own competitors. The dependency of the USGF on foreign superstars to fill an arena has recently diminished since publicizing of our own outstanding gymnasts (such as Kurt Thomas and Kathy Johnson) has proven successful. A recent gymnastic event was attended by 30,000 spectators, even though Nadia Comaneci was not entered. With the growth of the sport in America, the USGF has expanded the training opportunities for our future superstars by establishing the Junior Elite Training Program. The Junior Elite Training Program along with other USGF sponsored clinics for elite-level gymnasts provides new hope that American gymnasts soon will be elevated to their rightful place in international gymnastics.

TRAINING EXPENSE

In contrast to the Eastern European training programs, where, for example, East German gymnasts are trained at the expense of the state, American gymnasts must survive and train primarily on parental support. This approach has resulted in a random scattering of training facilities and opportunities for children to get involved in the sport. The United States Association of Independent Gymnastic Clubs (USAIGC) has done much to promote the expansion of independent clubs and provide safety guidelines. Future activities by the USAIGC will be in the area of developing standards for hiring gymnastics instructors. Although these activities are greatly needed, the basic fact remains that survival of an independent club hinges on donations and contributions from parents and merchants within the community.

The expenses endured to compete and train at the elite level of gymnastics falls within a range of from $9,500 to $12,000 yearly depending upon whether the gymnast belongs to a private club or competes unattached. Coaching and training facilities expenses range from a monthly low of $100 to several hundred dollars even in situations where the coaches donate significant time and effort. The following costs for year around training include participation in both invitational and qualifying meets to the National championships. Included are the necessary travel expenses for the coach to accompany and handle the gymnast at each competition.

Gymnast Training	$1,200.00
Gymnast Travel	
Transportation Home & Gym	2,050.00
8 Major Competitions (Air/Auto)	1,800.00
Food and Lodging (24 days)	750.00
Coach Travel/Food and Lodging	2,550.00
Competition Entry Fees	250.00
Sports Equipment & Clothing	400.00
Medical/X-Ray/Therapy	500.00
Total	**$9,500.00**

8

Get That Program Going!

Janice and William Freeman

Girls' gymnastics programs are in great demand today, so great that even when facilities are available, it is difficult to find enough instructors to meet the teaching needs. This is particularly true in smaller communities that have potential for beginning programs in their city recreational programs, YMCA's and YWCA's, and schools—especially elementary schools. These organizations often are willing to pay well and purchase apparatus and equipment, but they need teachers.

You do *not* have to be highly trained or skilled to teach gymnastics or start community gymnastics programs. Though a background in gymnastics is very helpful, and the better the background the more advantageous to your teaching, what *is* needed is people who are highly motivated. You must *want* to learn about gymnastics (rather than just be *willing* to learn). You must have a concern for your students and a love for gymnastics. Good starting places for potential programs are the local recreation organizations of smaller cities or counties, often called "the Parks and Recreation." Another good place is in elementary schools that would like to have an outsider come in to supplement their regular physical education program.

When we relocated from an urban community in Oregon to

a rural community in North Carolina, we were immediately struck by the nonexistence of gymnastics in the community. Numerous high school graduates entering college had never even attempted a forward roll. We had little experience in gymnastics beyond the usual required school programs, but we enjoyed watching gymnastics performances and admired the skills of the top gymnasts.

William Freeman relates his experiences in starting a program—and its impact once it was underway: I asked for the opportunity to teach gymnastics to women in some college physical education classes on a work-study basis and even coached a small women's team for one season. Not only had the girls never competed before, most had never even had classes in gymnastics before coming to college.

After one year the principal of an elementary school in the adjacent county asked me to teach lessons to his students after school hours. The school board provided generous funds, and the principal bought mats, uneven bars, a mini-tramp, and constructed a balance beam, in addition to offering fair pay for the teaching.

By reading resource materials and attending clinics, conferences, and competitions, I was able to supplement my gymnastics knowledge and further develop my teaching methods and spotting skills. For any student of gymnastics there is a wealth of information available about teaching and learning gymnastics.

A lack of funds ended the college gymnastics class at the end of the year, but because of that program, several potential gymnastics teachers began to develop. The women involved assisted at the elementary school, and I was able to turn the elementary program over to them entirely when I was contacted six months later by the local superintendent of City Parks and Recreation, who was anxious to start a girls' gymnastics program there. My work then shifted to all age groups, permitting the development of a program that provided almost ideal working conditions and the funds to finance FIG-approved apparatus.

The college women who worked as "apprentice" teachers in these programs have since taken jobs at a nearby YMCA and in programs in other community educational systems. All of this has happened in just three years! The fact is, we can't seem to meet the demand!

ADMINISTRATION

The following material is intended to help potential teachers who need a starting point. Of course everything is relative, but we thought it might be helpful to relate what has worked for us.

Registration in the park program was scheduled for one week before classes began for each of the three sessions during the year. Each student had to pay a fee, which was invested in new apparatus, audiovisual materials, chalk, etc. The fee also included insurance coverage for each girl in the program. Adjustments in the fees were made for families with financial problems and those with more than one daughter in the program. Reduced fees were also available for returning students. By having registration one week before the start of the session each child could be covered by insurance from the start of the program, and there was a minimum of lost time on the first class day.

Three sessions were held each year, each lasting for about 14 lessons: fall session (learning new skills); winter session (learning the USGF compulsory routines); and spring session (composing optional routines). There was a break of several weeks over Christmas, a one week break for spring vacation, and a summer vacation of about two months. Classes were held on Saturdays, and an exhibition was scheduled for the parents and the public on the last Saturday evening of each session. The parents were informed of the dates of the exhibitions as soon as possible, so they could keep those nights available.

Because the last session ended in late June, the final lessons were turned into a "prep week," preparation for the year's final exhibition. The gymnasts met daily, Monday through Friday, for the final week. This was the time of the greatest improvement in skills, for it was the only time when the girls could train daily, rather than weekly.

The program grew rapidly, reaching a total enrollment of 75 girls after one-and-a-half years of operation. The numbers involved made it necessary to divide the groups, so three groups were set up for the Saturday classes. The junior high school girls (grades seven through nine) met from 8:00 to 11:00 in the morning, the fourth through sixth graders met from 11:00 a.m. to 1:00 p.m., and the first through third graders met from 1:00 to 3:00 p.m. The next natural division would be into groups by level of skills.

The program has been successful to the point that its growth has required schedule changes, age grouping, and even placing newcomers on a waiting list until we can meet the demand by getting more teaching assistants and more apparatus. Of course, this growth has allowed the financing of quality FIG-approved apparatus, the reduction of lesson fees, and the opportunity to discover exceptional talent and schedule exclusive team classes to help the more highly-skilled individuals to develop their full potential.

EQUIPMENT AND SAFETY

The apparatus needed is standard in women's gymnastics. Major items are the balance beam, uneven parallel bars, vaulting horse, Reuther board, tumbling mats, and crash pads. (A mini-tramp is a welcome addition, as is a trampoline, which was not available for the programs described.)

A new program generally operates under the handicap of limited funds. Safety equipment, such as crash mats, is excessively-priced. However, foam rubber is relatively economical, sometimes inexpensive, and can easily substitute as a crash mat. Scraps of foam rubber can be accumulated and then stuffed together with a vinyl cover.

A balance beam can be well-padded by draping a tumbling mat over it for practicing numerous skills: rolls, cartwheels, walkovers, etc. Benches or bleachers are ideal to use as training beams and are usually readily available.

Rubber tubing, or towels, or even foam rubber strips can be wrapped around the bars for padding, and foam rubber scraps can be inserted under the leotard where bruises might occur from striking the bar. Such padding is ideal for wraps and stomach whips.

The program will progress more easily if it has the use of a full gymnasium, rather than a confining smaller activity room. (The area required for floor exercise alone is 42 feet on each side.) If a gymnasium is shared, as most are, the buyer should look at the weight and mobility of the apparatus and equipment. As an example, one popular beam weighs almost 400 pounds, compared to an approved foreign beam which weighs 80 pounds, yet is more stable. Which one would you rather try to move? The best way to test the movability is just that: find one and try to move it.

TEACHING METHODS

Our major objective has been to make the program fun. As long as the children are having fun, they will have an unquenchable desire to learn new things and then enjoy practicing what they have learned. We want to describe some of the methods that were used successfully in our local community programs as factors of motivation and in developing an enjoyable learning experience.

Each child's progress can be recorded on large progression charts, which list each child down the side and different skills in order of difficulty from the easier to the harder across the top. This chart gives you a record of how each child is progressing and a means of evaluation. But, primarily, it allows the child to work progressively and keep track of what skills she needs to work on next without having to depend upon the teacher to tell her.

One of the child's basic urges is to be active. Highly structured programs that require long waiting lines, long lecture periods, or that demand quiet participation tend to stifle this urge and make the program less fun. To avoid long lines, prepare several stations of activity.

An ideal alternative, especially for elementary school children, is playing "follow the leader." The children are led in a line through a circuit of skills which have been learned before: walks and runs on the beam, rolls over the beam, mounts and dismounts on the bars, over the vaulting horse, jumps on the mini-tramp, through a tumbling station at a row of mats. Of course everyone follows the leader's example or else substitutes harder or easier skills, depending upon each person's preferences and abilities. This game keeps everyone active, requires almost no explanation, and reinforces skills. Try it to music!

Children also like contests. They enjoy seeing who can hold a V-seat the longest or stand on their heads the longest, or who can do the most pike leg lifts at the bars or who can switch their legs the most times in a split handstand on the beam.

Try to teach good technique by introducing fun games. Hold a broomstick in front of you and do a forward roll through it to come up with it behind you. This teaches them to think about staying tucked and in control throughout. Throw a ball up in front of you, do a forward roll, and catch the ball before it lands. Do a dive roll over a rope (holding the ends loosely, so the rope will fall if hit) and raise it gradually to increase the height of the dive. Do a *tour jete* by stepping up to the rope with the near leg and kicking and turning over the top of the rope with the far leg. This teaches them to kick before turning. Do a back handspring with a piece of foam rubber between your legs, first between the thighs, then between the ankles. This teaches them to avoid straddling the legs. Incorporate this technique in other skills and on other apparatus. Perform a back or front hip circle on the unevens while holding a piece of paper (such as a dollar bill) between your ankles.

These games can be introduced at parties. Schedule several parties during the year—perhaps at Christmas or for Valentine's Day. Provide refreshments or let the children bring Christmas candy or cookies that their mothers made or perhaps the children took part in making.

Good public relations can easily be developed by exhibiting a current bulletin board. Posters of recent gymnastics superstars, such as Nadia Comaneci and Olga Korbut, tend to motivate your gymnasts and impress the public. But also include photos of your own gymnasts. Children do things you don't think they can do, when you bring out the camera. Young children love to have their pictures taken! Be as proud to display their accomplishments as you are to display Olga's.

EXHIBITIONS

There is nothing that will motivate gymnasts more than the opportunity to demonstrate or compete. It is difficult to construct a reasonably brief (one to 1½ hours) exhibition when 75 children are participating, but it can be done very successfully. Each child can have the opportunity to perform individually as well as within the group.

A relatively painless system of preparing for an exhibition—

which features a personal appearance by every gymnast—is by making it a tandem effort. Have the children construct *short* combinations that include skills they feel they do particularly well (mini-routines) in the event of their choice (bars, beam, or floor). Schedule your class time to allow yourself the opportunity to work at each station, to work with each gymnast, one at a time. Watch each routine, gradually modifying it until all the routines have been refined. It is much easier to *refine* 75 routines than it is to *compose* 75 routines.

Train spotters to work on isolated skills at the different stations (bars, beam, floor, and vault). Parents are ready to give and will supply free labor. While you work at one station refining routines, the other gymnasts work on isolated skills at the other stations, which are manned by your trained spotters. The free exercise group may work at stations manned with spotters, they may work independently, or they may take a break to have refreshments, or simply rest. When you have watched each gymnast once at a given station, then rotate to the next station. After the children have been through this procedure a number of times, they are prepared to present their compositions.

To keep the exhibition from becoming monotonous or too long, schedule a rehearsal that will make the procedure clear to the gymnasts. If you are lucky enough to have or be able to borrow a second set of apparatus for the occasion, then one girl can be setting up her station while the other is performing and, consequently, be prepared to mount as soon as the first girl dismounts. This procedure will shorten the program by about one-half and will avoid interruptions to change landing mats, move beat boards, and readjust the uneven bars. Parents enjoy seeing their child apart from the crowd, and this type of exhibition affords them this opportunity.

Prepare a warm-up session before the exhibition and possibly begin with a short dance prelude that involves everyone together, perhaps ending with a tumbling exhibition or a vaulting demonstration, or a mini-tramp and crash mat finale. Try to end the program with a fun event. If there is a shortage of mats, you may find it necessary to allow a five-minute intermission when changing from apparatus to floor exercise to allow time to move the mats to the floor area.

Always remember: If you need help, turn to the parents. They are possibly your strongest source of support. Not only can the parents supply aid as spotters, but they are potential typists, dance instructors, pianists or public relations personnel.

9

The Oregon Experience

Judy Niesslein

The Russians and Romanians have enrolled their athletic champions in long-term education and training programs for years. The United States, on the other hand, makes no such provision—except perhaps for the Oregon experience.

A unique, accredited training program coordinated between the National Academy of Artistic Gymnastics and the Eugene public school system provides a superior course for athletes who aspire to high levels of achievement. Master instructors Dick Mulvihill and Linda Metheny hope that the program will develop champion gymnasts, but they also believe that gymnastics is more than competition. "It is every student working to his or her potential," whether that is learning new skills, being a member of the high school team, or just having fun. Thus, they have developed one of the most complete gymnastics training centers in the US today.

The Oregon Academy of Artistic Gymnastics (OAAG) and the National Academy of Artistic Gymnastics (NAAG) are part of a dual program stressing individual achievement. The OAAG provides recreational and competitive gymnastics instruction for beginner, intermediate and advanced students, while the NAAG provides superior training for those who wish to excel in gymnastics.

The Academy combines the expertise of coaches, dancing teachers, choreographers, and pianists who work with 250 students each year. In only three years, the Academy has produced Elite and even Olympic level woman gymnasts.

A 15,000-square-feet gymnasium facility houses both the OAAG and NAAG. It is a maze of equipment—eight sets of bars, 12 balance beams, six trampolines, a floor exercise mat, tumbling runway and vaulting section, plus safety pads, custom-designed training devices, and men's apparatus. There is also a dance area equipped with mirrors and barres, a training room with the latest therapy units, office, observation deck, locker room facilities, and a pro shop where gymnasts can purchase tights, warm-ups, shoes, etc. A dormitory facility only a few blocks from the Academy is available for gymnasts who live away from home. Dick Mulvihill's mother runs the dorm and serves as chief cook and house mother for the girls.

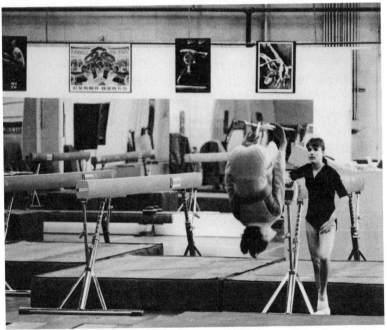

A gymnastic club—Oregon Gymnastics Academy (Marilou Sturges photo)

Dick Mulvihill, who oversees the entire program, has been coaching gymnastics for 15 years. He has helped coach many of our nation's international teams and has developed Olympic performers and Elite gymnasts since 1963. Linda Metheny, his wife, is one of America's foremost gymnasts. Having competed on three Olympic teams, she is well-known on the international scene. She was a premier gymnast on the beam and floor, US all-around champion for six years, and ranked in the top six all-around gymnasts in the world from 1970-72.

With this excellent program and top-ranking staff, students receive quality instruction in tumbling and apparatus, as well as motor learning, ballet, and modern dance. They learn compulsories, and optionals choreographed by the instructors. Classes meet as often as once a day for team members to once a week for recreational students. "Achievement is on an individual basis," explains Dick. "Students don't progress as a class, but as individuals. Thus, there must be personal contact between our coaches and our gymnasts."

Around 12:30 in the afternoon about 17 young gymnasts arrive at the National Academy to begin their warm-ups. The girls have just finished four hours of academic classes. The early arrival is unusual in comparison to most Elite gymnasts who don't begin their strenuous training until after school or evening.

At one o'clock Mulvihill begins the daily training by spotting each gymnast through a series of warm-up back handsprings. Next come sommies, layouts, full twists, and then handspring fronts. Several of the girls are working double fulls and arabians.

After tumbling, the team splits into groups of four for apparatus. Metheny coaches the advanced beam compulsory. "The arms move to here," she says, as she pushes Leslie Pyfer's arms into position. "I spend a lot of time correcting body line, pushing hips in, pressing shoulders down, and pulling rib cages up." The girls spend two hours repeating this routine 30 times. Afterward, they work on parts and new skills. Some of the gymnasts are performing phenomenal feats on this wooden plank. Would you believe a round-off back sommie mount? Or a full-twisting back on the beam? Metheny has a way of

Some clubs use sophisticated technology for teaching and safety
(Marilou Sturges photo)

combining these difficulties with dance to create beautifully choreographed routines.

Art Maddax, pianist for the Academy, helps Linda with the choreography of routines, and she thinks he's "terrific." His music is inspirational to floor exercise performers, but more than that, "Maddax has a good eye for movement," Metheny says.

Maddax works with his floor exercise group, accompanying each girl through three full optional routines, complete with tricks and without spots. Suddenly, the music stops as Art coaxes Karen Kelsall to put more expression into the middle of her routine. "Let's take it from that last tumbling pass," he says, and they begin again, perfecting the movement phrase.

Maddax, a Fulbright scholar, is not only the pianist-choreographer for the Academy, but has been the pianist and composer for the US National Teams since 1970.

Dean Barry handles the one-and-one-half hour bars workout. Each gymnast must perform six optional routines, as he assists them through handstands, twists, free-hips and maybe a stalter.

A graduate of the University of Oregon and the gymnastics coach at North Eugene High School, Dean choreographs all the gymnasts' bar routines.

The fourth group of gymnasts concentrates on vaulting. Dick spends forty-five minutes coaching the girls through about twenty vaults each. Most of the older girls do handspring-fulls or yami-fulls; however, the younger kids favor the Tsukahara. Dick speculates that a new category of vaults originating from a round-off off the reuther board (rather than a forward take-off) is up-and-coming.

In addition to their apparatus training, the gymnasts receive a one-hour ballet lesson each week. Their instructor, Sonya Robell, is a graduate of the Conservatory of Music in Kansas City, Missouri, and has danced professionally for many years.

"Dance has a lot to offer gymnastics," comments Linda. "Ballet teaches proper turn-out and body positions, while modern allows for the development of individual style."

The last half-hour of each workout day is devoted to power drills and warm-downs. All the gymnasts repeat the grueling sets of leg lifts, sit-ups, and pull-ups. In addition, the girls do back strengthening exercises, drills on a weight machine, and flexibilities.

By now, it's seven o'clock and the girls are ready for home and dinner.

"Linda and I have strong feelings on the values of working such long hours," Dick explains. "We hope to establish personal relationships between our coaches and gymnasts. We want to develop an appreciation for others' backgrounds and drives or lack of drives, as well as create an understanding of human nature. When you're working hard in such an intense training atmosphere these values become apparent."

The gymnast's performance is but the end result of
his or her training. This part covers step-by-step all aspects
of your training program:

Developing strength and stamina through weight training, so
vital for the strength events like the uneven and parallel bars,
rings, and pommel horse;

Increasing flexibility through traditional stretching exercises
and yoga, which is no longer a "mystical" Eastern meditation
practice but rather a balanced, effective method of developing
a flexible body and relaxed mind;

Forming an optimum diet to take into account the enormous
energy you will be burning during practices and competition.

3

PHYSICAL TRAINING

Mitsuo Tsukahara (Tony Duffy photo)

10

Warming Up

Valerie Braithwaite

For the best progress and stamina build up, you should keep to a strict routine. Plan your training schedule accordingly. Have a notebook and make a list of the movements and exercises that you intend doing, then vary it slightly from day to day, adding new moves and ideas. This is especially effective if you attend a class once or twice a week and practice alone the rest of the time.

Get into the habit of always starting with about fifteen minutes of warm-up exercises. (You may need to spend longer before attempting some of the more intricate moves.) Here is a variety of exercises that will stretch and loosen the muscles.

● **Figure One.** Lying stomach-down, place your palms on the floor next to your hips. Now push your head and shoulders back until your arms are straight. Hold the position. Having done this several times, bend the legs up behind you, and catching hold of each ankle, rock back and forth trying to lift the chest and thighs as high off the floor as possible. Put your hands back on the floor in the first position, still keeping the legs bent. Try bringing them up to touch the back of your head. This may seem difficult at first, especially if your back is stiff, but daily stretching will soon loosen it up.

71

● **Figure Two**. Stand in a normal position, knees straight and feet together. Bend forward until you can grasp your ankles. Keeping your knees absolutely straight, try to pull the head toward them. If you can get your head right against the knees without bending them and can hold the position for a few seconds, you will give the back of the legs a good stretch.

● **Figure Three.** Another stretch for the legs is to sit on the floor and with the legs in as wide a straddle as possible. Take both arms over to the right foot and hold, then repeat to the left, each time pulling the chest down to the leg. Still in the straddle position, reach forward with the arms as far as you can, trying to get the chest flat on the floor.

● **Figure Four.** Now for a slightly harder one—this time from a sitting position, feet together with both legs stretched out in front of you, bend forward and grasp the right ankle with both hands (**4A**). Now lift the leg right up until you are able to lie down still holding the ankle (**4B**). Hold the position. Return to the start. The important thing is to try to keep the other leg on the floor throughout the exercise, and of course, to keep both legs straight. Having done this three or four times with the right leg do exactly the same thing with the left.

4A

4B

Daily repetitions of these exercises will help loosen and strengthen the spine, legs and stomach muscles. Once you have conditioned the body there are no limitations to what you can achieve with some hard work.

The best and most progressive way to limber up is by "passive" stretching; that is, without bouncing. Practice and remember, anyone can practice when they feel like it; it's the gymnasts who practice when they don't feel like it that achieve success.

11

A Flexible Plan

Dr. Linda Carpenter

Flexibility, or the ability of a joint to move through an entire range of motion, is a critical quality for the gymnast to develop. Research on flexibility reveals several findings that should form the scientific basis for developing a program to improve flexibility.

First, we find a general agreement that flexibility can, in fact, be increased with the use of appropriate techniques. Some individuals will increase flexibility faster than others, but all can increase flexibility to a remarkable extent.

We find that males are generally less flexible than females. Pelvis structure adds to the female's innate advantage, but she is also more flexible in the back and shoulder areas where differences in skeletal structure do not seem to play a role. One might hypothesize that "socially related behavior patterns" (e.g., dance training in childhood, etc.) contribute to the flexibility differences between males and females. Therefore, the learning of skills requiring an extended range of motion may be more difficult for the male gymnast until sufficient flexibility is developed. (The requirement of a flexibility skill in men's floor exercise seems to acknowledge that the demonstration of flexibility is more difficult for the male than the female.)

Bart Conner demonstrates Olympic-caliber flexibility
(Marilou Sturges photo)

Flexibility is very specific to the joint involved. In other words, a gymnast who can perform splits with great ease may possibly have a particularly inflexible back or shoulder region. Thus, the gymnastics teacher or coach must design programs that develop flexibility in all areas of the body.

Generally, flexibility exercises are divided into two types: phasic and static. *Phasic* exercises include *ballistic* or "bobbing" type exercises such as toe-touching with a rhythmical up-and-down action. *Static* exercises may best be described as stretching the muscle in question until the "stretch pain" is reached, then holding that stretch pain position for a period of time without motion.

Research findings have demonstrated that the long-term flexibility is served equally well by phasic and static exercises. Even though phasic exercises may produce a larger increase in flexibility on a given day, they also produce discomfort the following day. In addition, the use of phasic exercises increases the risk of developing small muscle tears. Thus, the knowledgeable coach or teacher will generally avoid the use of phasic (bobbing) type exercises, being aware that static exercises will produce the same long-term result with less soreness and a smaller risk of injury.

Static flexibility exercises have been found to involve the stretch reflex (myostatic reflex) to a much smaller degree. Therefore, static exercises are less likely to produce muscular soreness or injury. The use of reciprocal inhibition (inhibition of the stretch reflex by voluntary contraction of the antagonist muscle) adds even greater weight to the research evidence supporting the use of static flexibility exercises. Put simply, the use of reciprocal inhibition means that the gymnast who is statically stretching the hamstrings will, at the same time, voluntarily contract the quadriceps (antagonist) area.

Although only sketchy tabular data are available, the incidence of injury resulting from two-person flexibility exercises is quite high. Using one gymnast to pull, push, or simply apply weight to another's flexibility exercise is to invite an excessive stretch. The stretching gymnast has relinquished voluntary control over the degree of stretching. Thus, if the second person is less than perceptive of the last eighth inch of stretching that can be safely tolerated, the gymnast will suffer tissue damage.

Some Practical Applications

Each movable joint in the body is capable of increased flexibility. However, for a gymnast there are six areas of the body which frequently must demonstrate an increased range of motion: hamstrings, leg adductors, quadriceps (hip flexors), ankle dorsa-flexors, lumbar region of the back and shoulders.

In order to increase flexibility in any of the above six areas, the muscles inhibiting the range of motion should he identified and then put on stretch according to the scientific principles relating to flexibility. It is important to remember that flexibility can be obtained through a variety of appropriate exercises. The exercises included below are intended as illustrations rather than exclusive programs.

● **Hamstrings.** Hamstring flexibility is necessary for any deep pike position. The hamstring area seems to be the region most frequently stretched in the search for flexibility. An appropriate exercise involves sitting on the floor with legs together and knees extended and locked. (See diagram 1.) While maintaining a straight back the gymnast reaches toward the feet and stops at the stretch pain. This position is held while consciously contracting the quadriceps (antagonist muscle). (See diagram 2.) Depending on the dedication and pain tolerance of the gymnast, this position may be held fifteen seconds, thirty seconds, or even one minute before relaxing. This exercise is rather straight-

forward and typical but it is important to remember that
(1) the back should not be rounded; (2) the knees should be
forcefully extended and locked during the exercise; and (3)
the exercise is a static one—*no bobbing*.

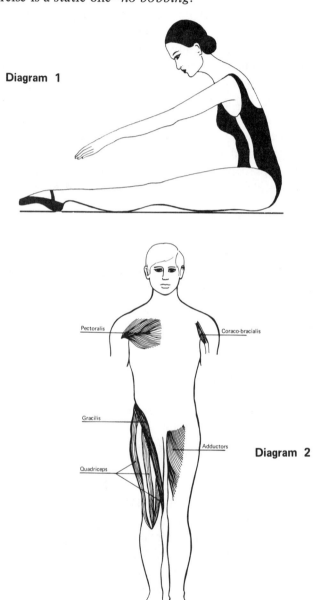

Diagram 1

Pectoralis

Coraco-bracialis

Gracilis

Adductors

Quadriceps

Diagram 2

● **Quadriceps.** Gymnasts who don't include splits in their routines still need split flexibility for correct and effective performance of such moves as walkovers, valdezes, and tinsicas. Any gymnast who can assume the starting position for the hamstring exercise has sufficient hamstring flexibility for the splits. The area generally needing increased flexibility is rather the quadriceps area or the big muscle in the front of the upper leg. (See diagram 3.) Most gymnasts who are unable to perform the splits will demonstrate a forward tilt of the hips caused by insufficient quadriceps flexibility.

A quadriceps exercise that follows the research-based principle discussed earlier involves the use of a pile of mats, a bed, or some such elevated platform about two-and-one-half feet above the ground. While sitting on the mats with the forward leg dropped down over the edge of the mats at the knee, the gymnast assumes a split position with the back leg. (See diagram 4.) The gymnast then simply tilts the pelvis backward until a stretch pain is felt in the quadriceps and gracilis area of the back leg. (See diagram 2.) This position of stretch pain is again held statically for fifteen, thirty, or a full sixty seconds depending on the gymnast. The quadriceps exercise should be repeated with the opposite leg forward.

Diagram 3

Diagram 4

● **Adductors.** Side splits are difficult to execute primarily because of insufficient flexibility in the adductor region of the inner thigh. (See diagram 2.) We have found the following exercise to be the most effective means of improving flexibility in the adductor region. While sitting on the floor, the gymnast slides the hips as close to the wall as possible. Then the gymnast lies down on the floor (head away from the wall) while putting the extended legs up the wall. The legs are then separated and allowed to proceed down the wall until a stretch pain is reached. (See diagram 5.) We have found that the pull of gravity provides a sufficient stretch if the static position is held for several minutes. The knees should remain extended but the gymnast should also concentrate on relaxing the adductor region.

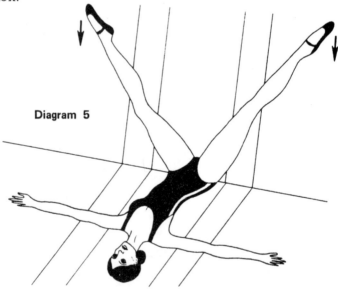

Diagram 5

● **Ankle Dorsa-flexors.** Inadequate ankle extension is a frequent problem for the male gymnast. He can work on ankle flexibility by assuming a kneeling position with the tips of the feet on the floor. Ankle flexibility is increased by simply shifting the weight backward so that the knees lift from the floor slightly. Assuming the starting position without lifting the knees may be a sufficient stretch for the particularly inflexible gymnast. Again, the longer the gymnast maintains the position, the greater the benefit. (See diagram 6.)

Diagram 6

● **Back flexibility**. Most female gymnasts have sufficient lumbar back flexibility, even though they frequently lack shoulder flexibility. Males are frequently quite inflexible in both regions and upper back is often referred to as an area needing particular improvement. However, a review of the vertebral skeletal structure reminds us that the lengthened spinous process of the thoracic vertebrae inhibits the upper back from extending much beyond a straight position. Therefore, with this in mind, the term "upper back flexibility" is of little importance. Rather the areas needing particular attention are the shoulder and lumbar regions. (See diagram 7.)

The typical bridge position with legs pushing the body weight slightly toward the arms is an exercise for developing both shoulder (coraco-brach/pectoral) and back flexibility. (See diagram 2.) The stretch pain should be particularly noticed in the coraco-brachialis region rather than only in the small of the back. This is even more important among female gymnasts who are usually sufficiently flexible in the lumbar region.

Diagram 7

● **Shoulders**. Insufficient shoulder flexibility inhibits the correct performance of almost all inverted movements. Tight shoulders are characterized in the hand-stand position by too much back arch or by the shoulders being located in front of the hands instead of directly over them.

An example of a static flexibility exercise that will improve flexibility involves standing about three feet from a blank wall and placing the hands on the wall at head height with the elbows straight. The gymnast then arches and attempts to force the shoulders toward the floor until the stretch pain is felt. Once again, this position can be maintained fifteen, thirty, or sixty seconds depending on the tolerance of the gymnast. (See diagram 8.)

Diagram 8

12

Weight Training for Gymnastics

Jack Einheber

Weight training is an activity that is often subjected to stereotype and myth. People tend to think of weight training as involving solely long bars with one or more spheres or plates at each end (barbells) or short bars or handles with one or more smaller plates at each each (dumbbells). What the stereotypers do not realize is that common household items such as books, chairs, and such can be employed as weights in weight training. There is nothing sacred about the weights seen in a weight room, except in terms of efficiency and maneuverability.

Many people stereotype users of weights. In the past "weight lifters" have been thought of as being big and stupid (perhaps the slang connotation of the word *dumbbell* originated here). What many people do not realize is that weight training is merely one of many forms of *resistance exercise* (working against an opposing or retarding force), and that weight training can be employed intelligently and strategically to enhance performance greatly in a vast variety of physical activities, including gymnastics.

Just as regular physical activity should be carefully integrated into one's life, weight training should be carefully integrated into gymnastics training. Everyone responds to exercise in a unique way. In other words, the same exercise or exercise regimen will not produce the same effect at all times. People go through daily, monthly, and seasonal variations. Therefore, it is essential to monitor the effects of weight training, since it is an activity that can take on many forms. Monitoring in this case means listening to sensory feedback from the body, looking in the mirror and touching (palpating) body parts to see how they are responding to the weight training.

Careful monitoring is not sufficient, however; interpretation of the findings is also essential. Proper planning and evaluation can expedite achievement and enjoyment, whereas lack of it can have the opposite result. For example, if gymnasts paid attention to non-painful sensations in the knee, they might prevent more serious injury by changing their routine or laying off altogether. In addition, the body's response to activity is often deceptive. Soreness or even injuries are often not detected until 24 or 48 hours or even more after the causal event.

Initial Phases

In the initial phases of weight training it is unwise to compare your ability or progress to someone else's. Each athlete has different levels and types of experience and each has a certain genetic endowment. It may not be fair (but unfortunately true) that these aspects play a major role in potential and achievement. Motivation and effort alone cannot compensate for all. This is not to say that a great deal cannot be done with the potential we all have. Few of us even come close to our potential, and it is not unusual for the one who starts at the lowest level to reach the highest achievement. Well-planned and wise weight training programs can make the difference between success and failure in a sport, and there is no substitute for hard, concentrated work. Of course, one can also work too hard (overtrain or incur injury) and therefore temperance and gradual progress are equally important.

In weight training the conscious mind imposes a certain workload on the body. Depending on the pattern and intensity of the workload, the part of the mind in charge of physiology and metabolism then alters the body to accommodate the work demand. Different work demands (bodybuilding exercise, powerlifting, olympic lifting, etc.) require different responses in the size and shape of the muscles, other soft tissue, and bone to these various forms of work demands.

Basic Principles of Weight Training

1. **Start with resistance you can handle easily.** At the beginning stages of weight training the muscles and other soft tissues learn or accommodate to perform the movements. For many people apparent progress in the beginning stages is quite rapid while the body is getting used to the exercise. Do not overdo it or injury becomes more likely.

2. **Build up gradually.** In ancient Greek history there is the story of Milo of Crotona, a wrestler who trained with a calf, which he carried on his shoulders every day until it grew to its full size. Each day the calf grew so little that the change in weight was hardly noticeable, and each day the man became imperceptably stronger. The man was very strong by the time the calf was fully grown. This story illustrates the principle of gradual buildup or progression in weight training. Give the body a chance to meet up to the work demand.

3. **Once you are accustomed to weight training, employ the principle of overload.** Applying the principle of overload means that you make your body perform work at a higher load than it was previously used to doing. After building a good foundation this principle is important for rapid and intensive progress. "Pumping out" those last few repetitions of an exercise, pushing the body past the point that it has previously gone, even sometimes past the point where you feel it can go—that is how rapid substantial progress is accomplished. It takes experience and careful analysis, however, not to over-exert. This is why progression is so important and also why the individual should take into account and accept fluctuations and "off days" or "off periods" when his or her performance level is not quite up to par.

Along similar lines there is often a fine line between training optimally and overtraining. Determining or getting a feel for this line can be an art, particularly in light of the myriad variables affecting human fluctuations. In addition to the daily, monthly, and seasonal fluctuations mentioned above (which incidentally are clearly manifested in temperature fluctuations and substantial changes in humoral or blood components)[1] performance can change through alterations in life situations that affect moods and motivations. Stress due to school or work, relationship problems, financial problems, may all affect physical performance.

Avoiding injury cannot be emphasized enough. Soft tissue injuries take only a fraction of a second to incur, but may take weeks, months, and even years to heal (if given adequate rest and care). If an initial injury is not given adequate opportunity to heal through rest and progressive re-education and reconstruction, it can become chronic and often does. Once the injury occurs a second time, it has a great chance of re-occuring periodically. Therefore it is important to avoid initial injury or to give an initial injury sufficient care and time to heal properly, and that means in some cases not using the affected part until a week or two after all pain has subsided, which could be many months after the initial injury. This is particularly important in soft tissue injury (muscle, tendon, ligament, and cartilege), which, unlike bone, may not be as functional as before the injury. Once an injury recurs, the quality of the damaged tissue often declines substantially.

4. Apply the principle of specificity. Weight training exercises should be designed to duplicate as nearly as possible the gymnastics movements you are training towards. Not only should the pattern of movement be similar, but the speed should also be similar. My own experience implies that weight training exercises performed rapidly have more carryover to movements at slower speeds than slow movements do to faster speeds. Although there has not been extensive research in this area, there have been some studies[2] to support this notion.

Rapidly executed training movements, however, may be jerky or too quick for all the tissue to accommodate, and thus there is a greater chance of injury in some persons. However, if principles (1) and (2) are followed, the chances of injury are reduced. Also, the danger of injury may be less in gymnasts than in most other sports, as gymnasts are generally accustomed to performing rapid, explosive movements.

5. Warm up before weight training and stretch after its completion. Warmup (raising the body temperature through physical activity) reduces inhibitions, making higher level of performance possible and reducing the chances of injury. Although scientific research in this area is not conclusive, my experience and that of colleagues support these notions.

6. Do not believe everything you read or hear about exercise with weights. This is very important. There are few areas where so much nonsense is perpetuated as in weight exercise. I have often heard people in capacities of instruction and other capacities of responsibility at well-known institutions dispense total nonsense. Be wary of patent prescriptions and gross generalizations. Be wary of prescriptions for rehabilitating injured areas, particularly knees, lower back, and shoulders. Few exercises are universally advantageous in the case of injury because injuries vary so greatly from person to person in the same body part. In addition, some exercises would be beneficial if the participant were ready for them, but if they are embarked on too soon they can be harmful. For example, back hyperextensions (arching the back) can be highly beneficial to persons with a certain amount of back strength, but on the other hand can be detrimental to those who do not possess a certain basic level of fitness. There is no substitute for good judgment based on careful self-analysis. One must be a detective to see if a certain exercise or routine works in his or her case.

Exercise Routine

Bearing in mind these principles, here is a basic weight training program. In the beginning stages it is often safer to use machine weight, such as the Universal-type or light free weights. For more advanced work free weights are probably superior, or a combination of free weights and machines (including isokinetic machines) may be optimal. Free weights have the advantage of employing stabilizing muscles; machine weights on the other hand assume much of the work load, but are in some ways safer.

Weight training can be particularly effective in building up weak areas. These areas can usually be spotted by coaches. This regimen can be followed for a total body program; following it there are specific exercises for particular movements and weaknesses. (A *repetition* refers to one complete movement; a *set* is a group of repetitions; the amount of weight to be finally employed is learned through trial and error, the suggested percentages are merely rough guidelines.)

Exercise	Routine during heavy gymnastics practice season	Routine during light gymnastics practice season
1. Power cleans	4 sets, 4-8 repetitions First set light, second intermediate, third heaviest, fourth intermediate. First set should be at about 40% bodyweight, take several weeks or months to build up to 100% to 150% of bodyweight for heavy set.	4-7 sets, 5-8 reps (Use more gradual progression over sets to reach maximum weight to be used in 4th and 5th sets, come down in weight during 6th and 7th sets.)

Power Clean

2. Power pulls   3 sets (second heaviest), 4-8 reps   4-6 sets, 5-8 reps

This exercise follows the power cleans progression and is of the same nature: start light, build up to heaviest, and then decrease weights progressively through the latter sets. Forty—50% bodyweight for 1st set building up to 100-175% bodyweight after some time for the heavy set.

3. Quarter jump squats   4 sets, 8-15 reps   5-7 sets, 8-20 reps

Position of lower body and feet should resemble the position of jumping to be used in the actual gymnastics movement. First set 40-50% of bodyweight buildup over time to 100-250% of bodyweight, but do not sacrifice speed and explosive movement for weight. These latter factors are the key in this exercise.

Do half of the sets with the leaper and one-half with the free weight barbell.

Or: use the isokinetic leaper machine if available as a supplement.

Quarter Jump Squat

4. Leg extension   4 sets, 10-15 reps   4-6 sets, 12-20 reps

---

5. Leg curl   4 sets, 10-12 reps   4-6 sets, 12-15 reps

First set of each is light, second one is heavier, try to maintain fairly rapid movement, but do not hyperextend the knee joint (do not extend past the straightening point); to be on the safe side stop the movement just before knee joint is totally straightened. Alternate with exercise 4.

Leg Curl

Exercises 1-5 can be performed 2-3 times per week, a good average being about 5 times during each two-week period.

**6. Bench
press or
chest
press**

4 sets, 8-12 reps
First set is light, build up to doing
heaviest weight during the 3rd set then
come down; sets 2 and 4 are intermediate weight. First set 50% of
bodyweight.

5-8 sets, 8-12 reps
Build up from
light 1st set to
heavy 4th and
5th sets then
come down pro-
gressively.

The latter half of this exercise should be exploded out and the
maximum weight to be employed is one which can be exploded outwardly.

Bench (Chest) Press

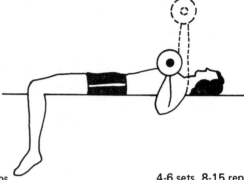

**7. Bar
dips**

4 sets, 8-12 reps
Alternate with exercise 6.

4-6 sets, 8-15 reps

**8. Front
lat
pull-
down**

3 sets, 6-12 reps
First set light, 2nd and 3rd heavy.
20% bodyweight, building over time to
50% or more, using explosive movement

3-6 sets, 8-15 reps
First set light,
build up to heavy
4th and 5th sets
with last set being
of intermediate
weight.

Front Lat Pulldown

Seated Lat Pulldown

9. Seated lat pull-downs
3 sets, 8-15 reps
Same progression as in 8, but starting with 40% and building over time to 100-110% of bodyweight. Alternate with exercise 8.

3-6 sets, 10-20 reps

---

10. Military press
4 sets, 8-10 reps using explosive force, 35% bodyweight, 1st set light, remainder maximum or near maximum with explosive force.

4-6 sets, 1st set light, 2nd and 6th intermediate, rest near maximum.

Military Press

11. Curls with barbell
4 sets, 8-12 reps
Explosive upward movement, slow controlled return; 1st set light 35% bodyweight building over time to maximum that can be handled. Alternate with exercise.

6-9 sets, 8-15 reps
Explosive upward movement, slow controlled return.

Curls with Barbell

12. Triceps extensions 3 double sets (one of each pictured below); 1st set light 50% bodyweight building over time to maximum that can be handled; use explosive extension and controlled return. Alternate the two exercises below and these constitute one group of triceps extensions within exercise 12. *Note:* elbows should be as fixed as possible and close together to isolate the triceps muscles.

4-6 double sets First set light 40% bodyweight and following sets near maximum or maximum that can be employed explosively.

In arm work there should be as little rest as possible between sets.

Triceps Extension

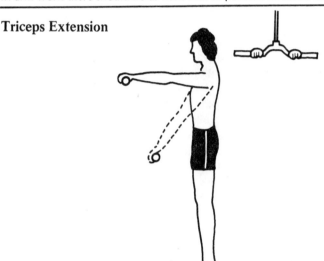

Exercises 6 through 12 should be done 3 times weekly.

For special purposes sample additional exercises can be incorporated into the program in addition to the above exercises or as substitutes for some of the above exercises. It is important to note that the routine described above, including the recommended weight percentages to be employed, the number of sets and repetitions, and the frequency of performance, are merely rough guidelines, and it is up to the gymnast to use a system of monitoring and analysis to determine whether these are meeting his purposes. It is with these thoughts in mind that the following additional exercises are also presented.

Supplementary Exercises

If adding the following to your routine, use 2-4 sets; if substituting them for some of the above use similar patterns of reps and sets to those listed above. In all cases the first set should be light building up to heavy weights in the later sets and using explosive movements in execution of the exercises.

Dislocate pulldowns. 8-10 reps.

Front dumbbell raises. 8-10 reps.

Incline bench press. 8-15 reps.

Side dumbbell raises. 8-12 reps. Movement is upward until hands are at shoulder level and then it is backward; in the backward portion of the movement the shoulder blades are brought closer together as though trying to make them touch.

Side pulley pulldowns. 8-12 reps.

Situps. 1-3 sets of 15-50 reps performed rapidly; if situps cause back pain they should be performed with knees bent.

Hanging leg raises. 2-3 sets 8-15 reps; 1st set rapid up and down movements, second set controlled up and down movements, slowly performed; 3rd set rapid up and slow controlled down movement.

Wrist curls (palms up). 15-30 reps or until burning sensation occurs (the exercise should be performed through at least several reps of the burning sensation). Supplement wrist curls with wrist turning exercises on the Universal machine wrist station where available and try to use it in all possible fashions (palms up turning away and then turning toward the body, palms down turning away and then toward the body, also rotating handle from the side).

Toe rises. Barbell is held behind the neck. These should be performed rapidly and explosively. 15-50 reps or until burning sensation occurs and persists through at least several repetitions. It is extremely important to stretch the calf muscle, even up to 5 or more times daily, since if it tightens, which it often does in athletes, it elongates the Achilles tendon and causes it to become thin.

Ankle builders. Use surgical tubing or a looped attachment which can fit over the foot and be attached to a pulley system such as one on the Universal machine. It is also possible to apply resistance to the normal ankle motions with the other foot or have a partner apply such resistance by hand. Start off with isometric exercise (applying force in a fixed position) in various positions, then as time goes on move the ankle through its range of motion against the resistance, both in an outward and up, and inward and upward direction (or in just the direction of the side that has a weakness). The latter steps should be employed initially in the case of a weak or rehabilitating ankle.

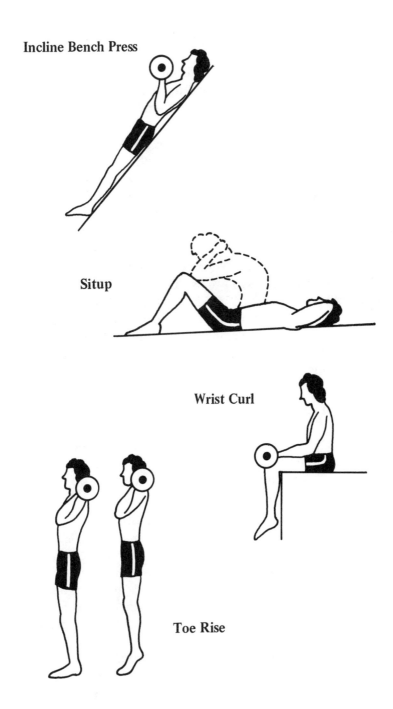

Incline Bench Press

Situp

Wrist Curl

Toe Rise

General Concepts

Rest. The less rest between sets, the more effective the exercise; however, less rest may mean more risk of injury. Too much rest, on the other hand, may also increase injury risk because the soft tissue may cool down and tighten. Depending on atmospheric temperature and other factors, one should not rest much more than two minutes between sets, nor much less than 30 seconds (unless you alternate, in which case there is little or no rest between the exercises being alternated).

Breathing. There is no proven correct way; just breathe as you feel comfortable.[3] (There are a few exercises in which a specific breathing pattern is advantageous, e.g., the stiff-arm pullover in which it is better to inhale while lowering the weight over your head toward the floor and exhale upon return, but in general there is no best way for most exercises.)

Recognizing fatigue symptoms. This is extremely important particularly when involved in a heavy gymnastics regimen. It is easy to overdo exercise and all individuals have different tolerances; moreover, these tolerances vary from time to time within an individual. It is also important to build up this tolerance, one reason for the importance of a slow start and gradual progression. Symptoms which *may* indicate excessive exercise are:

- Loss of appetite
- Irritability
- Inability to fall asleep; restlessness in bed at night
- Fuzziness or haziness in thought
- Shying away from exercise as a horse shies from a jump
- Restlessness and inability to concentrate

These symptoms could also indicate other conditions, of course, but they may be due to over-exercise. The gymnast's workload is often very demanding and it may be too much for some gymnasts to combine a gymnastics regimen with weight training program. Particularly during the heavy workout gymnastics season, the gymnast may have to work out very lightly with weights building up the weight routine very gradually over time.

What pattern of progress can be expected in weight training? Progress often looks like a slightly elevated roller coaster, i.e., peaks and valleys but moving always upward. Plateaus are also common, so the progress pattern may not include the "dip" or decrease in performance. In any case it is probably wisest to be reasonably patient with yourself. The body has innate wisdom and it improves at its own speed, often when one least expects such improvement.

Layoffs. Reynolds suggests varying one's routine every four to six weeks with a one-week rest period approximately every two months in order to allow the body to reconsolidate.[4] This seems to be an effective general notion, particularly if you can stay relaxed during the rest period. Also, it is highly recommended that you alter your routine (exercises) periodically to prevent staleness and regression.

Overcoming barriers in weight training. Partners can help with weights by allowing you to slowly lower the weight to its original position. This type of procedure often allows you eventually to get through the movement at the desired weight by yourself. For movements that do not require aid, such as bar dips or pullups where the person can jump up to the bar(s), lowering yourself slowly will help to achieve the upward movement. The same muscles that lower your body raise it in the initial phase of the movement.

Isokinetic exercise. Weight training exercises through a range of movement are known as isotonic exercises. (Contraction without movement or against an immovable object is *isometric exercise.*) Isokinetic exercise is force applied against resistance that is set to move only at a certain speed; this speed is adjustable but remains constant once it is set for a particular movement. In other words the speed can be set anywhere from (say) 0 to 216 degrees per second, but once it is set for a particular movement that is the maximum it will be for that movement. Therefore a person can exert maximum force throughout the range of motion because the lever arm of the isokinetic machine will not move any faster than it is set. Thus one can exert 3 lbs. or 300 lbs. of force and the machine's handle will still move only at the set speed. Therefore this type of exercise is known as *accommodative resistance* exercise. It can accommodate the moving body part through the various changes in its force exertion which occur as the leverage changes naturally through the range of movement. Because of leverage changes or changes in mechanics, the maximum force that a person can exert throughout the range of movement varies. With a free weight, you have to select one that is light enough to bring you through the weakest part of the movement, thus sacrificing the amount of resistance through the stronger parts of the movement, and not allowing the muscle groups involved to exert maximally throughout that range.

Isokinetic exercise may prove to be the safest form of rehabilitative exercise because you can let up during a weak range or range where an injury shows up most. The disadvantages may be that without sufficient motivation you may unconsciously slack off in applying force, possibly decreasing the benefits of the exercise, whereas with a weight you are usually motivated to complete the movement in total.

Although research regarding isokinetic exercise is scant, it may become very popular, either alone or in combination with free weights. Look for it.

In weight training as in all exercise, there is no substitute for sound logical reasoning based on complete knowledge. Get to know yourself. It often takes a good detective to formulate a good exercise program. Look to your coaches for advice, but remember not to sell your own analyses short. If properly employed, weight training and other adjunctive resistance exercise can be incredibly valuable tools for maximizing achievement in gymnastics.

References

1. Einheber, J. "Circadian Rhythms in Exercise," unpublished research review, 1977.

2. Pipes, T.V. and Wilmore, J.H., "Isokinetic versus Isotonic Strength Training in Adult Men"; **Medicine and Science in Sports;** 7(4): 262-274, Winter, 1975.

3. Reynolds, B., Unpublished Class Handout Notes at the University of California at Berkeley, 1976.

4. Ibid.

13

The Dynamic Yoga

Daniel Millman

Yoga is the ideal basis for gymnastics. Great sensitivity is required to achieve the refined timing, balance, and reflexes necessary to excel in gymnastics; the intense relaxation and concentration generated in yoga practice can give students this great sensitivity. G.S. Khalsa, Director of the Kundalini Research Institute, reports that after practicing meditation, one football player commented that he could "feel" whether the opposing lineman would move to the right or to the left. Research indicates that proper yoga warm-up can help balance all the body systems by opening up the flow of energy along the "classical meridians" described in acupuncture literature. This allows daily training to be more effective and can decrease the incidence of injuries.

Yet, yoga is far more than just a good warm-up. It is a way to reawaken our ultimate human potential by unifying our three centers, intellectual, emotional, and movement—vitality. As this occurs, a greater unity is experienced between ourselves and others, the world, and the entire universe.

To develop unity among the three centers requires the intense *involvement* of all three centers. Thus, merely an exclusively physical, mental, or emotional approach will not suffice. Whole-being activity is essential. Yoga, then, should not only be studied, it must be understood, felt, and brought into action as a *way of life.*

There are many yogas (many ways to unity) each suited to a particular temperament and psychology. For those who are inclined to deep, universal understanding and clarity, there is *jnana yoga* (the yoga of transcendental knowledge); for those of an emotional character, there is *bhakta yoga* (the yoga of loving surrender to the Source through a spiritual master); for those capable of selfless service to others, there is *karma yoga* (the yoga of working without reason, through love). Many yogis, saints, and sages of the past have followed one or more of these primary paths. Further, all true paths are one, and ultimately merge. One thing they have in common is the commitment to a way of life.

There are many other traditions, many paths toward unity. The best known yoga, however, and the primary subject of this article is *hatha yoga.* We normally refer to this form of yoga simply as "yoga." Hatha (*ha*—sun, *tha*—moon) refers to the "sun" and "moon" within the human body. The body is the "sun," and the mind, the "moon." Hatha means a balancing of the "sun" and "moon," or an approach to body-mind harmony.

Hatha yoga appears to be a kind of physical discipline. It consists of the practice of a series of postures (asanas), usually combined with *pranayama.* (*Prana* refers to breath or life-energy; *yama* means an observance. Thus pranayama, is breath-practice, or in a more esoteric sense, control of life energy). Hatha yoga involves a whole way of life, including all the elements of devotion, service, and understanding. Most specifically it is a way of developing a body of great suppleness, vitality, and energy to allow a high level of conscious awareness. In this way, the body becomes a fertile field from which grow seeds of clarity and love, to best serve humanity. Even on the most mundane level, hatha yoga can help develop superior health and well-being—a necessary requisite for gymnastics!

The development of *balance* permeates every aspect of hatha yoga: The postures are designed to develop symmetry and balance in the body (between back and front, right and left) and to balance the psyche (between pleasure and pain, between extremes of any kind).

If hatha yoga were only flexibility or relaxation exercises, most gymnasts would be instant yogis, because most gymnasts can perform many of the more advanced yoga postures better than many old yogis! Our gymnastics warm-up exercises incorporate many traditional yoga postures, in fact. To understand yoga, and to begin to see how gymnastics can be a yoga, it's necessary to understand the idea of a Way.

In our culture, practicality and directness is valued. When you make tea, you do it as simply and efficiently as possible so you can drink it. Nothing could be more obvious. In Japan, however, there is a tea ceremony, which creates a lengthy, serene, and graceful ritual out of preparing and serving tea. The practice of serving tea is treated not as an end in itself, but as a *way* of growth, as a yoga. When we play sports, we do it to *win.* This is fine. But many sports and physical disciplines in the East, especially the ancient martial arts, are respected as ways of growth, wherein the internal development is primary, the winning only incidental. If a Japanese sportsman happens to follow the ancient traditions, his sport, his hobby, and even his job become a way of life, a path for his ultimate liberation from disharmony of daily life. The concept of *way* is so inherent to ancient cultures, that it's built into the language. (In Japanese,—*do* means way. Look at the familiar terms, judo, aikido, kendo. In Chinese, tao means way.)

There are gymnasts in the West today, who instinctively use gymnastics as a yoga, as a *way.* It is nothing new or bizarre, then! You can instinctively recognize these people, because their life is, in some real sense, centered around this sport-art. It affects their diet, their daily habits. A significant amount of their time and energy and attention is directed to the way.

These individuals intuitively recognize the deep value of intense psycho-physical training, though they might not articulate it that way. They might just say, "I like it a lot. It's important to me." For the rest of the gymnasts, it's a pastime, a recreational or casual play they nominally engage in for a few hours a day, for a part of the year, during competitive season. Such people are not less than the "gymnast-yogis," but they have not yet seen the profound opportunity in commitment to a way of life. They have not yet found the capacity to give themselves wholly to an endeavor—with body, with mind, with emotions.

To gain this capacity, the average gymnast must cut through the usual social beliefs, spoon-fed to him from childhood, that "getting ahead" means developing the intellectual center above all else. For centuries our culture has been caught in the "mind-over-body" dichotomy, whereby the mind seems of ultimate status, and the body is only secondary. As you look around you, this imbalance is obvious. Institutions of "higher learning" (academic and intellectual pursuits) are multi-million dollar industries. Only a small percentage of the total budget goes to real physical education—or training of emotional strength. "P.E." is more often a term referring to physical fitness training or casual recreational play; enjoyable and useful enough, but not even approaching the potential of complete education. Many of our coaches and physical educators have forgotten their own bodies, and become "top-heavy" in their search for academic degrees. We're a culture that idolizes knowledge, yet mistreats the body through diet and excesses of every kind. Given this atmosphere, it's not surprising that few people are able to see the value in centering their lives around a sport or physical pursuit. Thus, the ancient meaning of a *way* has been lost. Athletes tend to participate in sport as an end in itself; intellectuals play their game without connecting it up to *whole*-body growth. One Chinese sage wrote a reminder:

> I hear and I forget.
> I see and I remember.
> I do and I understand.

There are some athletes who have cut through the conditioning and have intuited the whole-body truth. Many gymnasts have seen the potential of practicing gymnastics as a *way*. I was one. Perhaps you are too.

Gymnasts are doers; action is the game. When the game becomes a way of life; when it consumes you; when it becomes a passion, it can blossom into a true yoga.

Competitive gymnastics today, on its most intense levels, is a great opportunity to observe and learn about ourselves (and about others) in the fire and pressure of the Moment of Truth. The "way of gymnastics" shows us our latent weaknesses as well as our hidden strengths. Intense training develops impressive strength, suppleness, coordination, balance, courage, timing and stamina, physical qualities that surpass those of even the ancient yogis and martial artists. On the other hand, overzealous or hasty competitive endeavors can also contribute to injuries to the body, such as enflamed joints (especially knees, shoulders, wrists, elbows, or lower back).

Thus, the value of incorporating elements of yoga into gymnastics training to balance the explosive energy of our sport becomes obvious. Not only does yoga serve as an invigorating and complete warm-up (helping decrease various injuries and enhancing concentration), it gives the gymnast a wider approach to healthful, balanced training.

A YOGA ROUTINE FOR GYMNASTS

The following series of hatha yoga postures can be done either as a warm-up, warm-down, or even as evening or morning exercises. The movements should be done smoothly, flowing from one to the next, like a gymnastics routine. Bear in mind that for the following series to be of greatest benefit, you must practice them with complete muscular release, free of haste or tension. If you daydream while doing them to "get them over with," their effectiveness will be minimized. Then yoga becomes just a set of stretching exercises, which is fine, if that is all you want. But if you imagine that you are alone, lying on a warm secluded beach, with all the time in the world, and you just want to breathe deeply, stretch, and feel good like a lazy cat, then you have the proper attitude for the series.

The diagrams are the best guide for the postures, but accompanying the diagrams are general reminders about proper performance of the movements, with specific comments on each posture.

- Note that breathing should be full and natural, with inhalation through the nose, exhalation through the nose, mouth, or both, whichever feels more natural.
- Imagine that the breath is moving the body in all moving postures. This will help elevate the sense of relaxation and effortlessness with which you do the series.
- Do each posture as perfectly as you can, as if you are in a gymnastics meet. However, *do not strain*. Yoga is not de-

signed for unnecessary tension. Some of the postures do require strength, or muscular control (numbers 8 and 15, for example), but not unnecessary tension.

- It may take some time before you can do all the postures as drawn. Do not rush through them.
- After a few repetitions of the series, it is relatively easy to do, and takes only about fifteen minutes.
- The increased respiration serves to oxygenate the bloodstream and cells, thus invigorating you, and helps to retard the buildup of toxic residues that manifest as fatigue.

Sun Worship (5-25 reps)

out   in   out   in   hold   out   in   out   in   out

This is the "king" of yoga postures. Breathing is indicated beneath the figures. If you have no time for any other postures, the "sun salutation" is the best.

Circular Rotation (5-10 times each way)

Inhale as the head floats around and back, exhale around and forward.

Variation: Side Stretch (5-10 seconds each way)

Tree (1 minute or more each leg)

You might want to try this with eyes closed. Breathe naturally.

Downward Neck Pull (15 seconds or more)

Do this gently, breathing deeply.

Cobra (8-10 seconds or more)

Feel the upper back and chest stretching; not just the lower back.

Bow Pose (8-10 seconds)

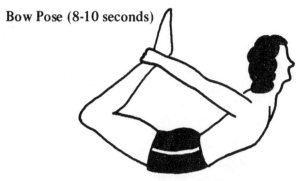

Hold the breath.

Locust (7 seconds or more)

Inhale up and hold breath. Only do this one a little ways up and for a short time at first.

Forward Bend (15 seconds or more)

Relax more with each exhalation. Do with feet flexed, then pointed.

Inclined Plane (5-10 seconds)

Deep breaths. A more advanced version, of course, is the back bridge.

Plow (2 minutes or more)

Slow, deep breathing.

Bridge (1 minute or more)

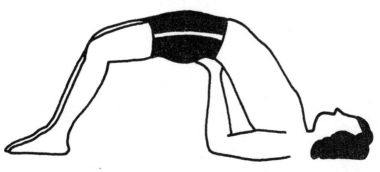

Deep breathing.

Fish (1 minute or more)

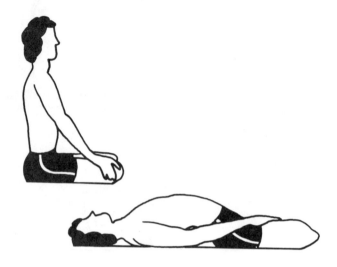

Head way back, breathe rapidly.

Peacock (10 seconds or more)

You may want to experiment; sometimes holding the breath; sometimes breathing into the belly region.

Camel (15 seconds or more)

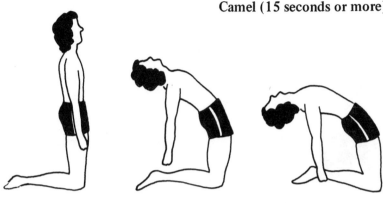

Feel a stretching in the front of the thighs; you may then want to lie back until your shoulders touch the ground. If you feel tension (in this or any posture), imagine your breath going to the point of tension, and letting it relax.

Yoga Mudra (10 seconds or more)

You may want to do this in a straddle position. Exhale. Hold.

14

Diet: Practical Nutrition for the Gymnast

Hardy Fink

More and more studies are showing that athletes as well as the general population are malnourished. Persons with multiple nutritional deficiencies have become the norm in our industrialized society. The reasons for this are many: the main ones being the general availability and desirability of non-foods, the over-refining of dietary staple foods, poor cooking habits and uninformed dieting. As a group these reasons indicate that nutritional ignorance is the prime reason for poor nutrition.

In the field of athletics many investigators are appalled at the poor nutritional habits of athletes and the nutritional ignorance of coaches. A recent study at the Fitness Institute in Toronto found that less than 5% of coaches concerned themselves with their athletes' nutrition, and that less than 10% of parents had any knowledge of an athlete's nutritional requirements. This study and other similar ones used gymnasts as a part of the population sample that was investigated. It would seem then that even we gymnasts could benefit from some nutritional information.

One commonly hears that regardless of one's activity level a well-balanced diet will lead to optimal well-being and optimal performance capacity. An active athlete will meet any possible increased dietary needs through the increased caloric intake. Nevertheless, as is shown by numerous nutritional studies, the "well-balanced diet" is a myth in our society. There is no doubt that nutrients supplied in optimum quantities will elicit optimum performances. Not many people seem to get these optimum quantities. Fewer yet can even guess at what these optimum quantities are. Nutritional requirements are difficult—perhaps impossible—to determine as they vary greatly from individual to individual or even within the same individual and vary considerably with environmental stress.

For athletes—in our case, for gymnasts—nutritional requirements may be even more difficult to determine. Athletes in general are subject to varying degrees of high physiological and psychological stress, are exposed to fatigue, are exposed to injury, and are in need of higher than average energy levels.

Although it seems obvious that the exact requirements of each nutrient for each gymnast under every condition will be impossible to state, it is possible to apply certain nutritional research findings to gymnastics and draw from them some useful conclusions.

The Soviet Team (*International Gymnast* photo)

Numerous studies of energy requirements for gymnasts have shown that caloric requirements are extremely high, varying from 15-40 k cal/min (some lower findings also exist) depending on the event and on the skill level of the performers. Most frequently, Horizontal Bar and Floor Exercise for men and Uneven Bars and Floor Exercise for women are quoted as those events involving the highest energy expenditures. In all cases, the least skilled performers use the most energy. At first glance it would appear that gymnastics involves considerable caloric needs inconsistent with its anaerobic nature, but even during a three or four hour workout a gymnast is not likely to do more than 15 minutes of intermittant work on the apparatus—during a competition, perhaps 5 minutes. The increased caloric intake above the basal requirements and requirements for other activity should only be in the order of 200-400 kcal for a full workout and 100-200 kcal for a competition. This would even provide for the fact that the metabolic rate remains slightly elevated (or might increase) for a while after an exercise bout.

In anaerobic activities such as gymnastics a limiting factor to performance is the accumulation of lactic acid in muscle. There is some evidence that certain dietary factors can help alleviate this problem. Alkaline reserve foods that have an alkaline reaction in the body may help to buffer partially the lactic acid. The best such foods are citrus fruits, tomatoes, apricots and green vegetables. Protein foods tend to have an acid reserve that might be undesirable especially before a competition. Protein should not be restricted during training. In fact protein needs are high for tissue repair and building, antibody formation, maintaining water balance, etc.

There is also some evidence that vitamin E reduces the accumulation of lactic acid and that vitamin C aids recovery by quickening the removal of lactic acid. As an aside it is interesting to note that the alkaline reserve foods are also the best natural sources of vitamin C. Furthermore, vitamin C and E are synergists.

There is mounting evidence that increased activity and increased stress (activity is a form of stress) increases one's requirements for all macronutrients (carbohydrate, fat, protein) and all micronutrients (vitamins and minerals). The macronutrients supply the additional calories and should supply the additional micronutrients, but the latter is not generally the case. It would seem then that the taking of supplements of all micronutrients would be prudent provided they are taken in reasonable proportions and in non-toxic dosages.

There are some aspects of gymnastics that suggest that participation requires an increased need of certain micronutrients over others.

As in all activities, participation in gymnastics frequently causes perspiration and therefore an increased need for water and electrolytes (potassium, sodium). Persons who are in good condition tend to lose fewer electrolytes in the sweat. These electrolytes must be replaced either by body stores or by ingestion. Water also should be replaced as needed. The water volume is maintained somewhat by the water liberated as carbohydrate is metabolized, but once the water loss approaches 1%, there is a loss of endurance accompanied by an increased heart rate.

Participation in gymnastics involves constant friction on the hands, and continuous pounding of the hands (Pommel Horse, Vaulting) and of the legs (Tumbling, Vaulting). These stresses often lead to a breakdown of red blood cells by hemolosis and crushing, resulting in possible anemia. Anemia may indicate increased requirements of iron, vitamin E, vitamin B-12 and folic acid.

Cramping of muscles may be due to inadequate intakes of calcium and magnesium (perhaps also riboflavin). These minerals also appear to be effective in reducing pain. For gymnasts who frequently have muscle cramps the solution should be obvious.

The fact that gymnastics participation acts as a stress on the whole body would indicate that the intake of all micronutrients pertaining to the stress state should be increased. In stress states the adrenal cortex begins to secrete adrenal hormones which serve to prepare the body to counteract the stress. In the early stages, potassium, and later, sodium are essential to prevent adrenal exhaustion. Some evidence suggests that vitamin C may delay the onset of adrenal exhaustion. In general vitamins A, C, E, B-2 and pantothenic acid act as anti-stress vitamins, and the essential fatty acid, linoleic acid, also appears to be implicated. All of these nutrients should be adequately supplied in a gymnast's diet.

Any improvement in circulation due to dietary factors should also deserve consideration. In this regard vitamin E appears to be especially useful, being implicated in improved circulation, increased capillarization, and reduced oxygen requirements. Other nutrients also have an effect. Niacin dilates blood vessels and thereby aids circulation. Certain volatile oils (phytoncides) contained in onions, garlic and horseradish strengthen the systole. As mentioned earlier iron, vitamins E and B-12, and folic acid may alleviate anemic symptoms and increase the oxygen carrying capacities of the blood.

Many of the vitamins appear to be effective in injury conditions that may result from gymnastic participation. Vitamins A, E and riboflavin are useful for various skin problems. Vitamin C and the bioflavanoids help prevent muscle pulls and tears by strengthening connective tissue, and to prevent bruises and hematoma by improving the integrity of capillaries. Vitamin E appears to be useful in the healing of wounds of all kinds and in preventing the formation of scar tissue. Vitamin K assures that blood clots properly. Vitamins such as vitamin A and C aid in preventing infections of all kinds.

In addition to all of this some vitamins (E, C and B complex) are useful in muscle contraction (also sodium) and proper metabolism of food stuffs.

There is little question that each of the aforementioned nutrients is important for the gymnast and must be supplied in optimum quantities. Some investigators suggest that for athletes, optimum quantities may be up to five times the normal intake of each micronutrient. Supplementation of these appears to enhance performance and reduce fatigue but supplementation should never be arbitrary. All micronutrients have far from understood synergistic and/or antagonistic chemical relationships with one another. As a consequence it may be unwise to increase only one or two nutrients at the expense of the others. Furthermore, supplements don't contain some vitamins that are as yet unknown and many minerals that are considered unimportant. For gymnasts, I personally would recommend supplementation of the diet with vitamins C and E, especially before a competition. As for the other nutrients I would recommend eating wisely in order to obtain them from the diet, although occasional supplementation may be indicated.

Perhaps the most important question is what is meant by eating wisely. In my opinion it means the elimination of all non-foods and the elimination of highly refined foods.

Tea, coffee, chocolate and Coca-Cola are drugs that may stimulate respiration and circulation but have enough undesirable side effects and antagonistic effects on certain vitamins that they should be eliminated or, at least, restricted. Perhaps the worst part of these non-foods (as well as of refined foods) is that they replace a real food that could have or would have been ingested.

Sugar products (candy, sugar, chocolate bars, etc.) should be completely eliminated from every diet and especially from athletes' diets. An intake of simple sugars causes a sudden rise in blood sugar which stimulates the pancreas to oversecrete insulin. The result is that the blood sugar is lowered excessively. The symptoms of this induced hypoglycemia include a full range of sub-clinical symptoms such as depression, moodiness, headaches, tiredness, insomnia, sore muscles, constipation, etc. In a sport such as gymnastics which requires a high level of vigilance and motivation hypoglycemia is certainly not desirable.

After having removed the non-foods and the highly refined foods, what remains? All the *foods* of course: fresh and unsweetened fruits and vegetables, meats (preferably untreated and organ meats), dairy products, eggs, nuts, whole grain products (whole wheat flour, brown rice, seeds) and specialty foods.

The group that I have called specialty foods should become a regular part of every diet for the reasons indicated.

Wheat germ: excellent and cheap source of protein, B vitamins and vitamin E.

Brewer's yeast (or turola): excellent source of protein and B vitamins.

Carob: replaces chocolate and has none of the undesirable effects, a source of trace minerals.

Kelp powder: excellent source of iodine and trace minerals.

Yogurt: an excellent food that has all the benefits of milk and provides beneficial intestinal bacteria that produce B vitamins.

Sprouts: an excellent and cheap fresh vegetable food that

provides high concentrations of all nutrients (depending on the seed) at any time of the year.

Most of these (wheat germ, yeast, kelp, sprouts) as well as seeds (another excellent food) can be added in quite large quantities to stews and soups without affecting the taste. Sprouts, seeds (sunflower, sesame, poppy), and wheat germ can similarly be added to salads. The seeds and wheat germ also go well in hot and cold cereals. I also recommend such foods as skim milk powder, rice polishing, desiccated liver, and lecithin. The most difficult part of using these specialty foods is to *begin* using them. Once you have convinced yourself that they are foods and once you have overcome your resistance to using them there will be no limit to where they can be added (i.e. scrambled eggs, milkshakes, casseroles, meat patties, special drinks, etc.). I find new ways of incorporating these foods in meals daily.

Specific nutrional advice aside, perhaps one of the most important factors in gymnastic nutrition is the pre-competitive meal. In general the pre-competitive meal is more important from a psychological point of view than from a physiological point of view, although, if possible, certain physiological aspects should be considered, especially in anaerobic sports. For high level competitors, it is not wise to become too stereotyped since a favorite dish or meal may be unavailable in foreign countries.

For gymnastics competitions the energy requirements are so low that the pre-competitive meal is not needed to supply liver and muscle glycogen stores. In fact these stores are established up to three days before the competition. The meal should be such as to make optimal use of the principles mentioned and several others. Some aspects to consider are:

1. The meal should be enjoyable, well prepared and not forced on the competitor. Unattractive meals inhibit the secretion of digestive enzymes.

2. The meal should be eaten two to four hours before the competition.

3. Saturated fat slows the emptying time of the stomach and should be avoided.

4. Foods that cause gastric disturbances should be avoided.

5. Avoid gas forming foods (onions, cabbage, beans). Gas mechanically distends the stomach which will interfere with the descent of the diaphragm during breathing.

6. Don't eat too much for the same reason.

7. Limit protein foods. These metabolize slowly and result in possible undesirable acid residues.

8. Avoid simple sugars (sucrose). These can lead to hypoglycemic symptoms such as fatigue and depression in 2-4 hours.

9. Alkaline reserve foods may be useful by buffering accumulated lactic acid.

10. Consider vitamin C and vitamin E supplementation.

11. If it is hot and humid, or if there is a chance of dehydration, drink water before and during competition and ingest salt tablets (preferably a sodium, potassium combination).

12. Eat less if you tend to be nervous.

13. If you wish to change your eating habits do so far in advance of the competition.

14. From a psychological point of view, if you really want it, eat it.

Day to day eating should include most of the considerations of the pre-competitive meal as well as some others. Generally meals should be distributed throughout the day. Protein should supply from 15-25% of the daily calories with the higher quantities being ingested during periods of hard training. Carbohydrate should supply 35-50% of the calories and fat from 30-45% of the calories (lowest before meet). Seventy percent of the fat intake should be relatively unsaturated.

The micronutrient intakes should, in my opinion, be in the following orders of magnitude.

Vitamin A: 10,000 IU (more under high stress)

B complex vitamins: although the quantities may be altered the proportions should remain as indicated.

B-1 (thiamine): 5 milligrams

B-2 (riboflavin): 5 milligrams

B-6 (pyridoxin): 5 milligrams

Folic acid: 5 milligrams, taken together with

    B-12 (cobalamin): 15 micrograms

    Pantothenic acid: 30 milligrams

    B-3 (niacin): 30 milligrams

    PABA: 30 milligrams

Biotin: 25 micrograms
Choline: 1 gram
Inostil: 1 gram

Vitamin B intakes can be reduced if yogurt is eaten frequently. They should be increased in the presence of agonists such as caffeine and alcohol.

Vitamin C: 1 gram—more in the present of agonists such as tobacco and more in high stress conditions or infections.

Vitamin E: 400 IU of dl—alpha tocopherol (acetate or succinate). Don't take at the same time as iron. Increase in injury conditions.

Calcium: 1.5 grams

Magnesium: 7.5 grams—magnesium should always be taken in quantities that are one half of the calcium intake.

Iron: 15 milligrams—extra iron is probably not wise as it is already supplemented in many foods. It should not be taken as iron sulfate.

Other minerals: use liberal quantities of kelp to supply the dozens of trace minerals that are necessary in human nutrition.

Many of the quantities mentioned here would be considered very excessive by official sources. They would also be considered far too little by other investigators, especially for athletes and during other stress conditions. I recommend that the reader go out of his way to become knowledgeable in this area and then apply knowledge to his own situation.

References

1. Adams, R. and F. Murray, Body, Mind and the B Vitamins, New York: Larchmont Books, 1972.

2. Astrand, P.O. "Diet and athletic performance," Federation Proceedings, 28:1772-1777; 1967.

3. Bailey, H., Vitamin E: Your Key to a Healthy Heart, New York: Arc Books, 1968.

4. Blochin, I.P. "Energy characteristics of male competitive gymnasts," Teoria Praktila fiz Kultury, 28: 32-38; 1965 (Russian).

5. Coaching Association of Canada - Proceedings of the 1st International Symposium on the Art and Science of Coaching (Volume 1) Toronto: F.I. Production, 1973.

6. Davis, A., Let's Get Well, New York: New American Library 1972.

7. Department of National Health and Welfare, Nutrition Canada: National Survey, Canadian Government, 1973.

8. Fink, H., "Vitamin E and Athletes" The Gymnastic Technician No. 7, October 1974.

9. Fredericks, C. and H. Bailey, Food Facts and Fallacies, New York: Arc Books, 1968.

10. Guthrie, H.A., Introductory Nutrition, Saint Louis: CV Mosby Co., 1971.

11. Keys, A. "Physical performance in relation to diet" Federation Proceedings 2: 164; 1943.

12. Prevention Magazine, Vitamin A: Everyone's Basic Bodyguard, Emmaus, PA: Rodale Press, Inc. 1973.

13. Seliger, V. et al., "Metabolisme energetique arc cours des exercises de gymnastique," Kinanthropologie, pp. 159-169; 1970.

14. Silander, H and H. Viri, "Der Stoffwerhselbeim Barrenturnen," Scandinavian Archives of Physiology, 60: 247-253, 1930.

15. Van Itallie, T.B. et al., "Nutrition and athletic performance," JAMA 162: 1120-1126; 1956.

16. Webster, J. Vitamin C: The Protective Vitamin, New York: Award Books, 1971.

17. Williams, J.C., "Nutrition in Sport" The Practitioner 201: 324-328; 1968.

Gymnastics, perhaps more than any other sport, makes intense psychological demands on its athletes. The powers of concentration must be nurtured and maintained, fear of height and apparatus must be overcome, and the fire for "psyching up" for a meet must be sparked.

Conquering the Fear *discusses methods that the coach may adopt in the first weeks of training.* Fear in Competition *treats the important aspect of gymnasts' nervous anxiety before a meet.* Staying on the Beam *addresses the special problems of the scariest event in women's gymnastics and proposes psychological training techniques to solve them.* The Psychology of Training for the Meet *is a theoretical piece, connecting the fear-anxiety problem to principles of experimental psychology.*

4

PSYCHOLOGICAL TRAINING

Ludmilla Tourischeva (Mark Shearman photo)

15

Conquering the Fear

Dr. Joe Massimo

How the athlete copes with fear is more important in the progress or lack of progress in gymnastics than any other variable. Very often, it is this emotional condition that separates the good from the great. In order to make our discussion more valuable, we should define this concept and a few related terms.

Fear, in the most general sense, always carries the connotation of "anxiety" and corresponding physiological responses; discharge of adrenalin, and increased heartbeat rate. On the positive side there is an increase in alertness and an overall tuning up of the sensory modalities such as visual perception and auditory acuity. It is important to be aware of the physical reactions the human being experiences in relationship to this emotional condition. Fear is defined in Webster and most psychiatric texts as an unpleasant and often strong emotion caused by the anticipation or awareness of a dangerous situation. Dread, which often accompanies the more general notion of fear, is represented by an intense reluctance to face a situation and suggests aversion (turning away) as well as anxiety. Phobia or exaggerated fearfulness is usually irrational and an over-determined psychological state which cannot be remediated except through prolonged therapeutic help. In the most

125

extreme form of fear, panic, all reasoning disappears and the person is often emotionally and physically crippled or out of control.

We will use the dictionary definition and address ourselves to the emotion experienced by gymnasts in coming to grips with the anticipation and awareness of acute or potential danger.

If a gymnast is dynamite during practice but turns to jelly in competition, we are dealing with "fear" in a different sense. In these situations we are confronted by a constellation which involves the social dimensions of competition, evaluation, exposure, and pressure created by a special set of circumstances rather than with a fundamental apprehension of danger. Helping the athlete with this kind of response is another topic and for now we will focus on the emotion of fear in the learning-training phase of gymnastics.

The level and degree of fear resident in a gymnast is a very individual matter. Basically timid people tend to be more fearful than those who operate out of a more aggressive stance. Being timid and being quiet are not, however, the same thing and only through getting to know an individual gymnast in a variety of situations can one begin to understand what their unique personal temperaments are and what kind of communication is appropriate insofar as fear and its performance ramifications are concerned.

The triggering mechanism and definition of "danger" which results in fear-behavior is different for everyone. What appears hazardous to one gymnast, another takes in stride. Some gymnasts are afraid of going backward while skills involving forward rotation, for example, present no problem. The reverse situation could be equally true. Some gymnasts appear fearful of everything and every event (a kind of diffuse anxiety) but somehow get through in a manner that is awe-inspiring to those who just can't quite handle it. Others appear relatively calm until that moment of decision when one discovers they are actually terrified. There are several signs to watch for but no infallible system of prediction other than experience. It is important to identify early the particular situation or circumstances that create the most fear behavior for any given gymnast in order to minimize its impact during the training. These observations are helpful in selecting what skills should be pursued on what kind of timetable, and under what conditions.

The individual response is a product of very personal experiences as well as the basic child-rearing practices of the parents. The youngster who has fallen on his head doing a particular skill will usually shy away from related movements especially if the fall resulted in some real physical trauma. The child who is continually reminded of the implicit danger in certain action is most likely hypersensitive to the signs of potential danger. This type of interaction coupled with our instinctive drive for self-preservation can produce some very fearful people. In any event, these individuals ordinarily do not tend to gravitate toward gymnastics as an avocation.

No one is without fear. We have often heard people speak of someone as being "without fear" but this is not accurate in the literal sense. What is being indicated is the gymnast who has developed a defensive system which enables him to manage this natural emotion and face dangerous situations successfully.

I have spoken to many gymnasts about fear and how they deal with it. Some can explain their defensive structure with amazing clarity. The most common position I have encountered we will refer to as the *fate* or *determinism* philosophy. The gymnast takes the position: "If I am going to get hurt it will happen no matter what I do, so I will prepare well and just won't waste energy and concern myself with it." This kind of gymnast is usually able to concentrate very well and, although fearful from time to time, which is often a source of personal aggravation and frustration, will most likely attempt the skill being approached with minimum support. My past interviews have suggested that this is a most popular stance for successful gymnasts when it comes to the control of fear. The problem is dealt with by placing the major responsibility for any mishap beyond the control of the physical world. It is not that fear is denied as a reality but that it is relegated to the sphere of destiny which is pre-determined. Obviously, this is easier said than done but its prevalence suggests a high success ratio.

I would be remiss not to indicate that many gymnasts overcome fear on the basis of plain old fortitude and guts. They recognize the potential danger but go after the skill despite this because of a high degree of motivation and old-fashioned courage. Such athletes make few excuses and are usually characterized as "taking the bull by the horns" when the moment of truth arrives. They are not oblivious to danger but are determined to overcome their fear as a special kind of challenge.

It should be noted that this is not the same kind of attitude as the gymnast who will try anything seemingly totally unconcerned about risk. A complete lack of appropriate apprehension is not a healthy sign and suggests a neurotic approach to anxiety-laden situations where fear is denied as a fact. Eventually such spurious bravery will most likely prove rather foolish if not fatal.

In the coaching situation we deal with fear every day. Assisting the gymnast to overcome and cope with this problem is a difficult and challenging task. There are some general guidelines which should be stressed at this point in our considerations.

First, the concept of progression should be used in approaching a new skill. A step-by-step method where each element needed for completion of the final skill is mastered in an orderly fashion. This block building technique reduces the amount of fear which accumulates around the learning of a difficult movement. This is a basic preventive technique which can virtually eliminate fear-behavior difficulties later in the training process.

Physical readiness is related to the idea of progressive learning. In a previous article we talked about the importance of proper conditioning not only to facilitate the learning of a new skill but to promote a positive mental attitude which is a by-product of "feeling good" about your physical condition and preparation. The coach who emphasizes this kind of readiness along with progressive teaching will automatically be assisting the gymnast with the management of related fear around the new move and routine.

A third basic guideline has to do with spotting and its role in the entire process. It isn't necessary to dwell on the importance of selective safety procedures with our readers but it should be pointed out that it is through good spotting that many gymnasts are helped to deal with specific fear-behavior as they approach a dangerous skill. It is not only important that the actual spotting be provided but in some cases it is of considerable help if the gymnast understands what the method will be and how it relates to the acquisition of the particular movement. For some gymnasts the only thing they want to know is that "you will get them" and the amount of explanation is an individual matter. Generally speaking, the more clearly the athlete understands the entire movement (mechanics and spotting) the less fear is associated with its performance.

In the next section I will address some specific procedures the coach can utilize to help the gymnast cope with fear. In addition, we will make some suggestions as to what to do with the athlete who simply cannot manage the situation despite all attempts to get them over the block.

FEAR IN COMPETITION

Previously we defined fear in gymnastics as a strong and often unpleasant emotion associated with the awareness or anticipation of danger. We can now discuss the more general anxiety that some gymnasts experience in relation to competition. We will discuss some specific procedures a coach can use in helping the gymnast manage fear as it relates to a particular skill. It should be remembered that the coach must first have a strong working relationship and an awareness of the psychological style of the gymnast as it relates to fear-behavior. Such acquired knowledge is indispensible and the best teacher for it will dictate in part how the coach approaches an individual gymnast. Obviously, the following approach must be modified to fit the communication pattern of the people involved but it does serve as a frame of reference that is both practical and psychologically sound.

1. Discuss with the gymnast that the time has come to attack the skill unaided. Emphasize that the skill has been learned and that you have confidence in the gymnast's ability to perform it.

Note: At times the gymnast will indicate readiness for the skill before you make the overture. Do not stifle this enthusiasm but be certain you agree with the position.

2. Review the progression that has occurred (low beam mastery, for example), the gradual improvement in the overall execution and the increasing physical readiness to perform the skill. If overt fear is expressed, pin point it in reality. Eliminate as many "unanswered" issues as possible.

3. Reflect the attitude that it is a given fact that they will be successful in their attempt and that the skill is ready for incorporation in a total exercise.

4. Begin any warm-up progression that has been used in relation to the skill. It is very important that the coach remain relaxed and low-keyed at this point. Excitement is fine but not over-anxious quivers.

5. Run the skill through with the usual spot used in learning. The gymnast should be assured that you will in fact provide the spot if necessary.

6. Perform the skill a second time (in sequence if appropriate) with a slightly reduced spot. Physical contact is often helpful at this time—an arm around the shoulder, or a pat on the back. Talking through it can also help. As in most training, auditory cluing is useful--i.e., an explosive sound—"GO," "NOW" with heavy accent. Much depends on the individual gymnast.

If the gymnast "freezes" at this point one should remain patient and encourage a second attempt and greater effort. Run through the warm-up procedure (do it on the floor, low beam, whatever) and then perform once more with the usual spot. In the majority of cases, if all other issues are equal, the gymnast will probably push at this point to get past that "first one" we are all familiar with in the sport. Peer support can often be very helpful to the acquisition of the new skill and in getting over the fear associated with the first attempt. This is particularly true if another member of the group has already mastered the skill under focus. Coaches will find that using the same gymnast in the training phase can speed up the learning of a skill since the coach cannot always relate to the skill along the same dimensions that the gymnast who performs it can. Of course, this depends on the individual gymnasts involved and the nature of their relationships. The same holds true for group encouragement and its effectiveness as part of the climate in the gym. Some gymnasts do not want any "audience" when they first learn a skill and prefer to struggle it through without any witnesses. Generally speaking, however, such verbal, spiritual support from teammates is a beneficial technique.

Once the skill has been performed, praise and celebration should be forthcoming. Such positive reinforcement can go a long way. With no further discussion repetitions should follow in rapid order. The skill should be drilled with the moves in and out of it progressively added. Successful repetitions should eliminate fear of the skill. Should a mishap occur during time it is usually a good idea to move back (depending on the individual) to a repeat of the progression and performance with a light spot. This prop should not be continued and the gymnast will usually get back into the swing of the execution with relative ease.

Psychotonic training (mental run-through of skills and routines) can be used for reinforcement. Simply encourage the gymnast to think about the movement before going to sleep at night and to picture it being executed flawlessly in the "mind's eye." Again, in this drill they should try to kinesthetically "feel" the skill as they picture themselves doing it.

Despite preparation, some skills and gymnasts do not mix at a particular time in space. Very often simply letting it go and returning several weeks or months later will result in success. This depends on how much fear and strain is associated with it and how neurotic the coach and gymnast are in training. Very often it is helpful to have a timeline for the acquisition of a new skill. The coach and gymnast decide when they feel the skill should be ready for execution and they work toward that date. This must remain somewhat flexible, but should strive for the target date.

What do you do when the gymnast simply won't go for the skill, even if deemed ready? There are several options at this point depending on the individual situation and past history. One option is to continue encouragement and gentle coaxing. Another is to raise appropriate hell. Overall the best approach is to restate the issues, set a termination date (two more workouts, or one hour, for example) and stick to it. Beyond that point the coach should indicate that the skill will be dropped and no more energy, physical or psychological, will be devoted to it. A return to the skill should not occur unless the impetus comes from the gymnast and then only with definite limits set. This usually does it. If the fear of execution persists, it must be recognized that the additional tension of competition would make the skill a high risk for a major break and that further investment is no longer worthwhile. It is important that the coach not rub the gymnast's face in the failure—after all, not all gymnasts can do everything.

Remember, fear is natural. Overcoming it in relation to the

ymnastics skills is a process involving progression, ness and scientific spotting. Have patience, per- ith. Above all, do not be afraid of fear. In a very knowledging this human emotion and struggling to master it can be a source of lasting inspiration.

NADIA

Nadia Comaneci was selected for training while she was in kindergarten (five years old). The test-basis for selection appears relatively simple and included a 15 meter sprint, a long jump, and a walk on the balance beam. From my own experience in Romania I happen to know that the evaluation methods are far more complex than Mr. Karolyi indicates. In any event, Karolyi notes, "If they are *afraid* on the beam, we send them home right away." At five years of age many children show very little overt fear—the connection between activity and harm has very often not occurred. In addition, the human being at this age is not yet completely differentiated; that is, the sensory-motor-receptive modalities (i.e. sight-hearing) are not totally separated by discrete function and the opportunity for kinesthetic learning is ideal. There is little doubt that getting them young is a real advantage.

There are two aspects of the *Sports Illustrated* interview with Nadia Comaneci which are most revealing and which I wish to discuss briefly. Ms. Comaneci is not famous for her elaborate answers. She is rather stern, very serious and to the point not only in her gymnastics but in her interviews. For the most part her responses are one word. When asked the question, "Have you ever been afraid?" Nadia's answer was simply, *"Never."* (It is interesting to note that the same one word answer was provided when she was asked if she ever cried!) Later in the interview Karolyi discussed the fact that the Secretary General of FIG, Max Bangerter, attempted to ban "dangerous acrobatics" (Korbut's tuck on beam) from the gymnastic performance. During this conversation Mr. Karolyi was asked how much danger he felt Comaneci was really in. His answer, "Ah, but Comaneci *never* falls." It is in these two excerpts from the interview that we catch a glimmer of the ultimate management of fear.

I have discussed some methods athletes use to cope with the

emotion. One involved the acceptance of fear coupled wₐ stance which relegated danger to the sphere of destiny and, simply stated, concludes—if it is going to happen it is beyond my control anyway, therefore I will not waste energy worrying about it. The comments of Comaneci and her coach quoted above go one giant step further. In essence, there is no fear since there cannot be a miss and, completing the circle, since Nadia never falls there is nothing to fear! It goes without saying that a coach-gymnast attitude which is based on an accepted faith and commitment to this position results in a working relationship with fantastic potential. In summation, what is suggested is that the things one fears in gymnastics can happen to others, but we (Comaneci-Karolyi) have transcended that limitation and stand at a different place. To make a long story short we are not subject to the disasters others may face, we are close to super-human. Of course, anyone can say this but to truly believe it and act as if it is fact is another matter. Since it is this author who has made this inference, not the people themselves, there is reason to believe that this philosophical position is part of Comaneci's basic personal fiber and not a facade which is flouted to others, as would be the case in megalomania. Only time will tell if such a braver version of infallibility is accurate and sustainable.

16

Staying on the Beam

Dr. Joe Massimo

Many coaches and gymnasts know that gym meets for girls are often won or lost on the beam. We all know there are three other events, but for some reason things often turn depending on how your team does on the beam. For many good individual all-around performers this is the event they like to get over successfully. Probably one of the important reasons this is so is because when you fall off the beam it costs you .5 each time and that can really add up when four girls from a team, for example, compete and all fall off once or more. So it would seem that staying on the beam is really very important. I have compiled some ideas you might want to think about. These might make you a better beam performer or at least reduce the number of times you mount and dismount during this event.

Some research has been done in techniques of staying on the beam. Some of the following suggestions come from research, but most come from experience.

• Time on the beam is crucial. There is absolutely no substitute for actual time working the beam. You do not have to do difficult skills all the time, although they need constant practice. But simply time walking across the 16 foot beam is very important. I feel the beam requires the most time and should be treated in this special way when you plan your workout schedule.

• Make sure you understand technical facts about staying on the beam. Make certain your coach has made the mechanics and techniques clear, especially those to help you maintain balance while performing moving skills. Know what keeping your body in line, eye spotting, and shoulders-down, long-neck means and how to do it.

• Think straight! Before you begin your workout on beam have a little conversation with yourself. Relax and think about the event you are about to do. Think in terms of a straight line; actually look at the beam as you do this and make up your mind that you can and will stay on. Think lift and a dignified carriage of your torso at all times and that you are in no way afraid and are proud of your improving ability. It is not that you are trying to go into an hypnotic trance, but you are trying to get all your mental energy directed into the job at hand. (Another idea about staying straight is referred to as the "4-inch theory." It appears that in the average young adult or teenage girl the measured distance between the bottom part of your rib cage is approximately the same width as the beam. You can stick your fingers in and locate this spot. In other words you kind of have a built-in ruler for thinking and keeping straight which may help you line yourself with the beam.)

• Although it is more fun to work routines, allow time to do difficult warm-up drills including side-focus movements, scale and jump drills, and alignment exercises while on the beam.

• Work the beam up at competition height as much as possible. Naturally there are things that should be practiced on the low beams. They are excellent for helping you get confidence in a new skill you are working. When it comes to actual long term work you should spend your walking and/or skill working time on the beam at regulation height. There is research to prove that figure-ground adjustment even for experienced performers is not easy. The more used to the high situation you become, the better will be your chances of keeping balanced while moving along a stable surface which is usually 49 inches above the ground.

• *Concentrate* at all times. Don't allow distractions. Some coaches talk to their girls while they are on the beam. If this is so, stop to listen to the suggestion. Most coaches who are cluing while you are moving do so with single words, not breaking your concentration. When on the beam, that's where you should be. Don't look around for any reason. Some girls talk quietly to themselves while they work or even hum. Another good method is to try to feel the beat of the movement, the rhythm of your body in the exercise. This often helps increase your overall concentration. If it works, use it.

• Another important thing to remember while working the beam is to stay up on the balls of your feet as much as possible during your training. This is not only technically and aesthetically better but it will help you control in an emergency. If you have trained well up on your toes then should you do a movement which requires a flat foot position or are forced into it by a mis-balance you will find your foot like a small vice because you have trained in a raised position most of the time. You will find it can really make a difference in your efforts to stay on.

• Whenever possible work the beam with the same footwear that you plan to use for competition. It is amazing how many good gymnasts use the "feel" of the beam to help them develop steadiness. So it makes sense to practice in a consistent way when it comes to what is on your feet. If you are working bare footed, okay, but do it all the time.

• Learn how to breathe properly. Breath control is very important in all events and the beam is no exception. Holding your breath can cause that little bit of dizziness which can mean a big bobble. Ventilation of your lungs with fresh oxygen causes your brain to function best and as a result your control and endurance improves. This does not happen by accident. You have to plan and practice it as well.

• A most interesting technique you might want to try, cautiously at first, is to put a small amount of cotton in your ears while on the beam. It should not be stuffed in tightly but just enough so that sound is less available as part of what you rely on when working beam. You will be very surprised how much gymnasts on the beam use sound (as well as feel referred to earlier) to help them orient themselves insofar as balance is concerned. With the cotton you will have to rely on your other senses, primarily sight and a total body awareness. You do not have to spend a great deal of time with this, perhaps five or ten minutes a workout, but you might find it a worthwhile activity. Of course, don't attempt your most difficult skills—simply walk, and dance, then gradually venture on. When first trying this it's a good idea to use the floor beam just to get the notion.

• When you are working the beam make yourself fight to stay on. Every gymnast has balance problems, but you should have the idea and set in your head that if it isn't perfectly steady you will not let yourself simply come off but will struggle to save the skill until you are hanging upside down under the beam if necessary before giving up. I have seen many girls, for example, execute a cartwheel and land with both feet on the beam and the upper torso perhaps slightly out of line. Instead of trying to save it they simply get off and jump back up again. Don't tolerate that in yourself. Scold yourself for falling off, but at the same time don't get so angry that you can no longer think.

• Don't hold back. Although you want to stay on you don't want to be so cautious that the exercise lacks pace and you lack confidence. Again, this does not happen by accident; it also must be practiced. Therefore when you work beam go for your movements all the way. Although high jumps may be scary they are impressive and dramatic and easier to manage than a little dinky leap. Constantly remember you are selling yourself and the routine. Make it big, show it off—it is a performance. Just as floor exercise is theater in the square, the beam is kind of a floor mat running in a straight line. Don't get preoccupied with the issue of falling off. Keep a positive attitude.

• If you have trouble, react quickly. Isolate your hips and try to line up as soon as possible. Eye spotting should not be a slow, dreamy thing; make it crisp. Although these are more coaching factors and this is a psychology article it is important to remember that no matter what you have been told by your trainer, unless your mind is with it and tuned-in, you won't be successful.

• Practice "recovery" behavior at all times. If you have a break, practice saving the move and going ahead in an unflustered way. Don't let a break blow your mind and lead to a collapse of the rest of your effort. It is very important to get it out of your head and continue.

• It is very important to pick a sure mount. No matter what the difficulty level be sure to start your beam routine with a mount that you have completely mastered. There is nothing so demoralizing than to fall off on your mount actually before you have really begun. You are then owing half a point and this can really affect your concentration for the rest of the routine. A good start is very important in all events but on beam a sure, confident opening is not only impressive to judges but gets your mind in the positive groove early and makes you feel good about your performance from the beginning.

• Put yourself under a certain amount of pressure. At least twice a week work your optional set with the stop watch. This is how it is going to be in competition and recreating the tick of the clock will help you with pace and to recover efficiently if you make a mistake. Keep track of your times to see how you are doing. Along the same line, compete with yourself and keep a record of your work. How many routines without a major break? Strive for the top expression and amplitude you are capable of and mentally reward yourself when you're doing a good job. It is a very sound way of self-evaluation and keeping your motivation up.

• If you're having an off-day on beam when nothing you do works and you simply can't stay on or get things turned around in your favor—*stop!* Nothing will be gained from drilling poor execution and your mental attitude will probably get worse. Walk away, take a rest, talk to your coach about it, and return later. Remember that if you have a very bad head cold or a sinus infection your inner ear (site of balance control) may be affected so it might be wise to work a bit less on such days.

• Ask your coach for some mental training drills that you can do alone or with the team. Exchange ideas with other gymnasts and coaches.

There is no substitute for time on the beam. This simply can't be emphasized enough. Think of it another way: Lots of people walk one, two, or three miles a day and think nothing of it. On the balance beam you have to make approximately 330 passes up and down the length of the beam to walk one mile. Allowing for about five (5 inches) seconds a pass that would take roughly 27 minutes of continuous work without a rest or break to go a mile on the beam. Surely walking two miles or more a day on beam is a reasonable goal so you can see, leaving time for rest and bobbles, you will need at least an hour and a half of beam to make it. Perhaps you could set yourself a challenge to see if you can do it in less time which would mean you are taking less rest and/or staying on with better control and pace.

I indicated previously in this article that I would return to the workout schedule as it relates to beam. Although this is the job of your coach there are some psychological implications connected with your training program on this event. In addition I have considerable direct experience in this area having coached several State and Regional as well as the 1976 USGF Sr. National Champion on Beam. Here are some recommendations you might want to consider in consultation with your coach. First, you must work the beam every day you practice. I don't mean just getting on it for ten minutes, I mean hard work. Second, I suggest that you do not work full optional and compulsory sets on the same day unless you have considerable time in between. Compulsory work requires a somewhat different mind-set. You are, for one thing, compelled to perform in a very specific and exact manner and there is no room for ad-lib as is the case with optional work. Assuming you don't have all day in the gym and time to have two complete beam workouts, I suggest that you work full compulsories one day and optional parts or sequences and full optionals the next day with compulsory parts. Depending on your meet schedule, three days per week for optional and three for compulsories (alternating and assuming you are working six days a week) makes the most sense. Extra concentration can occur, of course, depending on your level of mastery and personal objectives. Finally, although the number of routines is important, ultimately it is the quality of those sets that counts. The one that matters most is the one you do in the meet—that is what you are working toward. Ordinarily 25-35 compulsories a workout is sufficient and a fewer number of routines on optional days should do it.

17

Psychology of Training for the Meet

Dr. John H. Salmela

As Orlick points out, one of the most important roles played by the coach is that of establishing the *expectancies* for his gymnasts.[1] It is not uncommon for a coach who expects much of his gymnasts to have them subsequently realize these higher achievements. Conversely, one can see many a talented gymnast never reach his potential partially due to the fact that the coach was not expecting enough in relation to the gymnast's potential.

It should be pointed out that the coaches' expectations have powerful self-fulfilling tendencies. That is, if a coach perceives initially that a gymnast will do well, this gymnast will often do better than a more talented athlete who is not perceived as having potential by the coach. The coach, therefore, must be wary of these powerful forces that are in his control. He should be looking for certain qualities of worth in all of his gymnasts. By looking at each gymnast's best points, the athlete develops a *positive self-worth,* which can help performance in the long run. The expectancies of the coach are transmitted by verbal and non-verbal behaviors on his part, which create a positive non-threatening environment of acceptance for the gymnast.

Level of aspiration

Related to the expectancies of the coach is the *level of aspiration* of the gymnasts. Certain gymnasts, independent of the expectations of the coach, will not stop training until they have reached the top international level, while others are satisfied with a well-performed routine at the provincial level. Discrepancies between the two can lead to constant frustrations when the gymnast is not able to realize the performances to which he aspires.

It has been shown that the best performances occur when the probability of success is at about 50-50. Performance suffers when there is no chance of success, as well as when success is almost assured. Again we can see the importance of the goal-setting by the coach to keep the athlete at the optimum level of aspiration in comparison to the difficulty of the task. Three general findings on the levels of aspiration have been cited by Singer.[2]

● Success leads to a raising of the aspirational level, while failure encourages its lowering,

● The greater the success, the greater the probability in the rise in level,

● The level of aspiration is influenced more by success than by failure and these effects of success are more stable.

It may be appropriate at this moment to return to the concept of *goal-setting* that was originally presented on the section on psycho-motor learning. So that we can assure that both the coach and the gymnasts have the same goals, it is useful to sit down and translate the overall goals into precise objective short-term goals. Success on short-term goals has a stimulating effect on achieving future goals. The goals can be in terms of tricks, routines, consistency, length of workout, scores, or even strength and flexibility measures. It has been shown that preparing schedules and then having the gymnasts themselves plot their progress toward the goal has a beneficial effect on performance as well as increasing the interest in the activity.

Reinforcement

The term *reinforcement* refers to any event that increases the probability or maintains the strength of a particular behavior. In the early psychological literature, the pioneers such as Pavlov and Skinner used reinforcement in a very specific manner. However, the term will be used in a somewhat broader context in the present section. The initial work in behavioral psychology was interested in the particular schedules of reinforcement that were most efficient to maintain certain behaviors. While continual reinforcement is the best, it is not always practical. In general terms it has been shown that if continuous reinforcement was not possible for each effort, ("Nice stretch", "Good control", etc.) it was better to give the reinforcement on an unsystematic or variable schedule, rather than on a predictable basis (e.g., at the end of the practice). The relative value of the reinforcement, as will be seen in the next section, is also of great importance.

1. *Success and failure.* After any gymnastic performance, depending on the results and the *level of aspiration* of the gymnast, the outcome will be interpreted as being either a success or a failure. In terms of motivation, it is too simple to say that encouraging successes and avoiding failures should be attempted. As was pointed out earlier, motivation is quite low for tasks in which the probability of failure is high because of *frustration,* as well as, for tasks where the probability of success is high, because of *boredom.* It has been shown that about a 50% chance of failure may have positive reinforcing effects. It has been demonstrated, however, that high levels of success are important during the initial phases of learning. This indicates that careful preparation either of the gymnast, or modification of the gymnastic environment is extremely important to ensure success, a factor which may encourage the gymnasts to remain active after their preliminary experiences with the sport. This same principle would hold true for the initial attempts at a new skill of importance, such as giant swings or complex tumbling.

2. *Reward and punishment.* For the efficient reinforcement of different behaviors, lengthy discussions have occurred on the appropriateness of reward (praise) or punishment (criticism). In the earliest psychological literature, reward and punishment

were believed to have equal effects on the modification or maintenance of behavior. It was later shown that reward had stronger and more stable effects on behavior than did punishment. The effects of punishment were temporary and unpredictable, as Singer points out, since the performer is only told *what not to do*. Praise on the other hand tells the performer what he did while rewarding him at the same time. Orlick is of the opinion that high levels of positive feedback, or praise, in addition to aiding performance, also increase the gymnast's feeling of self-worth, his desire to continue to learn and thus to remain in the sport. The positive feedback is suggested to be displayed in a constructive manner that indicates to the athlete that he is improving different aspects of his performance or even his general behavior in the gym (cooperation in setting up the mats, for example). This positive approach to giving reinforcement can at the same time convey information feedback to the gymnast in terms of his performance, as well as establish genuine relationships of mutual respect between the gymnast and the coach.

3. *Intrinsic vs. Extrinsic Motivation.* The performance of any motor act can be done for its own sake, that is, it is *intrinsically motivated* or it can be performed for the material gain that will result from it; that is, it is *extrinsically motivated*. Intrinsic motivation reflects self-development and is characterized by the joy of performing and executing a skill for his satisfaction. Extrinsic motivation is characterized by performing to win a trophy, a title or even praise. From an educational point of view, intrinsic motivation would be preferred, but our culture tends to impose a structure of external reward for sport performance. Those individuals who participate for the joy of performing are more likely to continue in the activity once the external rewards have been withdrawn. It has been shown that intrinsically complex tasks, such as the variety of gymnastic skills, require high levels of intrinsic motivation while more simple tasks require higher levels of extrinsic reward. Some recent evidence shows that when extrinsic rewards are imposed upon the outcome of intrinsically interesting tasks, they can undermine the intrinsic motivation of the individuals. This means that the extrinsic reinforcement can be interpreted more as a *bribe* than a *reward*. Care should be taken in administer-

ing too many external rewards in an activity as captivating as gymnastics.

Arousal

To ensure that any motor task is performed at its maximal level, there is much evidence that indicates that the performer should be in the proper state of *arousal*, or activation for the task. Too little arousal, as exemplified by a lackadaisical attitude, will result in poor performance as will too much arousal, as is seen in different "freezing" or "choking" phenomena. It seems also that each task has its own specific amount of arousal necessary for maximal performance. Relatively simple tasks can be best done if the gymnast is "fired up," but the more complex tasks are best done with the gymnast in a state of calm control. Thus activities such as vaulting could permit higher levels of arousal than those more refined events such as pommel horse and balance beam. One only has to think of the difficulties that are so apparent when already anxious gymnasts start a competition by competing on pommel horse or the beam. The initial nervousness experienced by the gymnasts on entering a competition may cause disastrous results. Training sessions that approximate competition chaos may be one way of habituating gymnasts to perform well under these conditions. Providing a variety of gymnastic environment as well as emotional control techniques may be successful methods of overcoming this competition stress.

Fear

One final topic in this section deals with the overcoming of fear in gymnasts for different tricks. Fear can be considered to be an extreme emotional reaction in anticipation of physical or psychological harm. In most fear reactions, the gymnasts are faced with tasks that surpass by a great deal their perceived level of ability. Often coaches can alleviate these reactions by discussing the movement with the gymnast so that the exact reason for the fear can be detected. Use of "sure fire" spotting techniques (foam pits, overhead bells) can eliminate this fear reaction in a single stroke. However, it is often the case where more progressive methods should be used to alleviate gradually these reactions; for example, a gymnast may be afraid of jumping from ten feet in the air but not from two feet. In this case, an intermediate step of four feet could be adopted and discussed. Solving these problems in a gradual and concerned manner, rather than teaching by ridicule method, is preferred. The sources of fear of the same movement may be different for several gymnasts and should be evaluated through discussion.

References

1. Orlick, T.D. - Psychological Circles in Gymnastics - Dr. J.H. Salmela (ed.) *The Advanced Study of Gymnastics* - Springfield: Thomas, 1976.
2. Singer, R.N. - *Motor Learning and Human Performance* - (2 ed.) New York: Macmillan, 1975.

International competition has shown American gymnasts that dance education is a necessary component in their training programs. On floor exercise and balance beam, ballet, modern, and folk movements lend the artistic structure to the gymnast's overall routine.

Part 5 forms a basic dance program for both men and women, including warm-up exercises for dance training. The last chapter, written by one of America's best women's coaches, takes a look at an often neglected but nevertheless crucial subject—choosing the correct music for your floor exercise routine.

5

SPECIAL EDUCATION

Elvira Saadi (USSR) (Mark Shearman photo)

18

Learning Ballet Steps

Sandra Hammond

All ballet steps can be broken down into components. These components can and should be practiced before the complete step is attempted. There is a popular story among ballet dancers concerning a famous ballet teacher in Russia. She trained her students with great care, emphasizing preparatory exercises such as the ones described in this article. At one time, during an examination period for her students, she asked them to perform whipping turns on one leg, called *fouettes*. The students were surprised because she had never given them these turns in class. But she had given them all the component exercises. The story goes that the students performed the *fouettes* beautifully in their exam.

BALLET ALLEGRO

Perhaps the most distinguishing feature of ballet technique is the *allegro*. Taken from the musical term, allegro in ballet refers to rapid, lively movements such as jumps, leaps, spins, beats, and delicate connecting steps. The vocabulary of these movements is vast, but certain basic concepts can be learned which help simplify matters.

Fundamental movements of elevation. The dancer has five fundamental ways in which to get into the air.

149

● A spring from both feet to both feet. This is the first jumping movement learned in ballet, but even professional dancers will do dozens of these simple jumps (in first or second position) as part of their warm-up before a performance.

As in all jumps, the movement begins and ends with a good *demi-plie* (A bend of the knees with the heels remaining firmly on the ground). A good exercise to practice before attempting the jump is simply a demi-plie followed by a rise to the ball of the foot or half-toe and a return to the demi-plie. Repeat the exercise for eight or 16 times.

Later the jumps can be practiced in all five positions of the feet. Common variations are jumps from fifth position to fifth position with a change of feet in the air *(changement)*, or from a closed position (fifth) to an open position (second or fourth) and back to fifth position *(echappe saute)*.

● A spring from both feet to one foot. This is usually a traveling step, the most common example being *sissonne*. The sissonne begins from a demi-plie in fifth position. The spring is usually made forward or sideward onto the front foot, or backward or sideward onto the back foot. Since the landing is onto only one foot, the other leg can remain in the air in any desired pose (usually arabesque, attitude, or extended to second position) or it can close quickly after the first foot into fifth position.

A spring from both feet to one foot *(sissone)*.

Practicing brushes of the foot along the floor, known as *battements degages*, and finishing each one in demi-plie fifth position will help achieve the lightness of the feet necessary for good sissonnes.

● A spring from one foot to both feet. *Assemble* is the most elementary example of this movement. It begins by brushing one foot into the air (to the front, side, or back) as the supporting leg bends in demi-plie. Immediately the supporting foot pushes off the floor and both feet are brough together (or assembled) in the air before landing simultaneously in fifth position demi-plie.

A good practice for this step is the following exercise: from fifth position, brush the back foot to the side a few inches off the floor and at the same time demi-plie on the supporting leg, rise to half-toe on the supporting foot and then close the extended leg to fifth position front in demi-plie. Now begin the exercise with the other leg.

● A spring from one foot to the other. *Jete* is the general term for springs from one foot to the other. As with all allegro steps, there is a great variety of jetes, both small and large. The most common small jete begins by brushing the back foot to the side and into the air as the supporting leg bends in demi-plie. Immediately the supporting foot pushes off the floor so that for a moment both legs are straight in the air. The leg to the side then returns to the spot vacated by the supporting foot, which in turn arches just behind the other ankle.

A spring from one foot to the other *(jete)*.

This jete can be "broken down" into a practice exercise similar to the one described above for assemble. In this case, however, the ending will be a demi-plie on one foot instead of both, with the other foot arched near the supporting ankle.

The large split leap, or *grand jete*, is popular with both dancers and gymnasts. The secret to good split leaps is a strong forward brush with the front leg (practice quick high kicks forward with a rise on the half-toe on the supporting foot), and a strong push from the back foot as it leaves the floor. The back foot should literally try to push the floor away as it leads the back leg into the air.

● A spring or hop on one foot. The hop on one foot which is called *temps leve* requires considerable strength because the entire foot must arch completely several inches from the floor. The temps leve sometimes is added to another step, for instance, jete and temps leve, or sissonne and temps leve. A series of hops on one foot can be a challenging and strengthening exercise in its own right if done correctly. The other leg can be extended in any position or simply arched near the ankle of the working foot.

A spring or hop on one foot *(temps leve)*.

A good exercise for developing the articulation of the foot which is necessary for these hops is the following: standing in first position, lift the heel of one foot but keep the ball of that foot firmly on the floor; now arch the entire foot by firmly pointing the toes (the knee will be bent as the toes should lift slightly off the floor), return the ball of the foot to the floor and then lower the heel to first position. This exercise should be repeated many times on each foot, gradually increasing the tempo so that the action becomes very light and quick.

These, then, are the basic ballet movements of elevation and the most common steps associated with those movements. Helpful practice exercises such as the ones suggested above can be devised for any allegro step. To do so, first consider the components of the particular step. For instance, a *pas de chat* is a jump which consists of a rapid lift of one knee and then the other, so that for a moment both knees are sharply bent in the air. Preparatory exercises could be a rapid series of *retires* or *passes*, meaning the working foot is brought from fifth position up to the side of the supporting knee. The thigh of the raised leg should be well turned out to the side and the toes sharply pointed, just touching the inside of the supporting knee which remains straight. The exercise can also be done on half-toe. As the raised foot lowers to fifth position, the legs may bend in demi-plie, a further practice for the landing from a pas de chat.

Retire or *passe,* an exercise for *pas de chat.*

More complicated steps can also benefit from this sort of "dissection." An example is the large turning jump popularly known as *tour jete*. This lovely movement is often preceded by a three-step run which is a helpful preparation for the high lift of the legs off the floor. Before attempting the tour jete itself, take the three step run (left, right, left) and immediately throw the right leg high into the air to the front then spring high into the air off the left. Switch legs in the air but do not turn in the air (remember, this is a practice exercise, not the actual tour jete), then land on the right leg in a good demi-plie.

The use and timing of the arms are important to practice in this exercise. Arms often mean the difference between a good or weak tour jete. During the three-step preparatory run, keep the arms out to the side. But as the weight transfers to the third step, quickly lower the arms and then raise them overhead when the legs lift into the air. (Be sure the arms always raise past the face and overhead, not out to the side and overhead.)

Turns

Turns are one of the exciting features of ballet. The focus of the eyes and rapid turn of the head (known as "spotting") are the keys to most *pirouettes* and traveling turns. Probably the easiest way to practice spotting is to revolve in place while taking small steps on both feet. Keep the eyes focused on a fixed point as the body begins to revolve, then quickly snap the head around to finish the turn before the rest of the body.

Next try slow turning steps in second position across the room. Keep the eyes focused on a fixed point in the direction of the turns. The steps should result in even half-turns which may later become very rapid with legs close together when greater skill is achieved. These traveling turns are known as *chaines*.

For *pirouettes* or turns in place, it is usually wise to practice quarter-turns, then half-turns until the strength, balance and control necessary for single or multiple turns are developed. These quarter- and half-turns should be done in the exact position required for the full turn itself. For instance, if the ultimate turn is to be done with one leg out to the side *(a la second)* then each quarter or half turn should be done with the one leg to the side.

19
Dance Warm-up
Maria Bakos

The purpose of the dance warm-up is to prepare the muscles for the workout and to avoid injury. For best performance, the woman gymnast should learn basic conditioning exercises of the classical ballet and modern dance. Ballet provides exercise for the arms and legs, but not enough for the gymnast's body—an important factor for apparatus work. The dance aspect of modern rhythmic gymnastics and modern dance technique provide this exercise. The technique will differ because of the teacher's selection, knowledge, and background, but the "goals" should be the same:

● The exercises should build the strength and control essential for apparatus and floor work.

● The proper preparation and conditioning will avoid debilitating injury and pain.

● The warm-up should never be "gotten over with" with some short, fast exertion. A *slow* and deliberate stretch is necessary, beginning with the feet and toes and building to cover the entire body.

● Dance is not only an art form, but also an *education*. And physical education is only possible through *intellectual* education. Dance combines both dimensions, developing and refining

155

the body and spirit, courage, skill, timing, dynamics, rhythm, and sense of form.

The logical and proper dance exercises require concentration, discipline, and coordination. They teach how to isolate the muscles from each other properly; they should be executed intelligently, consistently, and precisely.

Whether you use the warm-up exercises given here or make up your own, the purpose should be the same: Warm up the body *honestly*, taking responsibility for your own body (or for the students' bodies) to avoid injury. Usually the time available before workouts, about fifteen minutes, is best for warm-ups. The exercises can be different each time, but the idea is the same: starting from the feet, up to the head and fingertips.

The Barre exercises from classical ballet are excellent for warm-up purposes, but usually require more time than fifteen minutes. As mentioned, ballet exercises emphasize mostly arm and leg work and not enough body warm-up for the gymnast. Thus, if the gymnast works out six days per week, three should be preceded by ballet warm-up and three by a free movement warm-up.

The dance exercises were chosen for training of competitive gymnasts. They include basic exercises to be practiced in the order given; the idea is to make variations, combinations, and compositions with them. I hope it will inspire the teacher's talent and creativity to invent new movements.

The exercises should be accompanied by the right music, not just background music. Background music is better than nothing, but does not serve any educational purpose. Both tempo and length should be designed specifically for the exercise.*

The fifteen-minute time limit for the entire warm-up was selected to coincide with time restrictions of each teaching period and a precise measure of the time for warming up the muscles of the body.

DANCE WARM-UP EXERCISES

Exercise 1. Locomotor Exercises (Circle)

Walk. Body is held erect with seat tucked under, abdomen held in tight, chest stretched high, shoulders back and down,

---

*The author's "Warm-up Fever," Statler Records SLP 1264, corresponds to the tempo and length of the following exercises.

arm down and relaxed, head held high giving the picture of the longest neckline possible. Arms are carried in opposition to the feet, swinging forward oblique to rear oblique, arms rounded to the side. Step on a pointed toe with legs rotated outward from the hip (knees turned out, heels turned inward and up). As weight is taken on the toe, allow heel to touch the floor. As body weight is shifted forward, lift heel first, extending foot to toe point before carrying foot forward in the pointed position to the next step. Allow knee to bend slightly as foot is carried forward, so that path of the foot makes a straight line forward.

Walk faster. Same as above, but speed up.

Runs. Body position held erect, as in the walk, but allow body to angle forward leading with the chest. Arms swinging in opposition, keep arms bent at elbows with palms up and slightly cupped. Run onto forward foot as in the walk but do not allow the heel to touch floor. As weight is shifted forward, push back against floor with ball of the foot extending to the toe, before allowing foot to leave the floor. Continue with the foot as close to the seat as possible, before bringing it forward with the knee bent ready to take the body weight again. Run with spring. Execute eight exercises. Body position held erect, but body leans slightly backward, while arms move from rear to sideward, turning palms upward. Execute eight runs kicking legs forward with straight knees and pointed toes. Repeat the first runs eight times again and then the second runs eight times also.

Walk.

Shuffle. Correct body position as in the walk, hands on hips. With feet parallel, shuffle feet forward (keep contact with floor) keeping knees bent and heels down.

Walk on toes. Body erect. Keeping legs straight and rotated outward, walk on extended toes. Be careful to keep ankles extended—heels directly above toes. Arms are carried in opposition but very straight, with hands bent so palms are turned to floor.

Repeat walk again as music requires.

Skip. (Step-hop). Step—bringing forward knee up to make high horizontal hop, foot just a bit above the ankle. Arms swing in opposition forward and back to a point slightly below the shoulders.

Chasse. Step onto ball of foot. Spring off of forward toe, bringing rear toe to forward heel in the air (fifth position). Land on rear toe. Step forward with right foot again, then switch and execute the same chasse starting with left foot. (*Chasse* means "chase," so one leg always chases the other one.) Eight chasses.

Straight jump. Body erect, feet in parallel position. Jump up from demi-plie, legs extended in the air and toes pointed. Travel a bit forward while jumping, but with motionless body position. Do not bounce. Force heels to floor, and in spite of fast tempo, stop on each landing.

Walk again. Slow down gradually and close your feet together for the last note.

Exercise 2 (Stretching and Bouncing)

Standing position in center of the gymnasium. Straight lines on floor. Feet together parallel. Stretching may be executed either with flat feet or on toes. With body erect, reach over head with one arm, and with the other try to reach higher than the time before. Counting one for each reach, continue stretching for four counts. Reach should be from the hips, with palms turned outward. Bounce forward, bringing head to knees and palms to floor for four counts. Feet flat.

Exercise 3 (Knee Bounces)

Four knee bounces in demi-plie (half squat). Four knee bounces in grand plie (deep squat). Repeat three more times. Body erect, feet parallel. Starting with heels on floor, extend onto toes and return heels to floor on each count. In deep squat, feet are also in parallel position, raise hips slightly on each bounce. Body remains motionless during the exercise. Hands on hips or arms may be varied, swinging in time with bounce. Could be done also in each position, ballet first, second, third, fourth, fifth.

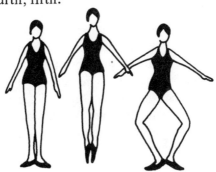

Exercise 4 (Marching in Place)

Right knee raises to chest four times (forward). Right knee raises to side four times. Four times left knee raises to chest (forward). Four times left knee raises to side. Then eight times only forward, switching legs always and in a faster tempo. Feet parallel, body erect, arms overhead with hands clasped. Body remains motionless during the whole exercise as knee picks up sharply. Feet in parallel starting position. In executing the march sideways, turn leg out from thigh, knees outward. Toes point while marching. Pick up knees for the fast and last eight march steps, one after the other, without leaving time for closing feet, as we had it before (staccato).

Exercise 5 (Slow Squats)

Four grand plies, feet parallel. Four grand plies in second position (straddle). Feet parallel, keeping body erect, squat slowly. Rise, forcing heels to the floor first. At second position plies, feet turned out but heels remain on floor throughout. Close to starting position for last note. Suggestions for arms: hands on hips, or arms to crown position overhead, while squatting. The first mentioned parallel-feet position could be substituted with ballet first, third or fifth position using the classical ballet's plie-arm movement.

Exercise 6 (Body Twisting–Swings)

Four with left hand to right foot. Four with right hand to left foot. Two with left hand to right foot. Two with right hand to left foot. Then left, right, left, right. Repeat the entire exercise one more time. Standing position, feet apart and arms extended to the sides. Twist the trunk to left, bend forward, placing left hand to right toes and bounce four times (upper body and right arm swing along with the motion). Switch arms, right hand to left foot, and follow the above order.

Exercise 7 (Body Waves and Body Circles)

Four body waves forward in standing position, feet parallel. Two body circles to the right, feet apart (straddle). Two body circles to left, feet apart. Four body bounces forward, feet apart. The whole exercise is flowing. Start body waves from contraction and finish in the contraction. Roll body forward and back into a deep body wave. Knees follow the movement. Demi-plie at contraction and straight knees at body wave with flat feet (or on toes). Press hips strongly forward and drop head back as finishing body wave backward. Show the contrast between the contractions forward and waves backward. Arms rounded overhead (crown) at starting position. While executing body wave, rotate arms at shoulders, inward, bringing elbows forward without shortening the arms. Lower arms downward, backward, and upward, beside the ears, then back to the crown position. Step out into a straddle position for body circles. Bend the body fluently forward, to the right side, backward, and then to the left side. Arms parallel by the ears and follow the motion of the body. Relaxed arms. Same to left side. As you bounce body forward, bring head between knees (straddle feet) and arms on floor. The bounces forward should be a relaxation exercise.

Exercise 8 (Legkicks—Sitting on Floor)

Eight with right leg, eight with left leg. Clasp elbows under right knee while bending it. Knee as near to the chest as possible, toes touching the floor. Left leg straight on floor. Body erect during the exercise. Kick right leg high, not allowing the knee to drop lower. Remember to keep body in correct position and supporting leg straight throughout. The exercise is sharp (staccato). Knee should be straightened out completely and toes pointed in the air. Try to kick the leg a bit higher each time.

Exercise 9 (Body Bounces Forward in Sitting Position)

Four bounces with soles together, in contraction. Four bounces with legs apart in straddle position, flat back. Repeat the exercise once again. Body erect, soles together and knees turned out completely, hands on knees. Push knees with hands downward and bounce also with knees toward floor as with body forward to floor. Head in front of the feet (contraction). Curl head forward until body is rounded, with head as close to floor as possible, body weight leaning forward. Return to erect position then straight and stretched body position, start to uncurl at the base of spine, lifting head last. Straddle, as wide as possible, body bounces forward with straight back, arms in tension by the ears. Show the difference between contraction and straight body, leaning forward.

Note: While straddling on floor, force heels forward, knees up, turn out legs as in ballet second position. Try touching floor with chest.

Exercise 10 (Hip Exercise—Hands and Knees on Floor)

One leg circle from front to rear, one leg circle from rear back to front (one element). Repeat it three more times with right leg; switch and do the same with left leg (total of four times). Remember to keep weight evenly distributed on palms throughout the entire exercise as in the starting position. Motionless body, only working leg moves. Starting position: right leg should be on floor with straight knee but turned forward on a diagonal (closer to the definition "front" than "side"). Circle leg backward to rear and cross it behind left leg, putting toes on floor. Circle back the same way, putting back to the starting position.

Note: Do not bend knee or lower leg. As high a circle as possible.

Exercise 11 (Abdominal Strengthening—Supine Position)

Four slow sit-ups. Supine position on the floor. Arms extended by ears, legs straight, toes pointed. Tense. First raise the head, then shoulders, as far as possible while keeping small of the back on the ground. Body contraction. While sitting up, knees bend too as a natural result of a strong contraction. Arms bend and elbows clasp in front of body. Hold this position, then start to uncurl at the base of spine, rolling body down to floor into starting position, sliding arms back to starting position on floor. Last is the head.

Exercise 12 (Back Strengthening—Prone Position)

Two baskets, two see-saws, and four hoops are needed.

Basket. Grasp ankles and straighten knees while lifting head, chest—hold. Only the stomach should remain on floor (big arch).

See-Saw. Extend arms and legs, arms next to the ears. Enact see-saw action by first lifting head and arms. Then lift legs, while simultaneously lowering arms and head. Smooth and gentle.

Hoop. Place hands on floor close to hips. Straighten arms, leaving stomach on floor. Extend head and shoulder back, while bending knees to touch feet to head.

Note: Elbows should be completely straight, otherwise it is not possible to reach the toes with head.

Exercise 13 (Waist Exercises—Sitting on Floor)

Three side-lean bounces to the right, then extend the body. Three forward bounces, body extends. Three side-lean bounces to the left, body extends. Three forward again, and body extends. Repeat exercise one more time. Sit with legs apart (straddle), arms extended to sides. Twist and bend your body into a side-lean in front of right leg, to the right toe, and curve left arm overhead and right arm in front of the body. Reach with left arm toward right toes. Bounce. Return to starting position. The bounces forward should be executed with flat back, arms by ears. Try to place the stomach on the floor and then the chest. No sense to bounce forward with curved back and with turned in knees. Repeat exercise to the opposite side, then forward again. As bouncing at side try to extend the body to a "long" side–lean and not short one with curved back.

Exercise 14 (Arm Warm-up)

Sitting or standing position, or walking. Four shoulder swings backward, arms overhead. Four shoulder swings backward, arms at sides (bounces). Repeat it one more time. One large arm circle and one forearm circle (vertical, in front of the body). Repeat it two more times, except the last forearm circle. Instead, push arms forward, arms extended, palms forward. Four wrist circles starting outward. Four wrist circles starting inward. (Elbows follow the wrist circle in a natural way.) Then two finger pushes with right hand to left. Two finger pushes with left hand to right. Repeat finger pushes one more time. Shake wrist and fingers.

Clasp hands overhead for the first shoulder bounces. Bounce backward without any body motion. Same as arms are at sides. Execute a large arm circle from shoulders, keeping arms straight in front of body. Continue with a forearm circle the same way, except keep elbows in place as arms bend. Instead of the last forearm circle, extend arms forward, but start wrist circle immediately. For finger pushes, bend left arm in front of body, elbow faces downward, hand in a vertical position, fingertips upward. Push fingers down with left hand, but don't allow any position changes in elbow. Shake wrist and fingers with arms in front of body, parallel position, elbows bent. Up and down movement from the wrists.

Exercise 15 (Ankle Strengthening and Balance Exercise— Standing Position)

Two knee bounces in demi-plie, one releve, hold. Repeat seven times. Body erect, feet parallel, hands on hips. Releve (getting up onto toes). Hold for a count with motionless body. Could be executed in ballet first, second, third, fourth and fifth position. For ballet position either ballet basic arm positions or optional arm movements. Body does not follow the movements, motionless during the exercise. Head remains forward.

Exercise 16 (Straight Jumps)

Four jumps, arm shaking and raising. Four jumps, arm shaking and lowering. Starting position: feet together parallel, demi-plie, arms down at body. As you jump, extend your knees and point the toes in the air. Body erect during the exercise. Shake the arms fast from shoulder throughout the whole arm to the fingertips and raise gradually and continually for the duration of the music. Shake arms and lower them the same way. After jump, land without rebound. Legs and arms require different rhythms and dynamics. Start with small jumps and gradually jump higher and higher, but keep the same tempo.

Exercise 17 (Relaxation)

Shake legs, arms in sitting, lying, or standing positions.

Exercise 18 (Leaps—Circle or Diagonal Optional)

Suggestions: Could be practiced as series of leaps or prepared with chasse. "Smaller leaps:" cat-leap, chasse cat-leap with turn (half or full), scissor leaps forward and backward, leg kick-turns (fouette), cabriole forward and backward. Different leaps in a row, as a combination.

"Big, wide leaps:" Most of ballet grand leaps could be used. Progression: When the leaps are executed high and well enough, then full turns in the air.

"Grand leaps:" Split leap, stag leap, split leap through stag leap, switched split leaps, sissonne, grand assemble, straight jump full or double turn *(tour en l'air)*, arch leap, "abstract leap," and side split. Leaps should be practiced both sides.

Exercise 19 (Optional Gymnastic Movements—Optional Formations)

For example: Stretching, limbering, flexing and extra exercises. Candle, bridge, splits, and handstand. Depends on the needs of the individual.

20

Movement for the Arms

Sandra Hammond

ort de bras is the term given to the carriage of the arms in ballet, but it has come to imply much more. Movement of the head and the focus of the eyes, the use of the shoulders, the relationship of the elbow to the wrist and of the fingers to the wrist—all are elements encompassed within the "umbrella phrase" *port de bras.*

The harmonious curves and graceful flow of the arms acquired through ballet practice can enhance a gymnastic routine. Interesting contrasts in movement textures between the lyrical curves of ballet arms and the extended arms typical of gymnastics can add new dimensions to floor exercise.

In addition, the practice of traditional ballet poses enables performer to move and to balance in efficient ways. That is, the head, arms, and shoulders complement the movement of the legs by working according to rules of alignment and opposition. Study of the 11 basic ballet positions of the body as well as the many poses of arabesque and attitude reveal the logic of the poses, carefully developed by ballet masters for over two centuries. (See illustrations 1-4.)

In all ballet poses the arms are gently rounded from shoulder to fingertip, thereby giving a fuller form to the already slight curve that arms naturally assume when they are relaxed at the

sides of the body. Even in arabesque, although the arms and
fingers are more extended, they still retain a slight curve so that
the pose will look effortless and without strain.

It is worthwhile to reflect that in ballet the grouping of the
fingers is essentially the natural position that the hand assumes
when the arms are relaxed at the sides. There is a slight separa-
tion between the fingers, all of which gently curve inward
toward the body. Ballet training stylizes this natural position so
that the thumb is brought closer to the third finger which is
slightly indented. This grouping of the fingers remains virtually
the same in arabesque with the only differences being that the
fingers are a bit more stretched and the palms face completely
downward instead of inward.

Undue tension is frequently revealed in the hands, warning the viewer of the difficulty of the movement being attempted and/or the lack of confidence of the performer. Too often attention is diverted to fingers spread stiffly apart and twisted out of alignment with the rest of the arm. Thus, an otherwise pleasing pose of exciting balance can become distorted.

Similar distractions can result from stiff or floppy elbows, hunched or raised shoulders, broken wrists, or poor head position. (See illustration 5.)

5

Control over these vital aspects of performing is gained through careful practice of ballet arm movements. An infinite variety of these combinations may be devised, but most are based on the following four fundamental positions of the arms:

• The initial position is one in which the arms form a low circle, the palms face each other and the fingers are gently curved.

• In the next position the circle formed by the arms is raised to the level of the diaphragm. In this position the arms have a gradual slope downward from shoulders to elbows, with the wrists slightly below the elbows.

• In the third pose the circle formed by the arms is raised overhead so that the hands are still within the line of vision of the performer. The fingertips should be only a few inches apart and the palms of the hands should face slightly downward.

• The last of the basic positions is one in which the arms are opened to the side in a gently curved line slightly below shoulder level.

A typical *port de bras* practiced in beginning classes utilizes these four basic arm positions in just the order described above. The arms are slowly raised from the low position, through the middle position, to overhead. Then the arms are opened to the side and gradually lowered to the beginning pose. The incline of the head and the focus of the eyes relate to the movement of the arms, thus bringing harmony to the exercise. (See illustration 6.)

6

Most arm exercises are performed while standing in fifth position *croise* where the performer faces one particular corner of the room and stands with the "downstage" foot crossed in front in fifth position.

For a more advanced *port de bras* exercise, begin in fifth position, feet crossed with the right foot front, head inclined to the left. Raise the arms from the initial position to the middle position, then continue to raise the left arm overhead as the right arm opens to the side. The gaze should follow the left hand. Open the left arm to the side and immediately turn the torso so that the left shoulder is brought behind and the right shoulder is brought forward of the body. The arms are thus extended as in an arabesque line, right arm forward, left arm back. The head inclines to the right and the feet remain in fifth position. Then, lower the right arm and bring the left arm forward to join it, thereby returning to the initial position, head inclined to the left. (See illustration number 7.) The exercise should be repeated several times then performed to the other side.

The arms should flow smoothly in these, and all other, *port de bras* exercises.

7

7 (cont'd)

21

Ballet for Floor Exercise and Balance Beam

Maria Bakos

A gymnast can only score well if her floor and beam work contain dance elements that are of sufficient difficulty and are executed extremely well. An important element in judging floor and beam routines is the gymnast's ability to show contrast between dance, acrobatic and tumbling movements. Yet, these elements must all combine; the dance must "dissolve" into the routine because it will be judged as a whole composition.

Expression is an important word in gymnastics. We know that without this important factor a gymnast has little character and becomes monotonous, mechanical, and boring, like a machine. Dance brings the refinement that makes gymnastics a sport and an *art*.

Dance and music belong together and affect each other. The melding of these two beautiful arts teaches us to express our emotional feelings. Music is deeply involved in floor exercise and therefore is essential to the study and practice of the dance. Learning dance takes some extra time on the part of the athlete, but the result can be great and the time spent worthwhile.

FLOOR EXERCISE

There are two ways to compose a floor exercise routine:

● Select the music first, inspiring the choreographer to compose the routine.

● Compose the routine first and look for a composer who can create the proper music for the composition.

The music helps with the choreography, the character of the piece gives style, the dynamics, and inspiration to the elements. Before choosing music, consider the personality and artistic talent of the gymnast in addition to the technical talent of the athlete. Decide where to include dance, tumbling passes, and acrobatic movements. Dance should be the graceful, relaxing side of the routine, using rhythm, tempo, and dynamic changes. Dance gives the gymnast the opportunity to cover the entire area and create an interesting floor pattern.

BALANCE BEAM

Routines for the balance beam contain many of the same techniques and ideas as floor exercises with added emphasis on balance and pose. Basic movements and combinations are similar adding the important limitations of space and direction.

Dancing on Beam

I emphasize this subject because it is not clear, and lack of knowledge of dance techniques can be dangerous; remember, the role of dance in the beam routine includes *the warm-up*, which, if not done properly or at all, can lead to serious injury.

Dance on beam should give the gymnast a secure, comfortable freedom of movement to walk, run, skip, leap, jump, turn, and dance on the beam. Ironically, the gymnast may fall off the beam doing the dance part, not the difficult "trick" part of the routine. This is usually because the gymnast concentrates so completely on the acrobatic movement, there is a lapse during the dance or during the connections between the acrobatic and dance movements. With proper dance instruction, the gymnast can learn how to get *into* a trick and how to get *out* of it with continuity, beauty, and safety.

For many years there have been international discussions on whether the beam routines should be accompanied by music.

I feel that instead of using so-called "background music," it is much more educational to use suitable music for each dance exercise. It helps to feel the dynamics of the movement and helps the gymnast to execute the dance technically well, and with the proper expression. [*Ed. Note:* The author's *On Beam* music is available on Statler Records SLP 1254 N.]

In my instruction I follow the successful educational methods of classical ballet. Most of the ballet barre exercises can be used as balance exercises on the beam, in the same logical warm-up order as in ballet. The difference is that the ballet requires completely turned out legs; on beam, moderated or even parallel positions are used.

Presented below are some dance exercises as samples for warm-up on the beam; they are also necessary steps to learn beam. These can be used for the beginner, intermediate, or advanced levels and with the help of the teacher's creativity, many different compositions are possible. It is not necessary to practice *all* of the following exercises. (It is not even possible time-wise.) Examine the grouping, then choose exercises among them; the same order should be followed, however. The beginner should be taught these exercises on the floor at first; intermediate level will depend on the gymnast's ability. Certain exercises may be executed on beam immediately (balance); others on the floor at first (traveling movements, turns). Advanced-level gymnasts should practice these on the beam, except if some problem shows up, in which case they should be polished on the floor before going to the beam.

Balance Exercises

Gymnasts should begin standing on beam (as many as the beam's size allows), leaving room for each individual to move freely.

1. Squats (plies)
2. Squat turn
3. Crossed leg squat with side lean
4. Releve
5. Releve turn (toe turn)
6. Slow squat turn and quick toe turn
7. Lunge-body circle with stops
8. Body wave

9.   Slides (battement tendu)
10. Slides with releve and leg kick
11. Lunge—Arm circles
12. Adagio (slow leg work)

Exercise with right foot in front four times, then change without stopping and continue four times with left foot in front. Arm movements for certain exercises are left open for the gymnast's choice.

Traveling Movements and Turns

Gymnasts should line up behind the beam. The instructor's choices include:

● One gymnast executes several passes, changing direction with a turn at the end of the beam, then finishes with dismount (like a short routine).

● Gymnasts follow each other, one at a time on beam, for *one* pass, and dismount.

Dismounts can be either dance or acrobatic elements. Examples of dance dismounts include straight jump, straight jump with half turn, straight jump with full turn, touch jump, and straddle jump. Most traveling elements can be executed backward.

13. Walks
14. Walking chasse with leg kick
15. Fast small runs
16. Runs
17. Releve-legkick in traveling form
18. Leg kick-lunge
19. "Czardas" step
20. Waltz
21. Polka
22. "Leap-hop" step
23. Pique turn
24. Small leaps
25. Big leaps
26. Stride jumps with bounces
27. Dance and acrobatic elements combination (slow)
28. Dance and acrobatic elements combination (bouncy)

The last two exercises are for improvisation or can be assigned with one or two tricks. Transitions should be executed fluently and properly. The gymnast should first practice the exercises several times on the floor, before executing them on beam with dismount. Arms and head movements are optional, but should be in harmony with the movement and style.

Exercise 1 (Slow Squats—Plies)

Feet parallel right foot in front. Squat all the way down, while arms go up to crown position overhead, palm in. Standing up, arms to side again. Feet on toes; this position remains throughout.

Note: Keep body erect while squatting. Rise, forcing heels to the beam first, but not changing the straight upper body position. After four counts change left foot, as it was mentioned before.

Exercise 2 (Squat Turn)

Based on Exercise 1. During squat, however, turn half to the left, focusing on the other end of the beam and standing there. Squat in this position and turn half to the right to get back to the starting position. Arms in crown position overhead during turn. As left foot steps in front, the first squat turn is executed to the right and the second to the left.

Exercise 3 (Crossed Leg Squat with Side-leans)

Keeping body erect, step across (right foot in front turned out, left leg bent, and foot on half toes). Squat down crossing knees to sit on left heel. Left arm moves from side starting position to overhead, curved. Right arm curved in front of body (low) while body is leaning to the right. Rise to opening position, releve (onto toes) and lean to the left side. Arms at side, palms downward. Head follows the same direction as the side leans.

Exercise 4 (Releve—On Toes)

Feet parallel right foot in front, arms at side. Sharp releve and hold (up onto toes) while arms go up to crown position overhead. Drop heels down and arms to the starting position. Knees remain straight throughout the whole exercise. Head forward.

Exercise 5 (Releve-Turn)

Based on exercise 4. While releve, execute a half turn. When right foot is in front, the first half turn will be executed to the left, when left foot is in front, the first turn will be to the right. (See exercise 2 for directions.)

Exercise 6 (Slow Squat Turn and Releve Turn)

Combination of Exercises 2 and 5 (one half squat turn and one half turn with releve). The difference is the following: Start squat with flat feet and after half-turn drop the heels down, to execute the releve-turn from flat feet position. At both turns arms in crown position overhead. Releve turn should be quick and sharp.

Exercise 7 (Lunge–Bodycircle with Stops)

Right foot in front in forward lunge. Starting position: Body leans slightly forward with flat back, arms stretched, and next to the ears. (Upper body stretched at 45 degrees.) Circle body to right side lowering to 90 degrees, then back to a backbend, and to the left side. Finish bodycircle in forward straight body position (as starting position). Repeat on the same side. After four bodycircles, switch legs.

Note: Lunge should remain as starting position all the way through. Do not extend leg in front while circling body.

Exercise 8 (Body Wave Forward, Back, and Sideways)

Starting position: Right foot in front, deep squat in parallel position, feet on half toes, sitting almost on left heel while body contracts. Arms rounded overhead. *Press hips forward*, knees still in plie. Roll body back (isolate your muscles inch by inch) into a *deep* bodywave, knees still in plie. Straighten legs, but keep the deepest possible body position, then extend the body gradually (releve position), and after stretching up return to deep squat and body contraction. Arm movements to bodywave forward. From starting arm position, rotate arms at shoulders inward, bringing elbows forward without shortening arms.

Lower arms down, back, and up, keeping arms bent until elbow is as high as possible and extend until arms are straight and beside ears. Arms follow body in wave with palms out. When starting contraction, turn palms inward to curved arm position over head. Bodywave backward: Reverse exercise above.

Note: As you roll the body back the head is always the last; as you roll the body forward back to the contraction, the head is again last. Otherwise, if the head is not dropped back and then forward, the bodywave will be unfinished.

Side bodywave with armwave: Same rules as forward and backward. Press the hips but now sideways, accompanied by an armwave. Armwave: shoulder, elbow, wrist, and fingers. Brush your body at side as long as you can, then extend (vertical arm position). Head follows hand throughout. Progression: Bodywave with leg extension forward. The combination of this exercise is up to the individual.

Exercise 9 (Slides–Tendu)

Starting in preparatory basic foot position (right knee bent and pointed, toes placed next to the left ankle), left leg straight, flat foot. Slide foot forward with strongly pointed toes, then pull it back to starting position. Continue it the same way but back (one forward, one back).

Exercise 10 (Slides with Releve and Legkick)

See starting position exercise 9, except left knee bent (demi-plie). Releve on left foot while right leg kicks forward to 45 degrees and hold for one second. After returning to starting position, same leg kick to 45 degrees backward and return again. Releve strong and sharp, demi-plie smooth. Progression: Leg kick to 90 or 135 degrees.

Note: Absolutely motionless body position while leg works.

Exercise 11 (Lunge–Armcircles)

Starting position: backward lunge (left knee demi-plie, right foot pointed on beam in front). Body leaning slightly back with chest lift. Arms oblique in front, curved, elbows pointed forward, palms face in, parallel arm position, head forward. Arm circle counter-clockwise (forward, down, rear, up, and finishing in rear) one-and-one-half armcircle paralleling. Arms should circle next to body, and all the way back. Transfer weight forward after one full arm circle and land into a forward lunge as you stop at rear. Body leans slightly forward, back straight, head turns to right. Armcircle clockwise (reverse it), transfer weight back, and land in the starting position. Only two on each side.

Exercise 12 (Adagio—Slow Legwork)

This could include every slow leg and arm motion possible from ballet and gymnastics. Make it a very difficult balance exercise on one foot. Suggestions: leg raising, develope, scales, legcircles. Stands: one leg stretched out vertically in front of the body or at the side with the help of hands, holding heel and then extending leg. Scale backward, scale forward, needle scale, stride stand with deep arch backward. Select a balance pose and let arms and body improvise dance movements.

Note: Do not miss head work; head and arm movements should not always follow the parallel line of the beam. Crossing arms or head turns make beam movements colorful and elegant.

Exercise 13 (Walks)

Body position is held erect with seat tucked under, abdomen held tight, chest stretched high, shoulders back and down, arm relaxed, head held high, giving the picture of the longest neckline possible. The gymnast is at the end of the beam and starts to travel forward. Walk with pointed toes forward, fluently. Improvise fluent movements with the arms also. For example: figure eights, arm and forearm circles, arm waves, etc. Not sharp movements. Get the feeling of moving proudly and elegantly on the beam, without stops or poses. Body and head follows naturally the optional movements.

Exercise 14 (Walking Chasse with Legkick)

Starting position: Third position but moderately turned out, right foot in front. Long step forward with right foot while left foot points behind on the beam and both knees are very straight. Close left foot to right to starting position. Demi-plie. Step forward again with right foot as you did before, then kick left leg forward as high as possible and hold it for a second. Body motionless during the exercise. Alternate left foot (four counts). Progression: as kicking leg forward, supporting leg executes a releve. Arms optional.

Exercise 15 (Fast Small Runs)

Starting position: releve, body erect, arms at side. Small fast runs forward on the ball of the foot, knees slightly bent. Then optional arms.

Exercise 16 (Runs)

Two runs traveling forward, picking up leg behind, then two runs with straight legs in front (45 degrees).

Note: Body position held erect as in the walk, but allow body to angle forward leading with the chest. Arms extended to the rear, head turned slightly either to right or left. Run onto forward foot as in the walk but do not allow the heel to touch the beam. As weight shifts forward, pick up the other foot close to the seat as possible (knee bent), toes pointed. Run with spring. After repetition, kick leg forward with straight knee, body leans slightly back while arms move from rear to side, turning palms up. Repeat once.

Exercise 17 (Releve Legkick in Traveling Form)

This exercise is based on exercise 10. Execute a legkick-releve, then step forward with right foot into a demi-plie, pulling left foot next to right ankle. Continue the same way with the left foot. Arms are in opposition. At starting position arms down relaxed next to the body. As right leg kicks forward left arm swings forward and right to rear. Switch at the next step. Arms loose, relaxed, swinging motion. Do not swing higher in front than stomach-level. Body can follow the movement with a small body wave (at the leg kick) and moderate contraction (at the "pull-in" position). Head drops forward at the contraction and turns to the side at the leg kick.

Exercise 18 (Legkick-Lunge)

Starting position: Body held erect, arms at sides, palms down, head forward. Kick right leg forward with straight knee as high as possible, while releve on left foot. "Fall" forward into a deep lunge. Lunge could be executed with flat feet, or left foot on half toe, or both feet on half toes. Lunge should be as deep as a deep squat. Kick left leg forward, but starting the kick from the deep lunge position. Alternate. Arms optional.

Exercise 19 ("Czardas" Step, Traveling Sideways)

Starting position: Standing on beam sideways, not facing the end of the beam. Feet together parallel, knees bent (demi-plie), flat feet on beam. Step out with right foot to side with straight knee, while left knee extends also (momentary small straddle position), then close left foot next to right foot in demi-plie, as the starting position was. Repeat (Step-close, step-close) until the end of the beam.

Note: Either both knees are straight or both are bent. Sharp, lively. Hands on hips the first time, then optional. Start also with left foot but then the starting position will be sideways but turning, facing the other way. Progression: stepping out with right foot, go onto toes, as close, flat feet on demi-plie. Speed up.

Exercise 20 (Waltz)

Waltz step: Step onto pointed toe, lower heel to floor, keeping knees and toes moderately turned outward, and bend knee. Step onto high toe with left foot and step again onto high toe with right foot again. Alternate. (3/4 rhythm).

On beam: Execute waltz steps with optional arm movements (flowing, lyrical style). Then combine waltz steps with body and arm waves, with turns, legkicks, etc.

Exercise 21 (Polka)

The polka step is a combination of a forward chasse and a small skip.

Chasse: Step onto ball of foot. Spring off of forward toe, bringing rear toe to forward heel in the air. Land on rear toe.

Skip: Step, hop. Bring forward knee up to make thigh horizontal on hop, foot just a bit above the ankle.

Polka step: Chasse forward (right, left, right), then step-hop (skip) on right foot. Alternate. Arms optional. Execute small gallops also (series of small cat-leaps); could be combined with polka.

Exercise 22 ("Leap-Hop" Step)

Prepare right foot forward with pointed toes, placing on beam, left knee in demi-plie, clasp hands behind the back. Leap forward with right foot like a small split leap, land in demi-plie, picking up left leg behind with knee bent (parallel), then hop on right foot kicking left leg straight forward to 45 degrees. Continue with left leg (alternate). Bouncy style. Speed up, arms at sides or out to help keep balance for the step.

Exercise 23 (Pique Turns)

I chose the pique turn as a sample for turn technique on the beam. Suggestion: Turns should be taught on floor until perfected. The gymnast has to know the spotting technique with the head *before* she goes up on the beam.

Preparation on the beam for pique turn: Right foot pointed in front, placed on beam, while left knee is in demi-plie. Right arm curved in front at stomach-level (leave space between your arm and body), palm inward, left arm at side, palm down.

Step onto the toe of right leg, bringing the rear pointed toe to the back of supporting ankle (a bit higher-calf). Lifted rear leg should be rotated outward with knee to side. Step back with left foot to the starting position. At the releve on right foot, the left arm turns suddenly inward into the same curved arm position to the right arm. While stepping back, arm also returns to starting position. Left arm movement should help to execute the turn precisely. Tension should be in the body, stomach pulled in; otherwise it is not possible to hold the balance on beam.

Execute the same exercise as above with a half turn as weight is taken on straight leg. Progression: Execute full turn, but still in place. Then travel with it, making passes and combinations.

Note: Head spotting, erect body position, the moving free arm is controlled for help. *Practice both sides.* Other suggested turns: Arabesque, attitude in front and behind, squat turns (executed in deep squat and the other leg extended straight in front or from side circling forward), chenee turn, leg kick half turn on toe, slow turns with body waves, body circles, etc. The order should be:

1. Preparation
2. Half turn
3. Full turn, but in place
4. Full turn, traveling forward

Exercise 24 (Small leaps)

Suggestions: Could be practiced as series of small leaps or prepared with chasse. For instance, chasse cat-leap, chasse cat-leap turn, chasse scissor leap forward, backward, kick-turns (fouettes), cabrioles, etc. Or, two leaps one after another, such as one cat-leap, one scissor-leap.

Exercise 25 (Big, Wide Leaps)

Suggestions: Most of ballet grand leaps could be used on beam.

Grand jetes (split leap), tour jete, etc. Stag leap, stag-split leap, switched split leaps, sissonne, grand assemble, straight jump half turn, arch-leap, "abstract" leap, side split, etc. Leaps should be practiced on both sides as well as turns.

Note: It is a dangerous and bad habit to start beam warm-up with big leap.

Exercise 26 (Stride Jumps with Bounces)

A. Starting position: Stride, parallel, right foot in front, feet on half toes. Weight is evenly on both feet. Arms at sides.

Counts 1 and 2: 2 knee bounces.

Counts 3 and 4: High straight jump in the air, keeping the same stride position and distance between the legs. Straight knees and pointed toes in the air. Landing on the next 1 count, as starting position—then continue it. Eight with right foot in front, then switch and eight with left in front (like sautees in ballet).

B. Based on exercise A, except while jumping up with legs in the air, switch and land on left foot. Repeat and alternate (like ballet changements).

C. Based on exercises A and B. While jumping up from right foot, switch in the air twice and land again on right foot (like entre chat quatre). Suggestions: The bounces could be used as preparation to other jumps. For example: Big squat jump, wide split jump, etc. Progression: Traveling with the jumps. Execute knee bounces in a deep squat.

Exercise 27 (Improvisation or Combination)

Make up a slow short sequence, which includes acrobatic elements also.

Exercise 28 (Improvisation or Combination)

Invent a short combination, but this time in a "bouncy" style. Should also include acrobatic elements.

Nadia Comaneci (*International Gymnast* photo)

22

Music for Floor Exercise

Ernestine Russell Weaver

Choosing music for floor exercise can be a very frustrating and time-consuming experience. At this point in the development of the sport, we do not have an abundance of pianists who are experienced in the composition of gymnastic music.

The music may come from private musicians or record albums that many recording companies are now providing for floor-exercise music. Either choice presents particular problems. Locating the experienced pianist can be very difficult. The truly talented gymnastic pianist is likely to be expensive. Because of pianists' creative pride, a piece of music may require many, many hours of work. For this reason they cannot produce the quantity needed to cover the many existing gymnastic programs. Clubs buying music for their programs often pass the music from gymnast to gymnast to defer the cost and difficulty of obtaining new music. Thus, the music may lose its impact and originality because gymnast, spectator, and judge have become tired of it.

If records are used, there is always the possibility that another gymnast in the meet will have the same music. This is undesirable, of course; the gymnast is usually handicapped psychologically by such an occurrence. She feels her routine is no longer unique.

Breaking in a pianist, whether it be for live performance or recording purposes, takes a great deal of patience on the part of the gymnast and coach. The language of gymnastics and the language of the musician may be worlds apart if they have not had experience with each other's area. The musician is not always willing to sacrifice what he feels is technically correct for his music to play what the gymnast desires for her routine.

Once a source of music has been established, the coach and gymnast must select the actual tune or tunes to be used for the exercise. Patricia Bissell, pianist for the 1972 Olympics, suggests that the following steps be considered when choosing a musical selection. First, listen to the melody without accompaniment. Secondly, look for strength and clarity in the rhythmic patterns of both the melody and the accompaniment.

When beginning exercise composition, one of the categories of character, ballet, or theme may be chosen. Character routines seem to be the most popular because they are entertaining and "fun;" the audience can "get into" the exercise. In character routine the gymnast portrays a particular object or person, such as a doll, puppet, shark, or soldier, or the music (such as "The Sting", "Let's Go Fly a Kite", or "Beer Barrel Polka") that lends itself to movements of a character nature. The gymnast plays to the audience. Their enjoyment and approval is a necessary catalyst to the success of the exercise.

The ballet or pure gymnastic type exercise blends with the music in such a way that neither is dependent totally on the other. The movements are usually of a ballet or rhythmic gymnastic variety. The gymnast enjoys her routine for its pure artistic qualities and not necessarily because the audience will enjoy it. The audience remains in the spectator role and does not join in with hand clapping as they might in a character routine.

The theme type of floor exercise is usually a gimmick. This is used for a special occasion such as a National Championship or an Olympic Games. The Mexican Hat Dance, for example, was used at the Mexico Games much to the delight of the audience who clapped and cheered their approval.

It is the job of the coach to see that the music fits the gymnast's personality. A tall, regal-looking gymnast should probably not try to perform a "cute" character routine. If the gymnast does not feel the music, she will not be able to put the exercise across successfully.

The music must also fit the morphology of the gymnast. A very young, tiny gymnast should probably not use a powerful, dramatic piece of music. The music would probably overpower the child's body. A strong muscular-looking gymnast should not use delicate soft music. She will probably look even more muscular or stocky in the presence of ballet music.

The gymnast's skill level should be enhanced by the music. A very fast, dynamic, strong piece of music will be a detriment to a young, ectomorphic, undeveloped gymnast. She must possess the strength and endurance to stay with the music to the last note.

It is my own belief that a variation of one tune is better than several tunes. Too many tunes or variations can be harmful because the judges' and spectators' attention is distracted trying to keep up with "name that tune."

The time limit for floor exercise is from one minute to one minute and thirty seconds. Beginner gymnasts will probably want to keep their time to a little over the minimum since their endurance and repertoire is small, while the Elite gymnast usually needs every second to include her many capabilities.

The music should be varied in dynamics: some slow phases, quick phases, and some accented phases. The music will ultimately decide where the acrobatic and tumbling skills are placed. The choice of elements such as rhythmic elements, acrobatic elements, dance leaps, and turns should be in harmony with the music. At no time should the movement deviate from the feel or style of the music.

The sound of the music is extremely important, so the recording of your music should be done by a professional. Too many times music is recorded on a small cassette player. When the volume is turned up for a big gym, the clarity of the music is highly distorted. The equipment used to play the music should be given special consideration. Get professional advice before purchasing equipment. Remember that you are usually competing in large gyms or arenas and you must be able to hear your music.

Part 6 is purposely wide in scope, skimming only the surface of gymnastics coaching. Notes for Beginning Coaches provides a good starting point for aspiring coaches. Linda Metheny's chapter gives insight into the coach's intangible, yet important, role of gaining the gymnast's trust and confidence in training.

Specificity of Stress and Training is a fancy title for the coach's responsibility for preparing gymnasts for meets psychologically.

Although space limitations prohibit extensive coverage of spotting technique, a general overview of the spotting skill is presented in the last chapter of this part.

6

COACHING GYMNASTICS

The indispensable coach (Lorraine Rorke photo)

23

Notes for Beginning Coaches

Sandy Thielz

Coaching and teaching gymnastics is an art. Not all of us can be good coaches even though we may have good performers. Enthusiasm is one of the most important ingredients to good coaching, along with knowledge of techniques, skill analysis, and spotting. Coaches must love their work and be willing to work very hard for very long hours. They should set certain standards for their gymnasts and enforce them as well.

Beginning coaches many times feel they are "experts" almost immediately. They do not attend clinics, meets, or workshops to learn—all of us can always learn. The best advice for any coach, gymnast, or judge is to keep an open mind and try to learn as much as possible from all sources.

Attend as many clinics and workshops as you can. Even though you may not agree with some of the material or it may seem "old hat" to you, try it. Read all available material, magazines and books.

Join the United States Gymnastics Federation. This organization is the governing body for gymnastics in the United States. By being a member, you will be kept up-to-date on most of the meets and clinics being held and on all information pertinent to gymnastics.

Attending meets can be very worthwhile. A coach can learn new skills and see different kinds of movement. Spotting new skills and teaching skills is a tremendous way to learn more about each skill (and the only way to become a good spotter is to do it).

Coaches should learn to recognize errors in technique. This comes from constant observation and work with gymnastics. Do not always use the same words to the students: if they do not understand, try to explain another way. Not all gymnasts respond to the same type of coaching. Use drills, warm-up exercises, specific conditioning programs for strength, flexibility, and endurance. These can be recommended by an athletic trainer.

When selecting your team, look for the following attributes:

• *Good body control.* What are their physical attributes? How well conditioned are they? Do they display good technique when working?

• *Ability to accept coaching.* Do they respond well to coaching? Are they enthusiastic about being helped?

• *Indication of potential ability on each event.* Even though a girl may not be particularly well-skilled, she may display talent potential.

• *Personal discipline.* Does the gymnast display a willingness to work? Is she capable of working on her own? Does she work to her fullest potential?

When training for the competitions, have your gymnasts work routines, including mounts and dismounts. After they finish full routines, then work on the parts that need polishing. Use all the available equipment. Lines on the floor or bleachers can substitute for balance beams. Single parallel bars can be used as an additional bar for single bar skills.

As a coach you should know the basic rules. Many times a coach's error can result in a penalty to the gymnast. Conduct practice meets so the gymnasts can practice marching, standing at attention, and the etiquette that is part of gymnastics.

As a beginning coach never be afraid to ask questions. Be willing to search for the answers—keep an open mind.

24

Motivation, Dedication, and Determination

Linda Metheny

What makes a champion in gymnastics is often not the physical ability, but something else, something apparently intangible, and not easily detected. This extra something lies deep within the individual and needs to be nurtured, coached and tested, just as the physical aspects need to be developed progressively.

Motivation is a personal trait that is primarily instilled by the coach. An important aspect in developing motivation is the setting of goals. To me that doesn't mean "you better stay on in this meet" or "we can win if you hit," but a more personal approach to the child's development. The gymnast probably has set long-range goals, or at this point more like dreams, such as being a national champion or making an Olympic team. This is great as long as the coach and the girl are realistically working toward short range goals also. These are the day-to-day accomplishments that really make working hard fun.

The coach and the gymnast will profit greatly through communicating with one another about what is expected in the near future. Such as sitting down on a Monday and saying "this week I would like to see straight legs on all kips". . . then concentrating on that. When that is accomplished go on to something else. We like to set goals for the summer (or goals for the season) such as getting new tricks or a new routine. Gymnasts, like everyone else, need things to look forward to. Even during competition season we like to have a few new skills for the girl to work on, so that there is always a challenge. Nothing is more tiring than doing the same thing over and over with no new incentive.

Besides setting goals and making challenges for the youngster, there is the motivating aspects of peer pressure. Keeping the girls in ability groupings is good, but if possible they should not always be the best one in the group. The gymnast will naturally strive to be as good as her teammates. You have all seen the "I can do it if she can" syndrome when one girl learns a trick and suddenly they all want to try. Everyone likes to feel that what they are doing is appreciated. A few words of honest praise from coach, judge or parent can mean so much to the gymnast who is trying her best to please. A coach must criticize constructively, but all correction and no encouragement will make anyone frustrated, as will meaningless criticism and false praise.

A coach can make travel to meets very inspiring if the team goes not just to win, but to learn from the competition. Seeing the new skills and styles of the other competitors can be exhilarating. This may carry over through weeks of practice, especially if the coach will evaluate the competition in terms of their performance (in relationship to others). This is a good opportunity to make any readjustment of individual and team goals. I feel that it is important for the coach and the gymnast to realize that competitions are for learning and not the end result. If a girl falls off the apparatus, that isn't the important thing. What is important is she learned something from the experience. Without this attitude the concept of failure may be too much for the girl to endure over the many years of practice that it takes to reach her potential in a sport.

Proficiency in anything requires a great deal of determination and self-discipline. These personal characteristics are learned by example and experience. If a few girls tend to sit around and talk instead of working, pretty soon most of the others will pick up this lazy attitude, or if the coach seems uninterested and "draggy" this will also rub off on the team. The whole team will benefit if there are a few girls to set the example of persistency and perseverance, especially if the coach praises their efforts. Many girls will work hard as long as they have direction but seem unable to work on their own. If this is the case, they need to be given specific direction as to the use of their time. This can be done with a strict workout schedule or by having them keep a workout diary. As the girls' self-discipline and stamina develop, so will their love of the sport.

An athlete learns to recognize the efforts of others and to follow in the direction that seems to be the most productive. Thus if a coach doesn't give 100 percent of his concern and energy, he can't expect total involvement from his students. Youngsters will also try to live up to the expectations of their leaders (coaches, parents, judges). So if not much is expected, not much will be produced. A coach can never "sell a youngster short." Everyone has hidden potential that may be developed to varying degrees. Often a girl who at first glance appears unathletic has the determination and love of movement to work hard at overcoming any weakness she might have.

A person's ability to cope with frustration is also an important factor in the life of an athlete. Recovery time from an injury and repeated failure at learning small skills may be too much for many physically talented would-be stars. The understanding of oneself and the determination to continue, with the realization that everything worthwhile takes a great deal of patience, is an essential requirement.

A coach can encourage and motivate the mind, install discipline and determination into the will, plus develop and train the body. These factors, together with inherent dedication and resource, will bring about the realization of individual gymnasts' aspirations. Through all of this it is not the triumph but the struggle that brings about the complete personal satisfaction in knowing that you as a coach, judge or gymnast, have given your all.

25
Hints on Coaching Techniques
Don Tonry

TWISTING-SOMERSAULTING SKILLS

Teaching a gymnast to twist while somersaulting poses special problems to the coach. Early twisting techniques, such as those used in Arabian Somersaults or the Barani, tend to retard salto action because the twist is executed in conjunction with initial salto thrust. The result, in the early stages of teaching, is usually under rotation of the somersault. To counter this problem, the coach must overemphasize *hip elevation* during the initial thrust of the somersault. The gymnast should be taught to twist as late as possible without destroying the character of the skill.

One excellent technique is to teach these early twisting skills in a layout position as a means of instilling a pattern of continuous hip drive throughout the movement. Breaking this coaching technique down even further would involve a dive with half twist in layout position, to a handstand (twisting belt). Once the performer masters the straight body drive to handstand with a twist, the coach can easily encourage a complete layout salto by lifting the gymnast off the floor for the second phase of rotation. Once the pattern of strong rotation has been achieved, the gymnast may be encouraged to change the layout position to a pike or trick.

Full twisting somersault may also be taught using this technique. In this case, the coach must be sure that the second half twist is in the same direction as the first one. Very briefly, the direction of the second half twist should be analogous to a "right hand first" round off if the first half twist is to the left (Arabian dive). Twisting from a left hand down first Barani should be to the right.

A general rule might be: Twisting tends to inhibit somersaulting rotation; therefore, a coach should anticipate this problem in advance.

HEAD PLACEMENT IN GYMNASTICS

The function of the head in gymnastics is somewhat illusive in terms of efficiency of motion. As a weight, the head probably has more influence on somersaulting than it does on twisting because of its location at the end of the body. During twisting skills, the weight of the head is relatively insignificant because of its location on the twisting axis.

It seems that the main function of the head is to carry the sensory organs that the gymnast relies on for orientation (eyes and ears). The head is turned or rotated into a particular position in order to allow the performer to perceive visually or to "feel" (inner ear balance) the directional thrust of the movement.

The head is attached to the upper end of the spinal column with the aid of various muscles and ligaments. When the head is turned or rotated, other portions of the upper half of the body are affected (twisted, rounded, or arched). This action can enhance (usual subtle) or inhibit the general theme of a movement.

When the head is *thrown* backward, on backward rotating skills, in order to perceive visually the ensuing final position, the joint structure of the upper back accommodates the motion. The result is generally a deemphasis of the drive or thrust of the lower portion of the body. This action is often desirable when the gymnast wishes to terminate his lower body thrust as in a flic-flac to handstand or a backward salto to handstand on the parallel bars.

On skills that require a continuation of drive throughout the movement, the head should be held in a forward or neutral position (varies on different skills) to promote continuation of the initial thrust. Once the "follow through" has been established, the head should be placed in position to provide visual orientation for the "catch" or landing. Generally, throwing the head backward or sideward early will result in weaker thrust (poor elevation) and form breaks in the lower body because an "early head" signifies over concern for the end portion of a skill rather than the thrusting (follow through) portion of the skill.

Follow-through often represents "daring," which is why judges reward points for virtuosity and difficulty. Most performers spend their entire gymnastics career trying to achieve a higher degree of "follow through" despite their innate feeling of self-preservation, which strongly suggests that making the trick is enough.

The use of the head in gymnastics skill performance has both physical and psychological implications that directly affect skill performance. Balance, visual orientation, and body alignment can be, to some degree, attributed to the use of the head during performance of all skills. An "early head" generally suggests emotional preoccupation with the final phase of a skill and therefore inhibits "follow through."

SPOTTING WITH THE EYES

Although there have not been any studies demonstrating the merits of eye orientation during the performance of gymnastics skills, there seems to be some practical evidence that spotting techniques are very important considerations particularly when learning new skills.

Spotting refers to the practice of visually focusing on one or more specific objects or body parts during the performance of specific skills. Coaches and competitors have long recognized the importance of this technique, but little or nothing has been written on the subject in relation to individual skills.

Balance Skills. Eyes focus on *one* spot that provides visual orientation in relation to general body position. Example: One arm handstand—focus on support hand and bar (parallel bars).

Forward Hand Springs (Aerial Walkover). Spot floor during first phase. Spot wall or floor during second phase.

Round Off (Aerial Cartwheels, Barani and Inverted Pirouettes. Spot floor throughout.

Backward Handspring. Spot floor until arms reach shoulder level. Spot floor between hands for second phase.

Forward Somersault. Spot floor or wall for first phase. Spot floor or wall for second phase.

Backward Somersault. Spot floor during first phase. Spot floor during second phase.

Backward Salto 1/1 Twist. Spot floor during take off. Spot wall or hips after take off. Spot floor during twist (under armpit).

Twisting Off a Pike. Spot legs in pike position. Spot landing area at end of twist.

Specific eye-spotting procedures should be incorporated in the teaching of all skills on all events. The coach must learn an acceptable spotting technique for all skills taught. Generally, always consider the surface of support as the first and last spot; intermediate spots should also enhance orientation.

FACILITATING THRUST THROUGH ARCHING & PIKING

The introduction of "new" concepts in gymnastics, especially if they are Japanese innovations, tend to be misused or "over accepted." Many coaches cannot determine when certain techniques are appropriate and therefore use a single "new" approach to all skills. A fair example is the straight body concept that has been with us for at least twenty years. This approach to gymnastics permeated American Gymnastics to the point where a gymnast was taught to perform like a jointless stick. For a while this technique was coupled with a "head down" approach that required orientation with one's navel rather than the apparatus. Currently, we are going through the "hunch" approach. Put these all together and you have a straight-hipped, round-shouldered, head-ducking gymnast.

All of these concepts have some merit functionally if not aesthetically; however, they are not the answer to most of our problems and therefore should be handled with caution.

Most backward rotating skills on the apparatus require a strong hip drive, which is characterized by a flexion of the hips or a pike. To do this effectively (power), the gymnast must arch the back before flexing the hips. If very little hip drive power is required, as on a horizontal bar giant swing, a straight body preliminary position is perfectly in order.

Forward rotating skills must often receive thrust from an arch. A preliminary pike position will enhance the power of the arch. An arch that is initiated from a straight body position will be considerably weaker. Horizontal Bar "hechts," back rise ring skills, and numerous forward somersaulting dismounts fall into this category.

Function and aesthetics are often confused. Many coaches, in their desire to achieve the straight line look, often fail to consider the main purpose of a skill which is, generally, to change position as effectively as possible with good form. Technical execution (style) should never inhibit the main objective. Consider also that style changes; thus, our concept of perfection.

Many gymnasts and coaches misinterpret and/or overemphasize the straight hip concept to the point of piking. Backward giant swings and forward parallel bar swings are often taught in an "archless" pattern which robs the gymnast of the potential for a strong hip lift at the front of the swing, where it is often necessary to drive the swing.

The straight body concept can also be a strong minus in tumbling where the power of a "snap down" from a flic-flac is derived from contracting the hip flexors in conjunction with elbow and shoulder extension. In this situation, the power of the snap down would be considerably less from a straight body position. The purpose of the flic-flac is to *gain power* for the ensuing somersault.

Gymnastics coaches must evaluate trends in body position with an eye on function or efficiency. Overemphasis in the area of straight, piked, or arched body positions can inhibit the main objective of performance.

26

Specificity of Stress and Training

James R. Brown

Stress physiology is a relatively new area of medical inquiry, but one which may be of great importance to those individuals who are interested in competitive athletics. It seems certain that in 1950, when Hans Selye published his first paper on stress physiology, he had little interest in competitive athletics. Indeed, at that time as a member of the faculty of the School of Medicine, McGill University, his interests were centered around medical illnesses. However, one of Selye's greatest contributions to medical knowledge was the finding that the body reacts uniformly and predictably to all different types of stresses (or stressors), and results in a predictable pattern of adaptation which Selye calls the "general adaptation syndrome."

During research aimed at discovering a new female sex hormone, Selye discovered that the injection of foreign chemicals into the body produced the same reactions, based on the level of toxicity rather than the composition of the foreign substance. This reaction to stress is commonly called the "fight or flight" reaction and consists of (1) loss of appetite, (2) dilation of the peripheral blood vessels, (3)ulceration of the duodenum, (4) enlargement of the pupils of the eyes, and (5) increased muscle tonus.

In athletics we typically refer to this condition as "nervousness;" and, for some forms of athletic competition, this nervousness serves to prepare the body for competition. Weight lifters, shot putters, and the like certainly benefit from the biochemical changes produced by the stress of competition. Unfortunately, there are some forms of athletic activities which do not benefit from this condition. Sports where there are no explosive actions, where there is a premium placed on steadiness and balance, can easily be adversely affected by an increase in muscle tonus and energy potential. Gymnastics certainly falls into this category; thus, the topic of this paper is to explore some of the ways that a basic understanding of the "general adaption syndrome" may be utilized to assist the coach in his task of preparing athletes for competition.

It does not take the beginning coach long to discover that the task of getting gymnasts through routines in practice is decidedly different than getting them through routines in a competition. Further, the more important the meet, the greater the possibility of missed routines seems to be. Indeed, one of the most frustrating (but challenging) problems which confronts the coach is the unusually talented athlete who constantly folds under the stress of competition; therefore, the task of the coach is more than teaching the gymnast moves incorporating them into routines. Perhaps even more important is his task of preparing for competition.

Selye describes the "general adaptation syndrome" as triphasic. The three phases are:

1. the alarm reaction;
2. the stage of resistance; and,
3. the stage of exhaustion.

In the usual practice situation there is little stress for the well-conditioned athlete, and the coach should have little difficulty in getting sufficient numbers of routines in preparation for forthcoming competitions. However, if a stress which is similar to competition has not been artificially imposed, it is likely that the athlete will not perform similarly. According to Selye's GAS (general adaptation syndrome), the gymnast would go into the alarm stage, to the stage of resistance, and how well he has learned to adapt to the stress is the key to success in competition. With this in mind I offer the following suggestion as the key to bridging the gap between the theoretical and the practical application of the GAS to competitive gymnasts.

Make the Meet Like the Practice or the Practice Like the Meet

This statement simply means that the athlete should train with the same types of stresses under which he competes, i.e., the meet should not be a new and different experience. Rather, it should be a continuation of the practice situation.

Environment

If the team generally trains in a pleasant, quiet environment, then meets should be conducted under similar conditions. If background music is utilized in the practices, it should also be allowed during the competition, and the music should be similar in both type and volume. It is not unknown for some teams to tape their practice music and play it softly during competition at away meets.

The importance of high intensity music has been recognized in other sports. In recent years, pep bands have been employed at basketball games as a psychological weapon. This has served to heighten the emotions of the games to the extent that spectators have had to be restrained. Obviously, this practice has no place at a gymnastics contest; however, the coach should be aware of the fact that loud or unusual music may have a detrimental effect on performance.

Although the principle "make the meet like the practice, or the practice like the meet" seems to provide two alternatives, actually the latter is more, for there are certain variables which are constant within the framework of the competition, i.e., certain stress-producing elements are inherent in competition. The most important of these are the effects of the crowd (and judges), performing alone on the floor (finals and dual meets), and most important, the realization of the importance of the individual relative to the team score. Since these are difficult to alter, the coach must adapt the team practice to take these sources of stress into account.

Formal Intra-Squad Meets

Here the gymnasts have the crowd, the judges, and are working alone on the floor. Further, and a point that is frequently overlooked, they are getting used to the competitive uniform. In a recent national competition, this writer witnessed six finalists "blow" their routines due to difficulty with uniforms. Suspender problems were the most frequent source of difficulty.

Of course, there are problems with utilizing formal intrasquads during practice periods. This is not as easy as it might sound, for to have one person performing in an intra-squad meet while the other members of the team sit and watch (spectators), represents a lot of wasted time for those not performing. As a result coaches tend to "take" routines so that the gymnasts can at least practice after doing routines. This is certainly a reasonable approach; however, if peer pressure is to be used to provide the stress of a meet, it would seem more effective to have all team members watch the routines.

Biological Rhythm

The time of competition is another factor in considering stress and athletic contests. According to Gartmann, man is governed by a "physiological clock," i.e., a biological rhythm which is commonly conditioned into the working man which describes his daily, patterned life. Gartmann's research discovered that the body temperature follows a pattern of being generally low early in the morning and gradually rising throughout the day. There is a slight remission following the dinner hour, but then it returns to the previous pattern. It was also found that efficiency followed a similar pattern, being greater in the early hours and tapering off as the day progresses. Perhaps more important was Gartmann's finding that extinction and reconditioning of this biological rhythm are difficult and time consuming. Every attempt should therefore be made to schedule practice at times of the day which are similar to contest times.

Since many secondary and college teams are generally "locked" into regular practice times due to facility scheduling, this factor must be taken into consideration in the seasonal scheduling of contests.

In advanced level competition, where the athlete competes in time zones different from his own, he could possibly be competing at a time when his body is usually resting (sleeping). In this situation, the coach must determine the difference in times in order to provide for an adjustment of the biological rhythm. According to Gartmann, this may take as long as three weeks, depending on the age and condition of the person.

Coaching Tactics

The attitude of the coach, both during practice and competition, is of great importance to a successful gymnastics program. Yet it is interesting to note that there is no single personality type which can be associated with continual success. There are many examples of very successful coaches who are softspoken and low key in their approach to working with athletes. Likewise, many outstanding coaches come to mind who are loud, outspoken, and not adverse to shouting at athletes during the course of a practice. The key of course is that the coach who maintains a low emotional level during practice should continue to do so during the meet situation. To do otherwise is to run the risk of adding additional stress which may have a detrimental effect on performance.

One outstanding coach at a large state university has had a great deal of success in perfecting routines by talking (or yelling) mistakes at his gymnasts during practice routines. If this practice is not to be disruptive, the gymnasts must perfect routines to the extent that their bodies seem to do the sets routinely while their minds are listening to the running critique. This practice seems to work for high level competitors when it is not done too often, but it should be considered that no one will be yelling during the actual meet situation!

The suggestions in this paper certainly do not exhaust the possibilities for "making the meet like the practice, or the practice like the meet;" however, it is hoped that they will provide a general understanding of the GAS and the relationship of stress to performance. In doing so, the coach can then make an effort to better align his practice and meet procedures!

27

Some Thoughts on Spotting

Hardy Fink

With the recent popularity and availability of such equipment as crash pads the emphasis on effective spotting has been reduced. Top spotters are now even more scarce than top gymnasts and are in danger of becoming scarcer yet. Nevertheless, good spotting is still essential to the development of good gymnastics and for the prevention of injuries.

There are, basically, two types of spotting: assistive spotting and protective spotting. *Assistive spotting* refers to the art of helping the gymnast to complete a particular movement successfully (thus, the occasional name of "kinesthetic" spotting). *Protective spotting*, of course, refers to preventing a gymnast from sustaining a serious injury during a fall or some other accident.

Both types of spotting require the spotter to have certain attributes and knowledge to be effective. Because a spotter must be capable of both types of spotting, he or she must have all of the attributes necessary to each. The spotter must be reasonably courageous by not fearing injury to himself; he must have quick reflexes, a desire to help, and must be thoroughly familiar with any special spotting apparatus he may be using,

210

with the movement or the routine he is spotting and with some specialized information from the sport sciences. In addition, the spotter, ideally, should know the performer and his reactions well and must, for the safety of the gymnast, know and admit to his own limitations. It is obvious, then, that spotting is no haphazard thing, but is a skilled activity like gymnastics and requires considerable learning, practice, and experience.

In terms of courage a spotter should not fear self-injury when a gymnast falls. A natural reflex to an object flying in one's direction is an avoidance response. To overcome this response takes some courage and practice and it takes more practice yet to react consistently and appropriately. This is not to say that a spotter should be reckless with his own safety. One of the responsibilities of a spotter is to keep himself safe. He need not catch a falling gymnast and thereby risk injury; he need only break the fall in such a way as to prevent serious injury to the gymnast, most frequently by preventing the head from hitting the ground. In both types of spotting he must place his limbs in such a way as to prevent them from being broken across the apparatus or injured in some other way. An occasional injury to a spotter is inevitable but the incidence and severity can be much reduced by common sense.

It is unknown to many that effective spotting requires some basic knowledge from the sport sciences. The spotter must know, for instance, where the center of gravity of a gymnast is located and how the location of the center of gravity changes as the relationship of various body parts changes. He should also know that the center of gravity of a female is located somewhat lower (about one inch) in the body than it is in the male. Any force applied directly through the center of gravity will cause the entire body to move in the direction of the force. An eccentric force—a force applied away from the center of gravity—will cause or modify rotation as well. A force applied at the wrong place can increase the risk of injury during a fall or prevent the gymnast from even approximately 'feeling' a movement during assistive spotting.

An understanding of other aspects of biomechanics will allow the spotter to analyze a movement and thereby predict where the greatest force and, therefore, greatest danger of a fall is likely to be. For instance the greatest pull on the hands during a giant swing is right at the bottom (not at forty-five degrees as is so often suggested) and a fall is most likely to occur just after this. In assistive spotting the spotter should know, from analysis, where, when and how external forces are most effectively applied for the successful completion of the stunt.

During assistive spotting the hands of the spotter are often in contact with the performer throughout the movement. It is important to know that the location of the spotter's hands may facilitate or inhibit the desired movement pattern. For instance stimulation of the skin over a muscle excites that muscle (meaning that it will tend to contract) while stimulation of a non-muscular area excites only extensor muscles. Furthermore, pressure over the belly of a muscle evokes a reflex contraction of that muscle. The spotter's hands should, therefore, not be placed in such a way as to elicit undesirable reflexes. A common example is the grasping of the performer's biceps during parallel bar work which may elicit an undesirable arm flexion, especially in beginners. Such reflexes are most likely to appear under conditions of stress or fatigue.

When an injury does occur—and it does—the spotter must have basic knowledge of athletic injuries and their treatment. There is no excuse for a coach (who is usually also the spotter) not to have any familiarity with basic first aid practices and not to have some basic diagnostic ability.

In order to be effective, it is the responsibility of the spotter to know what the gymnast is planning to do. He must also be aware of adverse effects, if any, that his assistance may have, especially on the technically correct execution of a movement. If assistance of some kind proves to be necessary it is essential, in many instances, that the assistance be continued to the end of the movement. All too often a gymnast, with help, successfully completes a movement only to find himself in an undesirable position just as the spotter lets him go.

The purpose of spotting is to beget confidences and, therefore, the spotter must be both confident and competent, as often a gymnast will only attempt a movement because of his faith in his spotter's ability. There is no faster way to lose a gymnast's confidence in you—and possibly in himself—than to be dropped unnecessarily. The spotter, however, must be aware of an impending overdependence on him and, occasionally, the opposite. Most gymnasts are accurate in the diagnosis of their ability and their opinion as to whether or not a spotter is required should be respected. Nevertheless, there are times when a gymnast must be weaned of a spotter or, conversely, when the coach must insist on spotting. These instances depend on many variables and must be diagnosed separately. Certainly, a thorough knowledge of the gymnast's ability and his possible reactions is necessary. A knowledge of some sport psychology would do no harm.

A final responsibility of a spotter is to teach others, especially his gymnasts, how to spot. This is an essential part of developing gymnasts as future coaches and will be an indispensible part of their future careers.

The dangerous nature of gymnastics makes the subject of safety a crucial one. Gymnastics equipment (the gymnasium itself, apparatus, mats, etc.) must be designed and built to ensure maximum protection for the gymnast. But the responsibility is also with the gymnast, who should know the intricasies of personal equipment such as tape, handguards, padding, and shoes.

First-aid equipment is indispensible to any program, and the chapter included here itemizes the complete gymnastics first-aid kit. Gymnasts habitually suffer from leg and foot injuries; the Injury Prevention *chapter concentrates on the problem of preventing shin splints with taping methods. Finally,* Injury Care *covers short- and long-term treatment for muscle strains and pulls, low-back pain, and the like.*

7
SAFETY

Bart Conner (Marilou Sturges photo)

28

Gymnastics Equipment

Charles Pond

THE GYMNASIUM

A gymnastics area should be solely a gymnastics area with no other activities or sports infringing. The gymnastics area should have national and international equipment that meets safety standards set up by the standards committee and upgraded from time to time by the standards committee of the equipment manufacturing group.

Ideal space dimensions should approximate 140 feet in length and 100 feet in width, all of which should be free space without supporting columns. The ideal height would be about twenty-four feet. The gymnastics area should have at least two pits, each pit two to three feet in depth measuring eight to nine feet in width and thirty feet in length.

The ceiling must provide for placement of mechanic hangs (spotting rigs) by either beam clamps or cable clamps for supporting these protective devices. Ideally, the floor area, if not made of wood, should be completely covered with mats. A wooden floating floor provides the perfect surface for gymnastics programs for all levels from beginner to the International Elite performer.

Lighting is vital to gymnasiums and must meet the highest standards of the safety committee. Entrances and exits are of vital importance to the gymnastics facility. A checklist should be provided for the safety committee or safety chairperson to use at predetermined time periods.

Maintenance of the proper temperature and humidity is very important to gymnasts. The use of bleachers must also maintain the proper space requirements for the gymnasts involved in the gymnastics facility. The physical plant of the building housing gymnastics must be alert to possible physical needs of the facility; that is, the constant surveillance of floor plates, the mechanic systems, the nylon mechanic lines, the varied wooden parallel and uneven parallel bar rails, in addition to the various attachments supporting the gymnastics equipment.

The placement of all gymnastics equipment in the gymnasium is of extreme importance. As most gymnastics programs in America now involve coeducational gymnastics with parallel classes and training times, the placing of equipment is vital to safety training, safety training aids, and the proper use of the gymnasium facility used for the field of gymnastics.

The gymnastics equipment manufacturing companies are making outstanding contributions to gymnastics through research and development programs directed not only to improvement but to safety as well. Rubber landing mats often many feet in thickness protect the performer from landings that otherwise might cause injury. Foam rubber in fishnet-type enclosures insure soft landings in the many pit areas constructed in the gymnastics gyms. Mats that vary in softness, thickness, resilience, and other factors have made the sport safe to the extent skills that could not have been attempted only a few short years ago may now be practiced and perfected with complete safety.

The floor plates, supporting cables, and all attachments for gymnastics equipment have been perfected by applying engineering methods to safety. Wooden rails on all type bars have been replaced with wooden laminated plastic bars that do not break. The equipment manufacturing companies also make major contributions to safety with their skills-learning charts from basic to higher level skills; personnel from these companies often provide outstanding gymnastics–trained clinicians to educational systems.

BELT MECHANICS SYSTEMS

Devices have been invented that have made major contributions not only to the safety and injury prevention phase of gymnastics, but also to learning efficiency by eliminating the gymnast's fear. The circus provided us with the first Overhead Mechanic System. This safety-training aid allows the "belt handler" to hold two lines in his hands and control the action of a performer so that falls cannot occur. The belt mechanic system and the art of "belt handling" is relatively unknown by gymnastics coaches.

There are several types of belt mechanics systems, though the principle of each system is the same. Different suspensions serve all gymnastics needs. Examples of mechanics systems are:

• *Fixed overhead suspension* for use with the trampoline, horizontal bar, rings and tumbling, vault, bars, floor exercise, and beam.

• *Traveling* or *trolley runway* system for use with tumbling, vaulting, and floor exercise. Serves also for trampoline, horizontal bars, bars, and rings, beam, tumbling, etc.

• *Pond Side Horse Suspension* for use especially for beginners on the side horse.

These mechanics systems may be attached to any type support such as ceiling girders of the "I" beam type or other ceiling support. The height and size of the gymnasium will determine the type and number of mechanics possible. Ceiling height is critical for the use of a mechanic system. A ceiling more than forty feet from the floor would prohibit the best use of a mechanic system. However, a portable mechanic system suitable for gymnastics could be installed in gymnasiums with ceiling height more than forty feet. The ideal height from ceiling attachment or suspension to the floor is approximately twenty-four feet.

The ideal width of the mechanic system is thirty feet. An absolute minimum could be fifteen feet, but the performer could become entangled in the system lines.

The mechanic system is secured to "I" beams or other attachment sites on the gymnasium ceiling. It could also be attached by eye swivel hooks that have been drilled through the ceiling. All beam clamp attachments should be swivelled. A double block and a single block are attached to the swivelled beam clamps, which are fixed to the ceiling area. Through these blocks are passed nylon lines 7/16 inch in diameter. The lines are preferably made of nylon. As nylon will unravel, tape should be used to secure the ends.

The fixed-belt mechanic system has lines about 120 feet long. A longer line runs up to the double block, across the block to the single block, and down to the mechanic belt. This line is approximately eighty to ninety feet long. The shorter line is approximately thirty to fifty feet long. The belt handler's position is directly below the double block where both lines terminate.

The traveling or trolley runway belt mechanic system has other additional functions. This system enables the belt handler to remain on a line paralleling the performer as the performer executes moving combinations not restricted to an area of the fixed mechanic system. The ability of the performer to travel distances of up to forty feet makes this device outstanding for use in several gymnastic events, such as tumbling, horizontal bar, trampoline, uneven bars, etc.

There are various types of mechanics belts used around the waist of the performer. Examples of these belts are:

● The plain mechanic has a "D" ring on each side of the belt through which may be attached swivel snaps that have been secured to the ends of the nylon lines. The purpose of the swivel snap is to prevent the lines from becoming tangled or from untwisting.

● The Pond twisting belt allows the performer to do either forward, sideward, or rearward somersaults with twisting movements, while the plain mechanic permits only forward and rearward somersaults not involving changes in direction. The Pond twisting belt allows the performer to spin in addition to the forward, sideward, or backward somersaults. The performer is not limited by lines or other restrictions. This belt mechanic system is not only a safety device; it has important functions as a teaching and training aid.

The instructor or student handling the lines of the belt mechanic system is called a "belt handler," on whom the performer is directly dependent. The belt handler should see that the mechanic system is working properly and thus is safe; however, the performer should also check the mechanic system for wear or damage for his own safety.

The belt handler must be trained in belt handling to materially assist the performer. One hand, called the "tight" hand, holds the lines taut as the student attempts tricks and sequences of actions in the air. This hand is held about three inches above shoulder level. The stroke of this hand, as the performer initiates tricks, is about fourteen inches above and below the shoulder.

As it is impossible to maintain tautness of the nylon lines throughout the action of the performance with this one hand, the other hand also has an important function. The other hand functions as the "slide" hand. The "slide" hand holds the lines above the "tight" hand, allowing the lines to slide through.

When the performer stands on the trampoline, the belt secured around his waist, and the belt handler holding the lines in his hands; this position is known as the standard position. The eyes of the belt handler should always be on the gymnast as he or she begins exercises on the apparatus. The belt handler's "tight" hand is outstretched upward and downward near the body to its fullest extent as the student performs. A swaying results in the lines as the "tight" hand reaches the fullest extent at the bottom of its stroke, and the belt handler must try to prevent this swaying. As the belt handler cannot hold the performer with only one hand, the slide hand assists in tightening the lines at the top of the bounce. The lines must be kept taut with direct mechanical contact with the body of the student as actions are attempted and exercises initiated. The belt handler may give power or force to the student or stop the action to support the student in the mechanic, should he fail to execute a skill.

The belt handler must be trained for other positions than the standard, such as landings on seat, front, and back of body. For example, the belt handler may allow both lines to slide yet still maintain contact with the performer as varied landings are being performed. The belt handler merely shifts hand positions on the lines from the standard to another position of a difference of approximately one or two feet in the lines, keeping eye contact to protect the performer. The same principle applies to the front drop position on the trampoline; the belt handler should make different adjustments in the lines to insure complete control of the student. As the performer returns to standard position, the belt handler uses both hands to take up the lines.

The fixed and traveling mechanic systems requires a belt handler, but the Pond side horse mechanic suspension does not require one. The gymnast places the twisting belt about his midsection or at chest height. A single strand line is attached to the gymnast's waist or back. This nylon line of 7/16 inch is further attached to a nine-foot length of four-strand, one-half inch exercise or elastic cord, which is flexible. Adjustments are possible with a strap to compensate for the gymnast's height, weight, and body type. This device allows a performer to work the length and breadth of the horse on either side without fear of falling from the horse.

Another device resulting in more efficient learning of gymnastics skills is the revolving ski deck, which because of its moving, padded carpet beneath the performer's feet, saves time and reduces fatigue. Shortening the learning time thus allows younger performers to reach skill levels unapproachable in the past. This device provides another safe "fixed" mechanic system as the deck (carpeted) moves and the performer stays in place while performing the gymnastics skills. The revolving ski deck can revolutionize the teaching of many gymnastics skills by decreasing to weeks what previously took months or years to teach.

Other safety-training aids:

• *Pond handstander,* a device with supporting arms to prevent the gymnast from falling from the handstand position; and

• *revolving horizontal bar system,* a ball-bearing device that allows for turning about the bar. A harness around the gymnast's waist provides the safety as the body is supported at all times in the action.

29

Personal Protective Equipment
Walter Zwickel

The best protection for a gymnast are his skills, his spotter, and his physical condition; these protect him best from physical injury. However, there are many areas of the body susceptible to special wear and tear during gymnastic practice and competition: the underarm area (in the men's parallel bar event), the forward pelvic area (in the women's uneven bars event), the lower legs (in the men's side horse event)—and the hands and feet in all gymnastics events.

HANDGUARDS

Hundreds of different kinds of handguards are available, but they generally fall into two basic categories:

Skin Protective

These handguards are designed to protect the skin against callouses and rips. They vary from super-soft doeskin type leather for women's activities to relatively stiff, heavy, chrome-tanned leathers for men's activities. This category also includes webbing and Lampwick versions.

All of these are designed to be worn with the finger loop

down at the base of the fingers for the purpose of protecting the palms of the hands. These are not designed for and never should be used in any of the fingertip configurations. Using them for this purpose may result in a break or an accident.

Fingertip and Supportive Handguards

These are specially designed handguards, generally used for men's still ring events only. They should be worn with the finger loops at the fingertip. The purpose of this design is to use the body weight pulling through the strap to increase the wearer's holding or gripping power.

This technique is very effective, and allows for longer workouts before "hot hands" set in. However, these *must* be handguards that are specifically designed for this job, and not oversized handguards as outlined in the section above. To design a handguard properly for this, the leathers must be super strong, virtually stretchproof, and all straps and finger loop areas must be of sufficient size and thickness to support the body weight. In addition, the buckles must be solid-piece forged or die-cast buckles because much of the strain of the exercise is placed on them.

This type of handguard should be carefully examined for signs of wear or impending breakage before each day's use. Failure to wear it could result in a serious injury.

UNDERARM

In some of the below-the-bar swing moves on men's parallel bars the bars themselves are actually the armpit of the gymnast. This can be abrasive and uncomfortable. Gymnastic jerseys do not cover the area, and whereas a jacket or T-shirt can be worn for practice, they cannot be worn in competition. If the gymnast is repeatedly going to use this move in practice, he should wear a T-shirt or a jacket, which should be made of a soft material at least on the surface in contact with the skin.

To avoid irritation in a meet, about the only thing that the gymnast can do is to be sure that the bars are clean (no chalk build-up) and that his underarm area is as dry as possible. Even a light inconspicuous dusting of talcom powder could be helpful. Although this underarm contact in a meet is only momentary with very few repetitions, it can be irritating to some types of skin.

FRONT PELVIC AREA

In women, this area is extremely sensitive to bruising, especially on the castaway-to-a-hip-circle. Several companies now offer practice shorts that have a pocket in the front where up to one inch padding can be slipped. Also, there are pads available for the lower bar for practicing this move. These bar or body pads can be used extensively in practice; however, they alter the "feel" of the bar, and the gymnast should practice without them so she can be familiar with the feel of the bar when protective gear is not there.

LOWER LEG PROTECTION (POMMEL HORSE)

During practice and during a meet, it is possible to brush the lower legs against the cover of the horse while doing circles. Of course, this is a break, and the object is not to brush, but many times brushing cannot be avoided. Because the horse covers are made of chrome tanned leather, they can be quite abrasive, and repeated contacts can be irritating. There are many garments designed for use in practice such as specific side horse pants ("farmer johns"), any pair of warmup pants, competition pants, or simply high sweat socks taped at the calf. In competition, the competition pants themselves offer protection. The important thing to remember here is that the legs should be protected during practice when repeated brushings are likely.

FEET AND ANKLES

This is the most crucial and controversial area for personal protective wear because of the many conflicting priorities. Since the appearance of the feet are part of the score, it is important that the foot covering be aesthetically flattering. This is in direct conflict with the need to pad the bottom of the feet against the shock of tumbling or dismounts; the heavier the padding the worse the appearance. Then, there is the matter of traction. In certain instances it is desirable that the shoe provide extreme traction, whereas in other cases such as the balance beam, controlled sliding or controlled lack of traction is desirable. The point is that there is no one shoe that is suitable for all events, and the gymnast must choose from the hundreds of available types the one that does the job for them in a specific event. Generally they are:

Apparatus Shoes

These are shoes used in the events where the only contact between the feet and anything else is primarily during the dismount (e.g., bars, side horse). The shoe may be of minimal weight and designed primarily to be flattering on the feet. Thin leather and stretch nylon are the most popular types. The soles of the shoes are generally a traction type of sole, because if the dismount is made properly, there will be no sliding, and if the dismount is made improperly the traction helps in the recovery.

Vaulting Shoes

In the days before the development of deep crash pads, a vaulting shoe was a heavy duty shoe with padding in the sole designed to absorb part of the shock of landing. Today with super thick and soft crash pads, a vault shoe can be an apparatus shoe. The only additional requirement is that the seaming at the toes be extra strong due to the bursting pressure at point of impact. Generally, a strong, soft, leather shoe is most successful in this event.

Floor Exercise Shoes

This type of shoe can vary greatly according to the routine that the individual gymnast has selected. All floor exercise routines must show a mixture of flexibility, tumbling, and dance, and each gymnast puts emphasis where their own individual strengths lie and does only the minimum in the areas where they are weakest. Therefore, a gymnast who does a lot of tumbling in the routine would prefer a shoe that is more heavily padded at the slight sacrifice of form. A gymnast with most emphasis on dance moves might want more sliding in the shoe. In general, an apparatus shoe is used according to the taste of the individual gymnast.

Balance Beam Shoe

This can be a specialized shoe according to the woman's tastes. One shoe that has been quite popular on the balance beam is a stretch nylon shoe with a soft leather sole. The advantage of the leather sole is that it can be used dry for a sliding effect, or it can be dampened by stepping on a moist towel for a traction effect. Similar results can be gotten by wearing the plain cotton ped. Used dry, it provides a sliding effect, and stepping into resin provides the traction when needed.

NEED FOR COACH'S ADVICE

All personal protective clothing can contribute in one way or another to the gymnast's comfort, safety, and performance. However, any of this equipment can be misused, and so it is strongly recommended that no individual gymnast should attempt to make his or her own decisions regarding shoes, handguards, or other protective or safety gear. The coach should always be consulted. The coach knows the needs of the individual based on the individual's skill level and physical conditioning.

It should also be remembered that gymnastics like any other sport can produce blisters, skin tears, calluses, sprains, and a broad assortment of minor irritations and injuries. Reliance on any one aspect for protection is foolish. Protection must be regarded as a comprehensive attitude comprising the personal equipment, the floor equipment, the physical conditioning, and the coach's skills—especially the coach, who will generally coordinate all of these factors.

30
First Aid Equipment
Holly Wilson

Could you respond to an accident? Is your gym equipped to handle an emergency? You may be improperly prepared for an emergency situation.

Your school or club's first aid kit should include the following:

• *Bandage scissors.* The 5½- or 7¼-inch size is good to cut tape from the roll. *Do not* use them to remove a strapping. Cutting through several thicknesses of tape quickly dulls the scissors. Chrome scissors are less expensive than stainless steel.

• *Tape cutter.* A tape cutter removes strappings. Although it is more expensive, the Shark is the most economical cutter because the blade remains sharper longer. Protective Products manufactures the Shark, but you can order it through some sporting goods dealers or medical supply companies such as School Health Supply.

• *Band-Aids.* Purchase plain strips without medication. (One of your gymnasts may be sensitive to iodine.) Several sizes are commercially available: strips, spots and patches. Strips are ¾" x 3", 1" x 3" and extra large. These should meet all your needs.

• *Sterile gauze pads.* It is more economical to purchase individually wrapped sterile gauze pads in boxes of 100. Use them to clean wounds or to protect a wound against further contamination while the gymnast is active. Three sizes, 2" x 2", 3" x 3", and 4" x 4" are useful. If your budget is limited, however, 3" x 3" is the most versatile size. You can cut the pad to the desired size or use more than one if a large wound needs to be covered.

● *Gauze rolls (2").* Roller gauze holds dressings in place, especially on moveable bony areas such as the knee or elbow. It's almost impossible to secure a gauze pad on a joint and prevent contamination with just tape. Encircle the joint with roller gauze to hold the dressing over the affected area, then secure with tape.

Though not as economical as other types, I prefer kling gauze (Johnson & Johnson) or a similar cohesive roller gauze because it is easier to use. It doesn't come unwound during application and it molds to the body part being covered.

● *Cleansing agents.* Bar soap is the easiest to obtain agent for cleaning out rips and mat or floor burns. It is also less irritating than green soap and less expensive. Cramer Products, Inc. produces an aerosol soap, Cinder Suds.

● *Antiseptics.* Hydrogen peroxide foams particles loose when it comes in contact with open skin such as a wound. Don't buy large amounts at one time. If the liquid doesn't foam the chemicals have dissociated. To prevent this, always store hydrogen peroxide in brown bottles.

Neither Ioprep or Betadine sting and are only dangerous if used on an athlete who is sensitive to iodine. Antiseptics in a solution foam are handy when treating an abrasion or a wound you want to dry quickly (blister or rip).

First Aid Cream (Johnson & Johnson) is an excellent antiseptic because it isn't too greasy and rarely does it irritate open skin. An oil base ointment may prevent air from reaching the wound and thus delay healing. If the wound is contaminated, it could become infected.

Before purchasing an eye irrigating solution, be sure the label says it is sterile. It should be sterile to avoid contamination of the eye when attempting to remove foreign objects.

If irrigation fails to remove a foreign object, or if you have something stuck in the eye, patch both eyes with sterile gauze pads and have the gymnast see an eye doctor immediately.

Isopropyl alcohol disinfects skin that is not open, for example, a blister before it is broken. It is too painful to apply alcohol to abraded skin. You should also use it to disinfect scissors and tweezers before using them on blisters and rips.

Petroleum jelly cuts down on friction between the foot and shoe when applied to the sole on the foot. Blisters are reduced in number or eliminated. When applied to the hands it keeps the skin soft and pliable and thus may prevent rips. It can also be applied to nonsterile sponges that are put on the heel and lace areas prior to strapping an ankle.

Purchase the least expensive brand of petroleum jelly. Amojell and Snow White Petrolatum are both available at Standard Oil Distribution Centers. If you contact the individual in charge you may be able to purchase it in small quantities such as five or ten pounds.

● *Mild analgesic.* An analgesic is a counterirritant that gives the athlete a local warming feeling. A water soluble analgesic—Johnson & Johnson's Heat Balm, Larson's MintGlo, or Mundy's Green Rub—is recommended rather than an oil base. Water soluble analgesics can be removed with cold water while an oil base must be removed with hot water to cut through the grease. If the analgesic is too hot, the athlete increases burning by using hot water.

● *Cotton-tipped applicators.*

● *Tongue depressors.*

● *Combine.* This roll of cotton sheeting has a gauze covering on both sides. You use it to cover an analgesic pack. If your budget is tight, you can substitute disposable diapers or pieces of old towel for the combine.

● *Elastic wraps.* These are used for compression after an injury to control swelling and also to hold dressings, analgesic packs or tape in place. They don't provide good support due to their elasticity. A four-inch elastic wrap is the handiest size. It can be applied to a newly sprained ankle or knee as well as a muscle strain.

● *Foam.* Vinyl foam is far superior to sponge rubber in its ability to dissipate force. Consequently, it is more expensive but a more useful product. In gymnastics I have used 3/8-inch vinyl foam pads to protect the hips from bruising when the athlete practices on the uneven parallel bars. It can also be used to pad the vertebrae of the neck when the gymnast executes rolls on the beam.

● *Felt.* Foot pads, arch pads and donuts for blister protection are the most common items cut from felt sheets. Since felt is used rather sparingly, it might be more economical to purchase specialty products such as the Dr. Scholl's line of foot products. Cramer Products, Inc. sells a felt variety pack that contains several different thicknesses of felt. One advantage of felt over vinyl foam, especially in the construction of arch pads, is felt can be split into different thicknesses just by tearing it apart. You need a knife or pair of scissors to cut vinyl foam and cannot always get a smooth cut.

● *Tweezers.*

● *Nail clippers.*

● *Pen light.* The pen light tests the reaction of the pupils to light following a blow to the head. If the athlete is conscious, tell him to close his eyes. This causes the pupils to dilate. After a few seconds, ask him to open his eyes and shine the light in one eye coming in from the side of the head. Both pupils should constrict; however, the one in which the light is shining should constrict more. Test the reaction of both eyes. If the eyes do not react, the athlete may have suffered a severe head injury. If the athlete is unconscious, call an ambulance.

If a pen light is not available, execute the test regardless. The pupils should constrict, although not as much, to room light.

● *Ammonia capsules.* Crush the capsule away from the athlete's face and pass the capsule across his face so he inhales the fumes. Do not hold the capsule below his nostrils. If you suspect a neck injury, use ammonia capsules with extreme caution. The athlete could jerk his head in response to the unpleasant odor of ammonia and the movement could sever the spinal cord.

● *Safety pins.*

● *Rubber bands.*

● *Needle and thread.*

● *Tampons.*

● *Contact lens wetting solution.* Purchase a sterile wetting solution to use instead of saliva when inserting lenses. Since saliva is contaminated with many hardy bacteria, a virulent eye infection could develop when it is used as a setting solution.

● *Hand mirror.* Use a mirror to find a contact lens that has moved out of place.

● *Tape.* The quantity and variety of tape needed will depend on the scope of your program, your philosophy of coaching, and of course, your budget.

Many different types of tape are available: white athletic, waterproof, elastic, plastic and hypoallergenic. If your budget is small, you can meet most of your needs by purchasing 1½-inch white tape in either a tube or case. White tape splits into whatever the desired width. There are different qualities of tape and your budget will determine what you can afford.

If tape is used infrequently, store it in a cool place, even in the refrigerator with each roll on its end.

Elastic tape is useful for strapping small bony parts such as the thumbs. Generally speaking, there are two types of elastic tape—that which can be torn and that which must be cut. An example of the first is Conform made by Kendall Products. It is ideal for anchoring a strapping and comes in a variety of widths. Elastikon (Johnson & Johnson) is also available in various widths, but unlike Conform, must be cut.

Waterproof and hypoallergenic tapes are rarely used. Plastic tape is used to prevent or protect blisters because its smooth surface cuts down on friction.

● *Tape adherent.* To protect the skin from the stress of the tape, spray or paint an adherent on the skin before taping. The adherent also helps the tape to stick to the skin, especially when the athlete begins to sweat. After applying the adherent allow it to dry, otherwise the tape will not stick.

● *Tape remover.* Always remove the tape residue and tape adherent after cutting off the strapping or the skin may become irritated. Use a commercially made tape remover, or use a readily available substitute. Standard Oil Company makes an inexpensive liquid called Stan-o-sol that can be used as a tape remover. It is available at a Standard Oil Distribution Center.

● *Gauze sponges.* You apply non-sterile 3" x 3" gauze sponges to the heel and lace areas before strapping an ankle to protect the tendon areas from skin lesions. In addition, non-sterile gauze sponges rather than cotton balls can be used for clean ups, like removing tape adherent. Remember, the gauze is not sterile so it should not be used to clean wounds.

● *Underwrap.* To protect the skin from tape, apply at least one layer of underwrap to the area to be strapped. Slightly stretch the underwrap during application but not too much, for it will roll up.

● *Aspirin.* Buy the cheapest brand of aspirin available. All aspirin has the same chemical formula, you just pay more for the brand name.

● *Ice cooler.* Over the long run the most economical cooler is that made by Igloo or Covey rather than the styrofoam type. Igloos come in 2-, 3-, 5- and 10-gallon sizes and, to the best of my knowledge, are still guaranteed indestructible. They can be purchased in many local sporting goods stores.

● *First aid kit.* Use a fishing tackle box or tool box. Check the kit before each practice and meet and restock it at least each week.

In addition, the trainer or coach should know where the nearest phone is located; he should have fifteen cents taped to the first aid kit to use in a pay phone. Carry a First Aid-Emergency Care Manual and know the procedure for securing an ambulance. Tape all emergency phone numbers, including the team physician's on the inside of the first aid kit or near the phone in your office. Carry a roster of gymnasts' parents' names and phone numbers if you are working with minors.

31

Leg and Foot Injury Prevention

Holly Wilson

SHIN SPLINTS

Shin splints may occur because the lower leg muscles are not strong enough to withstand the stress placed upon them. This series of isometric exercises will strengthen each specific muscle group in the lower leg and may eliminate shin splints from your gymnastics squad.

The exercises can be done with a partner or using the other foot for resistance; they should be done daily before practice.

Plantar Flexion. One gymnast attempts to point her toe while the other applies resistance, with one or both hands, to the sole of the foot.

Dorsal Flexion. The gymnast attempts to draw the top of the foot upward toward the shin. Resistance is applied by her partner to the top of the foot.

Inversion. Resistance is applied to the inside of the foot as the gymnast attempts to turn the sole of the foot inward.

Eversion. Resistance is applied to the outside of the foot as the gymnast attempts to turn the sole of the foot outward.

Work toward the goal of 10 repetitions of each exercise, holding each repetition for three seconds.

Another exercise that has proven beneficial in combating shin splints is the gastrocnemius stretch. (The gastrocnemius is the major superficial muscle forming the calf.) Stand approximately twelve inches away from a wall, facing it in a forward stride position. Extend your arms to shoulder height and place your palms flat on the wall. Lean into the wall by flexing your elbows. Keep your back straight and heels flat on the floor. You should feel a stretching sensation along the back of your leg. Switch forward foot and repeat five times on each foot. This exercise can also be done off the edge of a step. Stand erect with your heels protruding beyond the edge and hold onto something to maintain balance. Lower your body weight below the level of the step. Hold for a count of five and then return to starting position. Repeat ten times.

The gymnast should also include exercises to strengthen the small intrinsic muscles within the foot. Pick up marbles or small pieces of crumpled paper with your toes. Spread a towel out on the floor. Grasp the front edge of the towel with your toes, pick it up, bring it toward you, and then release it. Repeat the exercise until you reach the other end of the towel and it is piled up in front of you. Change feet. As the muscles become stronger, add a little resistance by placing a weight, i.e., book, brick, on the far end of the towel. These two exercises can be done as lower leg and foot conditioners to prevent shin splints. Start slowly and increase repetitions gradually. Do not strain muscles by doing too much too soon.

A word of caution, however; check the athlete who complains of lower leg pain carefully. Have her point out the area of maximum pain. If it is localized high on the leg, approximately two to three inches below the knee, suspect a fracture. There are many conditions that mimic shin splints and some are serious—a stress fracture and anterior compartment syndrome is a circulatory disturbance in the lower leg as a result of swelling within the compartment. It is usually seen in the unconditioned athlete following strenuous exercise. Symptoms include pain, muscle spasm, and numbness. Treatment by a doctor is required for both conditions.

Taping for shin splints is often beneficial if one ignores the skin and focuses instead on the arches of the foot. The lower leg muscles in addition to moving the foot also support the arches. If tape can help support the arches, then some stress may be taken off those muscles. The strapping shown below, plus exercises, has eliminated shin splints in many gymnasts I have treated. Do not rely on tape alone.

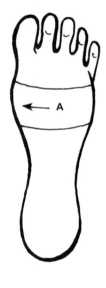

Materials Needed: Tape adherent, 1½-inch athletic tape.

Preparation:

  1. Instruct the athlete to hold her foot at a right angle throughout the strapping process.

  2. Spray or paint the area with tape adherent.

Strapping:

  1. Apply an anchor strip (A) loosely around the foot. The foot will spread out when weight is borne.

  2. Start at the anchor on the sole of the foot. From the little toe side, angle the tape across the sole, around the heel and along the little toe side of the foot as close to the sole as possible (B). End on the anchor strip.

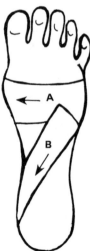

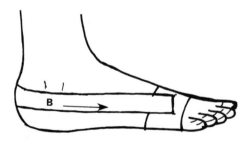

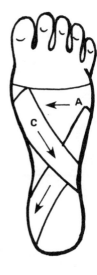

3. Start at the anchor on the sole of the foot. From the big toe side, angle the tape across the sole, around the heel, and along the big toe side of the foot as close to the sole as possible (C). End on the anchor strip.

4. Apply two to three lock strips loosely around the foot. Start at the anchor and go toward the heel. Overlap one-third to one-half. The foot will spread out when weight is borne.

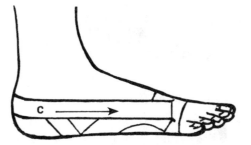

32

Injury Care

Holly Wilson

ICE APPLICATION

There are several methods of applying ice to an injured part. Immediately following an injury ice may be applied in the form of an ice pack, ice slush, chemical cold pack, or gel pack.

Ice Pack Technique. Fill a wet towel with ice cubes or shavings and fold the edges over. The towel is wet to hasten the cooling of the tissue. A dry towel would act as an insulator until it is dampened by the melting ice, consequently delaying the cooling effect. Wrap the injured part with a wet elastic wrap from approximately four inches below to four inches above the injury. Always wrap toward the heart. Apply the pack over the elastic wrap and secure it in place with a dry elastic wrap. Elevate the part if possible. Keep the pack in place for fifteen-thirty minutes.

The elastic wrap is applied to aid in compression and thus control swelling. Ice, a vasoconstricter, controls swelling by decreasing the size of the blood vessels. Drainage of the part is enhanced by elevation.

Ice Slush Immersion. Fill a deep pan or bucket with water and ice chips. Immerse the injured part in the ice slush until the athlete can no longer tolerate it, usually a few seconds. Continue repeating the immersion until the injured part is numb.

This technique can only be used for injures of distal joints such as the ankle or hand. Although it is extremely uncomfortable and the athlete forfeits the effects of elevation, ice slush does have certain advantages over the ice pack. The slush conforms to the bony anatomy of injured parts so more uniform cooling occurs. In addition, cooling appears to be more rapid.

Do not put salt in the water to hasten cooling because frostbite can result.

Chemical Cold Packs. If ice is unavailable, chemical cold packs do solve a problem; however, they are not too economical. Most can only be used once, remain cold for approximately twenty minutes and cost in the neighborhood of eighty-five cents each. If one leaks, which is not uncommon, the chemical solution can irritate the skin, especially if there is an open wound.

Gel Packs. Gel packs must be placed in a refrigerator or freezer where they can absorb the cold. Like the chemical pack, they remain cold for only a short period of time, but the gel pack has one advantage; it is reusable. If a refrigerator or freezer is available, however, it would be more economical to use ice. Besides, the ice cools tissue over a longer period of time.

Ice massage is used during the rehabilitation process to encourage range of motion as a result of the anaesthetic and muscle relaxing effects of ice.

Freeze water in non-waxed paper cups or styrofoam cups. Once frozen, cut away the edges of the cup and massage the injured area until numbness occurs. This requires approximately eight-ten minutes. The actual time is dependent on the area being treated. An area covered with bulky muscles such as the thigh will take longer than an area like the neck. After the part is numb, the athlete should work on range of motion and/or strengthening exercises; however, the part should never be forced beyond the point of discomfort. Ice massage is applied in sets of three 8/3, 8/3, 8/3 and if possible, three times a day.

SPECIFIC TREATMENTS FOR TROUBLE AREAS

Plantar Fascia Strain Taping. The strapping referred to is the same as that used for shin splints. A pad cut from 3/8" felt may be applied to the longitudinal arch for additional support. Be sure of proper placement of the pad. If the pad is improperly positioned, it could cause more pain than the condition for which it is applied.

Achilles Tendon Strain. The athlete can stretch out this tendon according to the instructions given on gastrocnemius stretching that appeared in Chapter 32. Cut the heel lift from vinyl foam or felt and place in the heel of both street and sport shoes. If the lift slides forward, it will be necessary to glue it to the inner-sole with rubber cement.

Muscle Strains or "Pulls." Tearing of muscle tissue, classified as a moderate-severe injury, responds best to rest and application of heat after swelling has been controlled. Do not attempt to stretch the muscle out or strengthen it until the blood has been absorbed and normal movement is pain-free. Only then should the athlete start on a slow strengthening and mild stretching program. When stretching, do not bounce, for the likelihood of tearing a muscle is greater with dynamic stretching than static stretching.

Low Back Problems-Muscular. The athlete with a low back problem should focus on strengthening the abdominal muscles to assure proper pelvic alignment. This can be accomplished through a daily program of sit-ups and double leg lifts providing the athlete can keep the small of his back flat against the floor during the execution of the leg lifts. In addition, he should also work on stretching the low back extensor muscles by performing other light back-strengthening exercises *daily*. He should sleep on a firm mattress or the floor.

A gymnastics meet is a multi-ringed circus of acrobatic thrills, dance, grace, courage, strength, stamina, and coordination.

The Active Spectator *is for the gymnastics fan, explaining what is happening on the floor (and above it), what those flashing cards with numbers mean, and how to enjoy it all.*

The next chapters, written by two judges of international stature, explain in simple terms the rules of judging in men's and women's gymnastics. The part concludes with three different viewpoints on the problems of judging, perhaps gymnastics most controversial aspect.

8

THE MEET

Nina Dronova (USSR) (Tony Duffy photo)

33

The Active Spectator

Dick Criley
Associate Editor, International Gymnast *Magazine*

Everyone knows what it feels like to put a ball through its
goal—the hoop, the uprights, or in a hole. The shaving of
seconds in a race or the absolute victory of a knockout are also
meaningful to our sports-oriented populace. Gymnastics,
however, presents a problem of identification for the sports fan
who has no idea of what it is like to be upside down and still
in control.

"I just can't imagine doing that," is a common reaction to
the gymnast's peregrinations on the apparatus. "I'd break into
little pieces if I tried it," is another expression of disbelief at
what sportswriter Jim Murray once called "the purest form of
athletics in the whole round . . . As a spectator event it combines the best elements of a field sport with *Swan Lake*."

Television, with its knowledgeable commentators and instant
replays has brought gymnastics into millions of living rooms.
In addition to creating stars, this medium has also been an
educational force for gymnastics.

There are three areas of a gymnastics meet to attempt to
understand: how it is conducted, what to look for in the events,
and that complex individual, the gymnast.

HOW IS A COMPETITION CONDUCTED?

There are several variations of two basic formats. One format is the dual meet or team competition; the other is an individualized competition represented by open meets, championships, or invitationals.

Gymnastics team competition often features two individual competitions, the all-around (overall event winner), and the individual events. At the highest level, the Olympic Games, the International Gymnastics Federation (FIG) has decreed three different competitions for the team, all-around, and individual events. At the national level, the all-around event is usually decided as a part of the team competition while the event champions are determined in a set of finals. In some national competitions, the team is omitted and everyone competes for him or herself.

The most enjoyable, however, is the dual meet. It is here, where the gymnasts are known personally by many in the audience, that excitement can build, the knot in the stomach be tied, and the tears shed for each individual triumph or failure and for the emotion we call team spirit in victory or defeat.

A gymnastics meet is a six-ring circus of activity (1978 NCAA Championships, Eugene, Oregon). (Marilou Sturges photo)

The scoring of a meet is comparatively simple. A key element is how many scores from each team will count towards the team score on each event. Whether it be 3, 4 or 5 scores, there is then a basis for determining how well the team has done. Multiply the number of scores to count by 10 for the theoretic maximum for the event: 30, 40 or 50 points. A score in excess of 27, 36, or 45 means an average above 9.0, which is very good indeed. The event scores are added, 6 for men and 4 for women, to determine the team total.

Here is one sport where hundredths of a point do count; meets have been won on the narrowest of margins, 0.05, and individual titles by as little as 0.005!

To the knowledgeable spectator then, a difference of two or three points means that it was a very close meet—that each event was closely contested to within half a point and only a few tenths separated individuals.

The same system of adding the points earned on each event holds for determining the all-around winner. A top-flight male gymnast should be able to score in excess of 54 points, a female gymnast about 36 points. In the championships where there are both compulsory and optional exercises, these totals would be doubled. The final rankings are determined on the basis of the compulsory plus optional totals.

To be an active spectator, one must learn what kind of competition is being held. How many scores will count if it is a team competition? Will there be a separate competition to sort out the very best on each event? Armed with this basic information, sidelights such as the number of entries on a team, the impact of an injury, or the truly outstanding effort by one individual can be appreciated.

It was little noticed in the 1976 Olympics in Montreal, when the Japanese men's team had to finish their last three events with all five scores to count following the withdrawal of an injured Shun Fujimoto, that Switzerland also had a similar predicament. Like the Japanese, they also rallied together to produce a fine team effort.

Similar excitement can be found in other great championships. The 1978 NCAA championships were won by the University of Oklahoma, a team consisting of only nine gymnasts; on several events they had available only the minimal four men.

A sprained ankle could have put them out of contention. Indeed, one of their gymnasts was seriously injured, yet he competed anyway, "for the team." Such drama adds dimension to a gymnastic meet.

In Montreal, thanks to the considerable resolving power of binoculars and telephoto camera lenses, spectators could observe the judges recording the scores. Bias was detected and the crowd was heard. Now that makes one an active spectator! Television, in this case, was *not* the next best thing to being there as it simply could not capture the electricity of being part of that crowd. This is not to suggest that one needs to bring a spyglass to the next meet. Even if one could see the judges' scoring sheets, they would be almost impossible to understand.

Judging is also conducted on the FIG system. Considerable evolution has taken place in the last two decades. The rules are codified into the FIG Code of Points, usually referred to as the "Code." Judges take courses, study, pass examinations, and judge at all levels for which they are qualified.

It has been written that a judge must have the hide of a rhinoceros, memory of an elephant, knowledge of an Einstein, endurance of an ox, wisdom of Solomon, smile of an angel, a complete disdain for money, a forgiving nature, and lots of love for gymnasts and gymnastics. To realize the time spent in mastering the intricacies of the sport by dedicated men and women is to take another step towards becoming an appreciative spectator.

WHAT TO LOOK FOR IN THE EVENTS

In many competitions, a program or announcer provides the guide to the requirements of each event. Beyond these guidelines are many details that raise or lower the quality of the performance. The systems used for men and women have been divergent for many years but are gradually approaching some common ground.

In Montreal, the scoring system used to evaluate the women permitted the perfect 10.0 score; the one used by the men did not. This was because the specifications differed. In 1976, a male gymnast was awarded a maximum of 9.4 points for meeting certain basic requirements; an additional 0.6 points could be earned by exceptional display of qualities called risk, originality, and virtuosity of performance (ROV). It was, and is, extremely difficult to satisfy the judges that all 0.6 should be awarded and that the performance itself was flawless enough to merit the 9.4. Different specifications for the women did permit a judge to conclude that all requirements had been met and that a 10.0 was in order. Since Montreal, however, the women, too, have accepted the ROV concept, making 9.5 their top score with a 10.0 much less attainable.

Components of the score for men and women.

Men (1976)	value	Women (1976)	value	Women (Revised)	value
Difficulty	3.4	Composition	5.0	Difficulty	3.0
Combination	1.6	value of parts	(3.0)	Originality &	
Execution	4.4	combinations	(1.5)	composition	1.5
	9.4	general		Execution	4.0
		composition	(0.5)	General	
Risk	.2	Execution	5.0	impression	.5
Originality	.2	execution		Rhythm &	
Virtuosity	.2	of parts	(2.0)	virtuosity	.5
	10.0	general			9.5
		impression	(1.0)		
		amplitude	(2.0)	Risk	.5
			10.0		10.0

Difficulty represents that portion of the exercise that can be shown to require skill, risk-taking, and danger of failure. To the spectator, it often occurs as a surprising element. Some gymnasts build their entire exercise around one Big Trick because of the possibility of enhancing their score should they pull it off successfully.

The difficulty elements are rated A, B, and C for men, with A=0.2, B=0.4, and C=0.6. Women's gymnastics rates only moves of medium (0.3) and superior (0.6) difficulty. Except for finals where requirements are highest, men must show four A, five B, and one C parts for a maximum of 3.4, while women must have 4 medium and 3 superior elements to achieve their 3.0 maximum. Spectators tend to over-value the moves they see performed and may disagree with the scores awarded by the judges. It is instructive to try to identify the moves of difficulty to see if there are enough of them, but only the most informed fan is likely to know the values as well as a judge.

The extra special moves of combinations of moves that involve risk, whether physical or in loss of points for failing, can contribute up to 0.2 points as a bonus after the judge arrives at a score. It is a very relative area: A move executed easily by an older, stronger, and more experienced gymnast may be very risky to the novice and intermediate gymnast.

Combination or *composition* are the standards that dictate what kinds of moves must be performed. In addition, 0.2 points may be gained as a bonus for new moves or unique combinations of moves as originality elements. It has nothing to do with difficulty, however, and extends the exercise beyond what is generally known or accepted.

Olga Korbut's back somersault to regrasp on the uneven bars illustrated both difficulty and originality in an era when these were not rewarded, but even condemned as too risky and out of character with the apparatus. On the men's side, the introduction of a spectacular single-leg flair by Stanford gymnast Ted Marcey was an example of originality that has been emulated and adapted by others.

Originality, however, has its time limitations. Usually a span of only one Olympiad will find a "new" move demoted and no longer eligible for originality credit. Originality is often expressed by naming a move for the gymnast who first performed it internationally—a way of remembering great athletes, but hardly easy for the uninitiated to understand. Today's young gymnasts scarcely know the origin of such moves as the Yamashita, Moore, Bailie, Ono, Takemoto, Koeste, Tsukahara, Voronin, Stalder, Radochla, Cuervo, Honma, Chaguinian, Carminucci, and Diamidov.

The final component of a gymnast's score is *execution*. There are at least two elements of execution that the spectator should try to discern: The easy one is the *form* with which an element is performed. A hooked toe, bent or straddled leg, bent arm or poor body line is a clue that something is awry. Gymnastics is *supposed* to look elegant, easy, effortless, and artistic. A visual display to the contrary shows that the gymnast has not yet mastered his or her body and the lack of discipline shows in the execution. The other element is much harder to catch: *tech-*

nique. Has the move been done properly? Does it meet the specifications for the move (shoulder height, straight arms, to the handstand position, length of hold, or whatever)? Is the gymnast going to extremes to reach the ultimate in execution? Should the ultimate actually be reached, a 0.2 bonus can be added for virtuosity of execution.

Writing on the art of gymnastics, Daniel Millman asked that we see gymnastics as a synthesis of bodily movement into an art form above and beyond competitive aspects. Artists choose their medium as brush and paint, instrument and note, paper, pen and ideas, while the artistic gymnast chooses the ground, the air, and the apparatus together with his body as a medium of expression. To enjoy gymnastics, the spectator, too, should have an aesthetic awareness and appreciation of the final product as a personal expression of the gymnast. The routine, then, has *meaning* as well as skill, and if this impression is caught, appreciation is gained no matter what the score.

CHARACTERISTICS OF THE GYMNASTIC EVENTS

Floor Exercise (men). Over an area twelve by twelve meters, the gymnast must perform elements of balance, hold, strength, jumps, kips, handsprings, and saltos (somersaults). Although a requirement for flexibility is no longer in the Code, it is commonly expressed by splits and back-bending moves. Men's floor exercise has gradually evolved from a harmonious and rhythmic whole to a series of tumbling passes connected with transition moves to satisfy the event requirements. In part, this is due to the renewed interest in tumbling by the Europeans, especially the Russians.

Spectator interest is easily captured by the complex and dynamic tumbling moves. The active spectator will look for other elements as well: an aesthetic line, an expression of flexibility, or a simple element done with harmony and rhythm. An artistic floor exercise evokes in the spectator a wordless joy as in the following word picture which conveys an image of gold medalist Franco Menichelli at the Tokyo Olympics: "He danced lightly as a flame over the floor, now here, now there, quiet for a moment, then exploding into a shower of brilliant sparks."

Floor Exercise (women). The same area is used by the women, but there is an important addition—music. The composition includes elements of tumbling, flexibility, dance, balance, and momentary poses. The personality of the gymnast is often best expressed in her creativeness and choice of music. Although there are restrictions (no vocals and only one instrument) that relegate the music to a background role, several themes and changes of pace provide an infinite variety of moods: drama, elegance, grace, youthfulness, and similar traits. Besides the images conveyed by the music and mime, there is also the pure joy and pleasure of the performer herself to watch. America's Cathy Rigby set the pace with her portrayal of a pixie at the Mexico Olympics, a trend since emulated by Olga Korbut, Nadia Comaneci, and Maria Filatova, to name a few.

Pommel Horse (men). A well-done pommel horse exercise, the most difficult of the men's events, is a joy to watch; a poorly executed work an agony. There are two kinds of motions required—circling and swinging or pendular elements. The performer must work all parts of the horse: the two ends and on the pommels in the middle. Most gymnasts have a preferred direction for their circles, either clockwise or counterclockwise, and it is an observant spectator who can detect a gymnast doing both in the same exercise.

This event is one in which light legs and long arms are an asset, and the individual who works this event exclusively is almost instantly identifiable. In the increasing trend for gymnasts to work all six events, the pommel horse specialist usually equals or betters the all-around man. Judging this event is difficult because of the speed at which the moves fly by and because combining two or three moves without extra circles can boost difficulty very quickly.

Among the more recognizable moves will be scissors, circles, travels, loops, and moores. There are other variations, including Ted Marcey's spectacular break into a full circle or more with one leg and a lightning-fast turn around the long axis of the body while circling, called a "spindle," which was shown by gold medalist Zoltan Magyar of Hungary. Key elements to look for include rhythm and balance, a minimum of banging into the horse, and an extended body line. Speed is of less importance, but watch the very fast exercises to detect loss of balance or control.

Balance Beam (women). If the pommel horse is considered the men's most difficult event, then the women's must be the balance beam. After all, it is only ten centimeters wide and 120 centimeters off the floor. In a sense the requirements resemble those of floor exercise, but the comparison is quickly over when you consider the spatial limitations of the apparatus. The full length of the beam must be used as the gymnast executes leaps, turns, jumps, poses, and some acrobatic and dance movements. Lying and sitting positions are used, but more than three stops are penalized so the modern trend is to acrobatics, like walkovers and tumbling. Although no musical accompaniment is used, the gymnast must still vary her pace—sometimes slow and rhythmic, sometimes dynamic and lively. Above all, however, balance is the key, and a fall from the beam is penalized .5.

Mounts and dismounts tend to be the more eye-catching parts of the exercise, but aerials, somersaults, and handsprings in mid-exercise are also worth watching for. Pivots in raised or crouched position, especially of 360 degrees or more, are a lot more difficult than they might seem because of the narrow width of the beam. Even simple moves may lead to falls should the gymnast's concentration be broken, and the successful completion of a turn, aerial, or handspring could be followed by a fall due to such lapses. Watch the gymnasts performing. Except for the most skilled and confident, the smiles will be forced and movements less fluid, and the intense concentration of the gymnast will be very apparent. Her expression on completion of the dismount can be a real clue to the poise of the gymnast.

Rings (men). The image of the ring man as a short, heavily muscled fellow with matchstick legs is an overdrawn stereotype. Today's ring man may well be an all-around gymnast who needs his leg strength and shoulder flexibility. The rings conjure up the image of power, with iron crosses held effortlessly and additional strength elements contributing to a "still," solid performance. Strength *is* a basic requirement on the rings but *swing* has become a far more prominent feature because of the all-around gymnast. Improved technique, using straight arms and the bounce and whip of the body has led to more varied performances as parallels were found with other events. The rings probably still remain the most limiting of events because of the need to grip the rings continuously until the dismount.

Strength moves such as crosses, planches, levers, and presses are easily recognizable. Hold positions are required and may or may not involve strength. The swinging moves are the counterpoint as the overall effect must be to keep the rings from swinging. Precise techniques and control accomplish this end. Among the most recognizable swing moves will be dislocates, giant swings from handstand to handstand, uprises, and felges (or shoots or flanges, as they are sometimes called). Dismounts are in a class by themselves on this event as each year gymnasts find some new way to turn topsy-turvy in space. The double salto is still considered good for high school, but at the higher levels extra twist is put into one or both saltos; this increased risk to the gymnast usually merits the award of the bonus tenths.

Mitsu Tsukahara (Mark Shearman photo)

Vaulting (men and women). This is the one event of gymnastics to stress leg power, yet contact with the horse is with the hands and much of the control is exerted through the arms and shoulders. In contrast to the other events, the vault is a single move and more difficult to compare with other apparatus events. Men vault lengthwise with the horse and women over its narrow dimension. The vault is aided by a take-off board, which provides a rebound or ricocheting action from coiled springs, a rubber air bag, leaf springs, or the resiliency of bowed wood. The maximum runway for men is twenty meters, while the women are not bound to a maximum distance.

A vault has seven phases, but only the parts after leaving the take-off board are evaluated. The run contributes momentum for continuing direction of the vault and for conversion into height. Considering their all-around reputation, gymnasts too often use poor running technique. This is not hard to detect and can serve as a predictor to the spectator for a poorly done vault. Contact with the board is the next phase. The board is best used for ricochet rather than spring as it is not constructed for use like a diving board. The last step before the gymnast makes contact with the board is the hurdle. It should be a long, low, skipping step rather than a high pounding jump.

The period between leaving the board and making contact with the horse is *preflight*. Unless the gymnast has improperly used the take-off board, he/she will have lifted the hips and heels overhead and extended the arms to make contact with the horse. Some women vaulters are capable of executing a half or full twist in preflight. However, they have a broader zone in which to place their hands than do the men. Ideally, the body is extended and the legs straight in preflight, but certain vaults which require somersaulting are entered with arms bent and legs bending to initiate the rotation.

Push-off from the horse is critical in several ways. The men have to have achieved a certain angle of contact or be penalized. Both height and distance are controlled by the timing of the force and direction of the push. The body must be tight or the force of the push is lost in loose body position. The phase after push-off and until the landing is called *postflight*. Height and distance are important components as well as control of form and extension before landing. An error meriting penalty is the failure to continue the vault in a straight line. Depending on the vault, preflight may be sacrificed for good postflight, and present day judging seems to support this trend. The last phase of the vault is the *landing*—the body is on balance with good posture and no steps are taken when vaults are properly done.

The values of vaults are preassigned to include the difficulty and combination aspects. Only virtuosity, usually for height or distance, will merit bonus tenths. Now men's vaults are given a base score of 9.4 and bonus tenths assigned for ROV factors. The more difficult vaults being shown are a handspring followed by 1½ forward saltos, the Tsukahara, which looks like a round-off, back salto, and handsprings with at least 360 degrees of twist. Even the two former vaults are being upgraded with the addition of twists.

Parallel Bars (men). The exercise consists of swinging, flight, and hold parts, which may also embody a certain measure of strength. The swinging and flight parts should predominate. The gymnast must release and regrasp the bars simultaneously either above or below them. A maximum of three stops is allowed. Shoulder strength is necessary on this event, and a good gymnast uses this strength and the resilience of the bars to achieve the swing, flight and release/regrasp elements.

Bart Conner (Marilou Sturges photo)

Despite the apparent limitation of the two wood rails, the parallel bars offer a great range of possible moves because of their length and the flight potential. Some gymnasts will even cast over the side of the apparatus, glide, and kip or stoop back up to a supported position again.

The handstand is a prominent feature both for satisfying the hold requirement and for the moves in which it is a beginning, transition, or concluding part. The arched handstand is *out*; the straight body is *in*. The parallel bars offer a variety of difficulty elements composed of two or more elements of value. Swinging moves with a twisting flight component are called "stutzes" and may be done on either forward or back swing. There are saltos forward and backward between the bars and off the side as dismounts.

Like the other apparatus, the parallel bars are a good place to look for technique. Technique is subtle, and it takes a keen-eyed spectator to detect the differences among gymnasts. A few things to look for, however, include the use of the shoulders in consonance with the rebound of the bars, where and when the body pikes (bends) in swing, the hips-to-shoulders position of the body when dropping below the bars, and the timing of the release on stutzes, saltos, and other release/regrasp moves.

Uneven Parallel Bars (women). This event rivals women's floor exercise for spectator appeal. Swinging moves should predominate as the gymnast works her way from hangs and supports on the two bars, changing grip and direction, now up, now down, extended, piked, in a handstand or with the feet touching the bar. Women have borrowed and adapted horizontal bar moves from the men and in doing so have made this their strength event. Olga Korbut astonished the Japanese in Tokyo almost a year before the Munich Olympics with her back salto in layout position to regrasp the high bar, but saltos between the bars—from low to high and high to low—had preceded this element. Nadia Comaneci executed a front salto on a back swing to regrasp the high bar. These moves have similar counterparts in the men's horizontal bar event. Still, the rapid twists about the long axis of the body as the gymnast bounces off the low bar or disengages from a partial sole circle have not been duplicated by men on the horizontal bar.

Technique shows on this event for women more than any other. Casting to the handstand with full extension seems almost obligatory as do straight-armed free hip circles, the pirouette turns, the somersaults, and powerful kips. Stops for poses are no longer countenanced; the exercise must keep moving, and the dismount will "ride the rails" for height.

Horizontal Bar (men). The requirements of the horizontal bar (or high bar) seem too simple. All the gymnast has to do is swing around the bar, have at least one release/regrasp with simultaneous hand action, and display some sort of contorted shoulder position while swinging. No strength moves and no stops are permitted. A well-constructed exercise will show giant swings in both directions, some in-bar work, stalders, the dorsal-cubital grip requirement, grip changes, the release/re-grasp, and a C-level dismount. It is possible, as Eizo Kenmotsu of Japan has demonstrated, to do a whole routine without one complete normal giant swing.

Although all of gymnastics has its own language, the horizontal bar has picked up the greatest collection of named moves: Higgins change, California hop, inverteds, look-in giants, German, Czech and Russian giants, Voronin, Ono, Takemoto, Staldershoot, Endoshoot, Koeste, eagles, blind change, and many others. Like the pommel horse, it all goes by too fast to catch the individual moves. Only the dismounts tend to remain in the mind's eye—the last free-flight element with saltos or twists or both to an early opening to a stable landing.

So far as technique is concerned, points to watch include the relative "looseness" of the body in giant swings—neither like a stick nor boiled spaghetti, but a sort of relaxed tenseness; also shoulder flexibility; flexibility to stoop in without bending the knees; no extra body wiggles to "make" the giant swings; sureness in grip changes; and control in flight elements such as vaults, twists, and dismounts. A good horizontal bar perform-ance should leave one exhilarated, not tied in knots or sitting on the edge of the bleacher.

UNDERSTANDING THE GYMNAST

Gymnastic meets are—well, erratic. Like track, either nothing is happening, or there are too many attractions. Indeed, it is why gymnastic exhibitions and TV-condensed meets have been so well-received. One way to endure is to become an active spectator studying the gymnast's performance.

Keep in mind that the mental challenges of gymnastics are equally as real as the physical challenges. The greatest challenge, however, is to combine these successfully.

Sports psychologists try to figure out the influences that motivate a gymnast. In some cases, even a spectator can detect clues to the *need* of the gymnast to achieve, to be successful, and to accomplish tasks of great skill. The dedicated gymnast seems to need a sense of order. He follows directions and accepts for himself the blame for miscalculation rather than project it on someone else or the apparatus. In this light the maturity of gymnasts is discernible, and it is where the youth, however talented they may be, cannot keep up with the veterans of the sport.

Gymnasts' performances can show the light, artistic elements of ballet, the suspense of circus aerialists, the dynamics of an auto race, and the fluid grace of a champion ice-skater. This is as it should be: Make the difficult look easy. The 1968 Men's Code of Points states "When the gymnast succeeds in blending elegance of execution, difficulty and risk in an impressionable dynamic [theme], he creates a presentation which radiates a brilliant inner experience and harmony which characterize the virtuoso. He is able to capture the soul of spectators and to fill their hearts with joy."

Steve Hug, U.S. Olympian in 1972 and 1976, expressed it, "How incredible it can be to move the body in so many ways . . . One of the greatest joys I have experienced in my life has been at a gymnastics competition or exhibition when we were all trying to do something with our bodies that we can communicate to each other, and also possibly, to spectators."

The active spectator should look for the characteristics that permit an aesthetic performance of a gymnast. Instead of "Man versus Apparatus," he should look for the harmonious blending of Man *with* Apparatus. A move that does not "fit" the routine will often be obvious just as a whole routine that does not suit the gymnast's personality will somehow seem awkward, out of character, jarring the spectator's attention.

The active spectator will watch a gymnast do a move and try to "feel" it in a sort of muscular empathy. It takes time to develop the feel of muscles tensing and relaxing and to feel the correct rhythm of the move. It is not the sort of capability one can develop in viewing just a few competitions; an appreciation of the artistic qualities of the performance is easier to gain.

Gymnastics is an art, as earlier chapters have illustrated. The same kinds of elements that make a great piece of art make gymnastics an artistic communication. Like loud-soft, fast-slow, or high-low notes, tempo, or change of pace, exists in great routines. But it is the *choice* of tempo elements that reveal the artist and the *emphasis* that builds the character of the exercise.

The dramatic quality of an exercise catches the spectator's attention. What makes the performance dramatic? Expressions and gestures and the music create a dramatic image in women's floor exercise. There is the dramatic contrast of rapid, powerful strides in a vaulting run, the explosive thrust into flight, and the sudden, dead stop of the landing. In movement, too, drama can be a component of amplitude—the long, easy giant swings on horizontal bar, the continuation of a back toss through a handstand and drop immediately below the bars and up again on the parallel bars, or the sole circle to pirouette catches on uneven bars.

Three aspects of suppleness characterize elegant gymnastics: shoulder extension, hip flexion, and groin extension. The potential of a tight gymnast is limited. It is not enough to be supple; the gymnast also needs the strength to control his or her body in extended positions. How a gymnast "swings" or works freely in an extended body position contributes to the appearance of ease.

When you start to understand the beauty of rhythm and perfect body line and how suppleness, strength, and swing interact, you are receiving the message the gymnast is trying to communicate.

You have learned how to become an active spectator.

34

Judging Men's Gymnastics
William Roetzheim

After years of lagging behind other gymnastics functions, judging has finally come of age. The system employed to determine the winners of a gymnastic meet has fluctuated radically in the past sixty years.

I remember my early days as a competitor: Officials sat around a huge table, beer steins in hand; evaluating performance was secondary to the socializing this format provided. Each gymnast knew that how high he scored him was directly related to the volume of beer consumed by the judge. The tools used by the officials for evaluation were completely subjective based on the experience he may or may not have had in the past.

Numerically, the value of a routine has fluctuated also. At one time a perfect routine was worth 15 points, and later, 100 points. Under the 100 point system, 50 points were awarded for form and 50 points on the basis of difficulty. It was never determined what was difficult or how a performer should be penalized for lack of execution.

In 1964, the International Gymnastic Federation (F.I.G.) developed a comprehensive rules book to gain a higher level of consistency in judging. The theory was advanced that officiating would be a subjective judgment based on very objective standards. The system was based on a 10-point maximum score. It subdivided these ten points into three categories, Execution (5.0), Difficulty (3.4), and Combination (1.6). In 1968 and 1976 these rules were refined once again.

In this country we then possessed a more objective system for evaluation, but still had no control over the evaluators themselves. Judges were still called out of the stands five minutes before the meet. Coaches still chose their own officials and based their choice on how high they scored their teams rather than on the basis of competence. It was quite obvious that a national organization was needed to establish standards for judges in the United States.

Mike Carter (Lorraine Rorke photo)

In the late 60s, the National Gymnastic Judges Association was formed. They developed a testing procedure for judges that is now used nationally. This organization is also responsible for assigning officials to all major competitions. After an individual is tested he can be awarded a National or Regional Card based on his test score. National and Regional judges must meet the following requirements:

1. He must be nineteen years of age for a National Card and eighteen years old for a Regional Card.
2. For a National rating he must have two years experience as a gymnastics competitor, coach, instructor, or judge. For a Regional rating this requirement is reduced to one year.
3. For either card the candidate must attend a fifteen-hour course given by the National Gymnastic Judges Association.
4. He must take a 100-question written test and score at least a seventy for a National Card, or a sixty for a Regional Card.
5. He must recognize at least sixty percent of all of the "B" and "C" moves performed in live routines for a National rating and fifty percent of these same moves for a Regional Card.
6. He must judge a minimum of sixteen routines, including the current Compulsory, and score within a given range of an expert panel also evaluating these exercises. At least four different events must be used.

A National or Regional Card is valid for four years or until the F.I.G. has a major rule change. To keep this card actively valid a refresher course of four hours must be taken each year and a written test passed. National Cards are good in the United States and territories, while a Regional Card is only valid in the geographic area where it was awarded.

To maintain uniform standards in testing, a member of the National Technical Committee must be present at all courses. This individual must also go through the entire testing procedure each year.

The first Code of Points was very restrictive in how a judge could award points. It was computer-oriented, i.e., the official applied the Code to the routine in a clerical operation. It was very quickly established that this system lacked the ability to distinguish the top performers. In 1968, the category of Spiritual Expression was added to give the judge some type of latitude in the decision-making process. The 1976 edition continued this same trend when three new elements were introduced: Risk, Originality, and Virtuosity.

Although the International Code of Points is the backbone of the United States system, a supplementary manual is also used. It is titled *National Gymnastic Judges Association Rules Interpretation* (Blue Book) and published yearly. This text goes farther than the Code of Points in the rating of moves. It also attempts to tackle the many gray areas in officiating to create consistent interpretation throughout the country.

Now let us examine the present Code of Points and determine how it is applied in rating gymnastic routines. The present code is based on a ten-point system, and these points are broken down in the following categories:

4.4	Execution
1.6	Combination
3.4	Difficulty
.2	Originality
.2	Virtuosity
.2	Risk
10.0	Total

We will now attempt to reduce each of these elements into its basic, component parts.

EXECUTION (4.4)

This segment is based on how well the gymnast technically performs the routine. It is subtractive in nature. Every gymnast begins with a 4.4 and as he makes mistakes in body position, points are taken away from this starting point.

The following is a list of deductions that appear in the International Code. The gymnast may be penalized:

1. If he stops or hestitates in a routine he will lose 0.1 to 0.3 depending on the difficulty of the move before.
2. If he sits down on the equipment, deduct 0.1 to 0.3.
3. For falling on the apparatus he will lose from 0.3 to 0.5.
4. If he fails to point his toes, bends his legs or has poor position of any body part, he will lose up to 0.3.
5. For a light touch of the equipment with any part of the body where it was not intended, deduct 0.1 to 0.3.

6. If he starts for a move and stops before once again moving to the finished position, deduct 0.1 to 0.3.
7. He may lose 0.1 for each step taken in a handstand position, but not more than 0.5 on any one handstand.
8. If he starts for a move, misses, comes down and must start again, deduct 0.2 to 0.5.
9. If he is attempting a swing part and uses exercise strength, or if he is executing astrength part and uses a great deal of swing, deduct 0.1 to 0.3.
10. If he holds a strength part one second instead of the required two seconds; if he needs the move you can give it to him with a 0.2 deduction.
11. If the move is held over three seconds, deduct 0.1 to 0.3.
12. If when dismounting he takes one or two steps, deduct up to 0.2. For many steps or touching the floor with his hands deduct up to 0.3, and for falling to the floor or using his hands for support he loses up to 0.5.
13. If he does not have the correct body position on any move, deduct up to 0.3.
14. He is allowed one preliminary swing on the Horizontal Bar, but if he exercises this option on Rings he loses 0.3.
15. The gymnast can be lifted onto the rings and horizontal bar, but if he fails to hold form during this action, deduct up to 0.2.

There are also some specific execution deductions on some of the individual events:

Pommel Horse
1. He may lose up to 0.2 for each scissor where the hip does not obtain a height equal to the shoulder of the supporting arm.
2. If he reaches back for additional support on any move, with the exception of the downhill stochli backward, deduct 0.3.
3. If his circles lack amplitude, a total deduction of up to 0.5 can be made.

Floor Exercise
1. For lack of rhythm harmony and low tumbling skills deduct up to 0.2. (This deduction can accumulate up to 1 full point.)
2. When the gymnast uses poor transitional moves between major passes deduct up to 0.5.
3. For poor position in scales deduct up to 0.2.

Yaseo Tomita (Marilou Sturges photo)

Rings

1. For poor body position when holding crosses, deduct up to 0.5.
2. If the rings begin to swing, deduct 0.1 to 0.3 per move executed while they are in motion.
3. If he falls from a handstand, deduct 0.2 to 0.5.
4. For bent arms in a handstand, deduct 0.2 to 0.3.
5. If his arms are bent and also touching the straps, deduct 0.3 to 0.5.

The last execution deduction is falling from the equipment. If this happens, the gymnast loses 0.5, but he has thirty seconds to begin his routine once again. The Head Judges must call out a ten to twenty second warning and the gymnast upon remounting the equipment is allowed one move to get himself back to the point where he became separated from the apparatus.

DIFFICULTY (3.4)

Moves are classified by degrees of difficulty. The *A* moves are the easiest, *B* moves are intermediate and *C* moves are considered superior in difficulty. The F.I.G. Code of Points has almost all moves pictured with their values. Each of these moves has a value, *A*'s 0.2, *B*'s 0.4 and *C*'s 0.6. In any routine, a *B* may be substituted for a *C* move with a 0.2 loss, but an *A* move cannot take the place of any other letter.

Gymnasts compete in three different formats, each of which have different requirements. However, all must have 11 letters to be complete.

Competition I. This is used for team competition. The gymnast must have a routine consisting of 1 *C*, 5 *B*'s, and 4 *A*'s.

Competition II. This competition is used in the all-around finals. The exercise must have 2 *C*'s, 4 *B*'s, and 3 *A*'s.

Competition III. This applies to individual finals competition. The gymnast must show 3 *C*'s, 3 *B*'s, and 2 *A*'s.

If you add up the value parts in each of these groups, you will find they all total 3.4. But we said earlier a routine must have 11 elements and these exercises are all short of that requirement. The deduction for short routines is made under combination in the following manner. If he does a ten part routine in Competition I deduct 0.2. In Competition II you may deduct up to 0.3 and in Competition III up to 0.4 for short routines.

This is by far the most objective category the judge has in making his decisions. For example, if a performer demonstrates 1 *C* (0.6), 4 *B*'s (0.4) and 3 *A*'s (0.2), his difficulty score would be 2.8. When judges confer they seldom have discrepancies in difficulty.

COMBINATION (1.6)

Combinations are requirements placed upon a gymnast when he structures his routine. If he fails to meet these criteria he is penalized. We can classify them into two categories, general requirements and specific requirements, in each event.

General Requirements

1. The routine must begin with a commensurate mount and end with a dismount of equal value. Failure to meet these standards will penalize the gymnast 0.1 to 0.3.
2. If the routine does not end with a dismount, deduct 0.3 to 0.5.
3. For an open swing when no trick is performed deduct 0.3.
4. If the exercise is poorly constructed, deduct 0.1 to 0.3.

5. If the routine resembles the compulsory, deduct up to 0.5.
6. If the routine ends with the compulsory dismount, deduct 0.3.
7. If your optional routine is the same as the compulsory you receive a score of zero.
8. For a move of no value, deduct up to 0.2.
   (a) Any move meeting the move's specification is valued as seen. No deduction.
   (b) A move performed the second time with a different preceding or succeeding part is valued as seen. No deduction.
   (c) A move performed the second time with the same preceding and succeeding parts is not given any value, but is not a move of no value and cannot meet any combination requirements.
   (d) A move performed the third time regardless of the preceding or succeeding parts is given no value as in (c) and is deducted 0.2.

Event requirements are in some cases specific deductions and in others general in nature. When the exact deduction is not given, subtract 0.1 to 0.3 for missing combination parts. In an event where the combination requirements are few, the general rule of thumb is to deduct the entire 0.3. For each event the general requirements are listed first, then the specific deductions.

Floor Exercises

The routine must move in a smooth rhythmic pattern covering all segments of the competitive area. It should contain hold, balance, strength, jumps, kips, handsprings, and aerials. The body should always be in the correct technical position. Only two steps may proceed any tumbling pass. In Competition I, one C must be swinging and in Competition III, 2 C's must fall into this category. The exercise must be performed between fifty and seventy seconds. All holds must be two seconds.

1. Failure to have a swing C in Competition I, deduct 0.2.
2. Failure to have one swing C in Competition III, deduct 0.2.
3. Failure to have two swing C's in Competition III, deduct 0.3.
4. More than two running steps before a tumbling pass, deduct up to 0.3.
5. For a routine that is too short or long up to two seconds deduct 0.1, up to five seconds deduct 0.2, up to nine seconds deduct 0.3, and for more than nine seconds deduct 0.5.
6. Touching out of the area without support, deduct 0.1.
7. Supporting your weight out of the area, deduct up to 0.2.
8. Executing tricks out of the area, deduct 0.1.

Pommel Horse

The predominant skill must be double leg circles. Forward and reverse scissors must be shown and one type must be executed twice in succession. All three portions of the horse must be utilized.

1. If the routine has one forward and one backward scissors, but none executed successfully, deduct 0.3.
2. If a forward or reverse scissors is missing, deduct 0.3.
3. If there is only one scissors, deduct 0.5.
4. If there are no scissors performed, deduct 0.6.

Rings

The exercise must show movements of swing, strength, and hold, but the swinging parts must predominate. There must be at least two handstands, one executed with strength and the other with swing. A second commensurate strength part must be used. In Competition II one of the *C* parts must be of a swinging nature, and in Competition III two of the *C* moves must fall into this classification. All holds must be two seconds.

1. No commensurate strength part, deduct 0.3.
2. Failure to have a swinging *C* in Competition II, deduct 0.2.
3. Failure to have two swinging *C* parts in Competition III, deduct 0.3.
4. If the routine is overbalanced with strength moves deduct up to 0.3.
5. If a handstand is missing either execution with swing or strength, deduct 0.2 to 0.3.

Parallel Bars

The exercise must flow between parts of swing, releases, and hold parts. Moving parts must predominate. In Competition I a *B* or *C* release must be executed below or above the bars. The hands during this move must leave the bars at the same time. In Competition III this *B* release move must be executed above and below the bar. In Competition I, one swinging *C* is required and in Competition III two *C*'s in this category must be performed. All holds are two seconds.

1. In Competition I, failure to have one swinging *C* move, deduct 0.2.
2. In Competition III, having only one swinging *C*, deduct 0.2.
3. In Competition III, having no swinging *C* move, deduct 0.3.
4. In Competition I, no *B* release above or below the bars, deduct 0.3.

5. In Competition III, only one *B* release above or below the bars, deduct 0.3.
6. In Competition III, having no *B* release above or below the bars, deduct 0.6.
7. Having more than three hold moves, deduct up to 0.3.

Horizontal Bar

The exercise must be free flowing without stops. It should consist of a variety of giant swings with turns, grip changes, and twists. It should have in-bar work and at no time should the routine stop. It must show a move done in the dorsal hang or el grip and must have at least one stunt where the hands release the bar at the same time and regrasp the bar.

1. For any hold part, deduct up to 0.2.
2. If it has only one move that meets the release and dorsal requirement, deduct 0.3.
3. If neither the dorsal nor release requirement are met, deduct 0.6.

The last 0.6 of a point is rewarded for originality, risk, and virtuosity. These points can be earned for one skill or may be applied to the overall performance in the entire routine. Let us take them individually. Because of the specialized judging procedure of the vaulting event, it will be discussed separately after the description of virtuosity.

ORIGINALITY (0.2)

This is self-explanatory. If a gymnast does a trick or combination the judge has never seen before, he can be awarded this 0.2 of a point. In international competition a move is considered original over the entire competition where it was introduced. In this country a new stunt is original the first year it was shown in competition, and if after the first year only one gymnast continues to perform the skill, it remains original.

RISK (0.2)

This applies to any move the gymnast performs in which he has an extreme chance of missing. An example would be free hips to a perfect handstand, triply flyaway off the horizontal bar.

VIRTUOSITY (0.2)

The virtuosity award applies to moves done higher than the Code requires (a piked salto instead of tucked, or straight arms on skills usually performed with bent arms would be good examples of virtuosity).

I did not mention Spiritual Expression when we discussed Combination. It is impossible for anyone but the extremely highly experienced judge to apply these deductions fairly. A spiritual performance is one that flows in a masterful way. If applied, it should never penalize a gymnast under Combination more than 0.4 of a point.

Vaulting

Instead of *A, B,* and *C* moves, each vault has a numerical value ranging from 7.0 to 9.8. These values are listed in the F.I.G. text. Two-tenths can be awarded for virtuosity, which we have already discussed. The horse is subdivided into two sections, the neck and the croup. If a gymnast places his hand on the line dividing these sections, he is penalized 0.5. He is allowed a twenty-meter run, and if he takes more than this distance he loses 0.3 points. Although the run is not scored, after his first step he is obligated to finish the jump or receive a zero. The two main elements judged are pre-flight and post-flight.

Pre-Flight
1. Low pre-flight, deduct up to 1.5.

Post-Flight
1. If the gymnast does not rise to a position where his buttocks are at an elevation 4/5 the height of the horse, and if he does not travel away from the horse on a croup vault one length of the horse or on a neck vault 4/5 the horse's length, he can lose up to 1.5.
2. If he is out of alignment while in the air, deduct up to 0.3.
3. If his lack of alignment is not corrected by the time he lands, he loses up to an additional 0.2.
4. If his body position is poor, deduct up to 0.3.
5. If his body position is poor throughout the vault, deduct 0.4 to 1.0.
6. For bending the arms on a vault deduct 0.3 to 1.0.
7. For deduction on landing it is the same as dismount deductions listed under Execution with the exception that for a complete fall the deduction is 0.3 to 0.5.

Meets are judged by four judges and overseen by a Superior Judge. The high and low score are dropped and the two middle scores averaged. The two middle scores must be in the ranges listed below:

> 0.10 with an average of 9.60 and higher.
> 0.20 with an average of 9.00 to 9.55.
> 0.30 with an average of 8.00 to 8.95.
> 0.50 with an average of 6.50 to 7.95.
> 0.80 with an average of 4.00 to 6.45.
> 1.00 in all other cases.

If the two middle scores do not fall within these ranges it is up to the Superior Judge to intervene and force one official to change his score so the average is acceptable.

35

Judging Women's Gymnastics: New FIG Code of Points Changes

Jackie Fie

The distribution of the ten points in judging of optional exercises on uneven bars, balance beam, and floor exercise is as follows:

The optional exercises must include three elements of superior difficulty and four elements of medium difficulty. The medium difficulties can be replaced by elements of superior difficulty. However, two medium difficulties may not replace one superior difficulty.

Optional Formula (Ten-Point Distribution)

Three elements of superior difficulty	
.60 points each =	1.80 points
Four elements of medium difficulty	
.30 points each =	1.20 points
Composition at .50 and originality and value of the	
connections at 1.50 =	2.00 points
Composition Total	5.00 points
Execution and amplitude =	4.00 points

General impression =   <u>1.00 points</u>

  Execution Total   5.00 points

USGF redistribution of FIG formula for areas of composition
and execution—effective for the Elite and JOAGP Competitions. A detailed explanation of Level of Difficulty and/or Risk
Elements is available from the USGF Women's Technical
Committee.

Composition (5.0)

Difficulty	3.00
3 Superiors (.6 each)	
4 Mediums (.3 each)	
Originality of all elements	0.30
Technical value of connections	0.30
Risk/level of difficulty (formerly difficulty level	
of competition)	0.50
Choice of elements (variations of structure	
groups, mount and dismount level of	
difficulty, repetition, series requirements, etc.)	0.50
Distribution: order of elements	0.20
Spacing/placement of elements in relation to	
use of apparatus or floor	<u>0.20</u>
Composition Total	5.00

Execution (5.0)

Execution, amplitude, rhythm	
(deductions for specific and general	
faults—small, medium and large errors)	4.00
General impression (elegance, maturity, poise,	
personality, projection)	0.50
Virtuosity (ultimate in technique, amplitude	
and ease of execution)	0.20
General rhythm and pace	<u>0.30</u>
Execution Total	<u>5.00</u>
Total	10.00

COMPULSORY EXERCISES (ELITE LEVEL ONLY)

The Compulsory Exercise is evaluated from 0 to 10 points
for each of the four events. The text of the international
(Elite) exercises will not be accompanied by a list of specific
deductions. (The USA has, however, established such a list for

USGF Elite Competitions.) The time duration for both beam and floor exercise will be published with the text of the exercises. All faults are to be penalized as indicated in the Table of General Faults and Penalties and Specific Deductions for each event in the FIG Code of Points.

When a prescribed element is omitted in the exercise, the deduction will be:

For a superior difficulty	0.60 point
For a medium difficulty	0.30 point
For a basic difficulty (not listed in the Code of Points)	0.20 point

The compulsory elements may be reversed totally or in part. However, the direction of the exercise may not be changed or there will be a 0.2 deduction each time. When reversing an element on beam or on floor, it is permissible to add or eliminate up to two steps.

SERIES (DEFINITION AND APPLICATION FOR BALANCE BEAM AND FLOOR EXERCISE)

A series is the total of all medium and superior elements executed in continuity without an intervening stop. Medium difficulties executed in a series on the beam are not repetitions,

Sandy Thielz, FIG judge

but are counted as one superior difficulty. Elements of superior difficulty executed in a series on the beam and floor are also not repetitions; they are counted as two or more superior difficulties.

The series can be *simple* when the same element is repeated two or three times in succession. Examples of simple series credited as one superior (beam):

1. Two walkovers forward or two walkovers backward
2. Two repetitions of the same medium element turn
3. Two split leaps

Examples of simple series credited as two superiors (beam):

1. Two one-arm walkovers forward or backward
2. Two flic-flacs
3. Two aerial walkovers forward

Examples of simple series credited as two or more superiors on floor:

1. Two or more stretched somersaults backward
2. Roundoff, flic-flac, (flic-flac without hand support)
3. Two or more tucked somersaults forward

The series can be *compound* when different elements from different structure groups are repeated in succession. When only one element in a compound series is a superior, the series is credited with one superior difficulty. However, when a compound series is composed of two or more superior difficulties, the series will have a value of two or more superior difficulties.

Examples of compound series credited as one superior (beam):

1. Cartwheel ¼ turn outward, walkover forward
2. Backward roll to handstand step-out into walkover backward
3. One-arm walkover backward, tinsica backward
4. Walkover forward, aerial walkover
5. Two different medium leaps in succession
6. Walkover backward, flic-flac

Examples of compound series credited as two superiors (beam):

1. One-arm walkover backward, walkover backward to split sit

2. One-arm cartwheel on far arm, aerial cartwheel
3. Valdez walk-out, walkover backward to handstand—lowering to clear straddle support
4. Press to cross handstand—walkover forward, kick to cross handstand with 180° turn into roll forward
5. Flic-flac, tuck somersault backward (salto)
6. Two different superior leaps in succession

Examples of compound series credited as two superiors (floor):

1. Roundoff, two flic-flacs, somersault backward stretched (salto)
2. Roundoff, Arabian somersault forward, aerial walkover
3. Handspring, somersault forward, round-off, stretched somersault backward (salto)

VAULT

Vaulting horse height is 120 cm (USGF Juniors and children may lower to 110 cm).

The following vaults have been eliminated from the FIG Code of Points (Numbers indicated are from the 1970 "old" Code:

1. Straddle (Horizontal)
2. Layout Squat (8.0)*
3. Layout Straddle (8.5)*
4. Stoop (Horizontal)
5. Layout Stoop (8.5)*
8. High Front Vault through Handstand
14. Handstand ¼ turn

USGF values of other lower level vaults are:
    Handspring-½ turn (8.8)
    ½ turn on Handspring (8.8)

New vault evaluations are as follows:

1. Hecht (9.40)
3. Handspring (9.20)
4. Yamashita (9.40)
5. Giant cartwheel (9.0)

*These vaults have been assigned values as indicated by the WTC USGF for use in the Age Group Program.

6. Cartwheel-¼ turn (9.0)
7. Cartwheel-½ turn (9.20)
8. Cartwheel-¾ turn (9.40)
12. ½ on-½ off (9.40)
16. Yamashita-½ turn (9.60)

New vault numbers:
    22 and 24 = 22
    23 and 25 = 23
    26 and 27 = 26

The ¼ turn on and ½ turn on Tsukahara vaults are now evaluated as the same vault. Number 19: Handspring-1½ tucked and also piked somersaults forward is the same vault. Number 30 indicates any vault that does not appear in the FIG Code Table of Vaults. Regulations for the *final* competition in vaulting (Elite level only):

1. The gymnast must perform two different vaults.
2. The counting mark will be the average mark of both vaults.
3. The gymnast is expected to perform two vaults. When she executes only one vault, the valid counting mark will be 50% of the score of the performed vault.
4. When the gymnast performs the same vault twice, the second vault is evaluated as 0, and the counting mark will be 50% of the average of the first vault.
5. Vaults 22, 23, 24, and 25 will be evaluated as the same vault 24. Therefore, tucks and pikes will be the same vault in finals.

Note: Complete USGF Elite Vaulting Regulations available from USGF Women's Technical Committee.

Team Vaulting. Of the 12 vaults executed by each team not more than 6 may be the same. The penalty is 0.3 for each vault in excess of 6 that is the same.

Penalties for landings (applicable to vaulting, floor exercise, balance beam and uneven bars for both compulsory and optional exercises):

1. Fall from the apparatus or during the dismount   0.5 point
2. Fall on the buttocks or knees   0.5 point
3. Fall against the apparatus   0.5 point
4. Distinct support with one or two hands   0.5 point

5. Touching the floor with one or two hands	0.3 point
6. Steps and hops	0.1-0.2 point

Vaulting Penalties and Deductions (General)

First flight phase (all 5 groups)

1. Insufficient pre-flight according to the technique of the vault	up to 1.00 point
2. Body bent	up to 0.50 point
3. Legs bent, straddled or open	up to 0.50 point

Support phase (all 5 groups)

1. Too long in support	0.20 point
2. Support with arched body	up to 0.30 point
3. Arms slightly bent	0.20 point
4. Arms fully bent	1.00 point

Second flight phase (all 5 groups)

1. Insufficient height	up to 0.50 point
2. Insufficient stretch of body before landing	up to 0.50 point
3. Poor direction	up to 0.50 point
4. Poor body position (legs bent, straddled or open)	up to 0.50 point
5. Turn too early or too late	0.30 point
6. Turn not completed	0.50 point

USGF additions

7. Insufficient distance	up to 0.50 point
8. Lack of dynamics	up to 0.50 point

Vaulting Penalties and Deductions (Specific)

Group 1 - Straight (Upright) Vaults (1, 2)

1. Body under horizontal in first flight phase	up to 1.00 point
2. Body piked too much in first flight phase	up to 0.50 point
3. Support alternate	0.30 point
4. Insufficient push-off	up to 1.00 point
5. Touching horse with feet	0.50 point

USGF Additions

6. Shoulders too far forward in support	0.30 - 0.50 point
7. Piking in first phase 45°—90° is a stoop vault	Wrong Vault—0 (Elite Level only)

Group II - Handsprings, Yamashita (3, 4)

1. Arched or piked body during first flight phase	up to 0.50 point
2. Support or repulsion alternate	0.30 point

3. Arched or piked in second flight phase (handspring)   up to 0.50 point
4. Insufficient angle or too early an angle (Yamashita)   0.50 point

Group III - Vault with turns around the Longitudinal Axis (5—18)

1. Arched during first or second flight phase   up to 0.30 point
2. Poor body position during the turn   up to 0.50 point

Group IV - Vaults with turns around the Horizontal Axis (19—21)

1. Insufficient tuck or pike movement   0.30 point
2. Technical fault in the turn   0.30 point
3. Legs opened during the turn   up to 0.50 point

Group V - Vaults with combinations of turns around more than one body axis (22-29)

1. Incorrect support   0.30 point
2. Turns too soon or too late   0.30 point
3. Insufficient tuck or pike   0.30 point
4. Legs opened during the turn   up to 0.50 point

UNEVEN BARS

New distance between the bars is 55—90 cm with a base at 70 cm. Dismounts with push-off from the feet (saltos) starting from a straight or crouched vertical position are not allowed if preceded by a stop. From a straight or crouched position on the low bar to establishment of a handstand position on the high bar will be considered a medium difficulty. A ½-pirouette in the handstand position into another element makes the element a superior. From a straight or crouched position on the low bar, using a second spring to continue the exercise, will be considered as an intermediate swing with a penalty of 0.50 point. The ¾ sole circle forward to somersault backward dismount is a superior difficulty.

Penalties (1975 edition):

1. Release of one hand with supplementary support of foot   0.50 point
2. Release of one hand without supplementary support   0.30 point
3. Touching the bar or the floor   up to 0.50 point
4. Intermediate swing (from the knees)   0.50 point
5. Stop in the exercise (each time)   0.20 point
6. Dismount from a stationary position   0.40 point

Deduction 11 ("Running underneath apparatus after completion of exercise") is eliminated.

BALANCE BEAM

It is forbidden to use chalk or resin on the covered beam.

The time duration is as follows: 1:15 minutes (75 seconds) minimum to 1:35 minutes (95 seconds) maximum.

Compositional regulations for the optional exercise are: The same element may be performed only once. The element may be performed in a series or as a single element.

An element already featured in a series and presented as an independent element in the exact form will be considered a repetition. The penalty will be 0.20 point. However, it is permissible for the same element to be presented in a modified form from a different starting position or into another possible exit.

An unnecessary lack of continuity between the elements of a series will incur a penalty of up to 0.20 point.

Two to three static elements are still allowed, but not before or after a difficult acrobatic element. The penalty will be 0.20 point each time.

A series is not mandatory for the beam exercise. The exercise must, however, contain the following minimum elements: 3 superior and 4 medium elements including a mount, dismount, 1 large leap, 1 full turn, and 3 acrobatic elements.

Penalties (1975 edition):

1. One full turn missing	0.20 point
2. One large leap missing	0.20 point
3. Hand support to maintain balance	0.50 point
4. Hand touch to maintain balance	0.30 point
5. Foot against side of the beam for balance	0.20 point

FLOOR EXERCISE

Penalties (1975 edition):

1. Hand support on the floor for balance	0.50 point
2. Hand touch on floor for balance	0.30 point
3. Absence of acrobatic series (2 required)	0.20 point
4. Not ending with music	0.30 point
5. Pianist aids gymnast (each time)	0.20 point
6. Beginning of exercise missed by personal error	0.50 point
7. Start of exercise without music	0.20 point

FAULTS RELATED TO BEHAVIOR OF COACH AND GYMNAST

Coaching Faults

1. Assistance from coach during exercise	1.00 point
2. Assistance during landing	0.50 point
3. Assistance during vault	Vault void
4. Coach between board and horse	0.50 point
5. Coach between rails or runs under apparatus	0.50 point
6. Coach on podium during beam or floor	0.50 point

(Coach may remove board and position mat for landing in Elite and JOAGP Competitions; coach may spot a difficult element in JOAGP, but may not walk the length of the beam or 0.5 point penalty.)

7. Coach talks to gymnast during exercise	0.50 point

(Coach may talk to gymnast after fall from apparatus, if gymnast appears injured.)

8. Coach gives signals to gymnast	0.30 point

Behavior of Gymnast

1. Lack of presentation to head judge before or after the exercise	0.20 point
2. Leaving competition area without permission of head judge	0.50 point
3. Starting exercise when red signal is flashed	Exercise Void
4. Absent in competition hall without permission of head judge	Disqualification
5. Warming up when green light is on	0.50 point

New springboard regulations:

The springboard for the Uneven Bars and Balance Beam may be placed on one or both mats for mounting. (Two mats at 6 cm each not to exceed 12 cm, if stable.) The new height of the springboard is 15 cm + 1 cm.

Space does not provide for listing of a complete vault classification by group and all medium and superior difficulties on bars, beam, and floor. See 1975 Code of Points available from: USGF, Box 12713, Tucson, Arizona 85711, price $10.00, and Corrections and Small Changes in the Code of Points for January 1, 1978. Also, USGF Supplement on FIG Difficulties Classification 1977 Fall Edition, price $1.00.

36

Dance and Gymnastics: Notes from an Official

Noreen Connell

The excitement is over; the stellar gymnast has been recognized, appraised, and classified by the judges; and the medals have been awarded. Of course, I'm referring to the 21st Olympiad in Montreal, which I attended [in 1976].

Each exercise in the competition demonstrated the importance of dance in making the performance a memorable one—and underlined how the professional dance teacher benefits the gymnast.

Gymnastics has decidedly progressed from a recital of acrobatic ability. In fact, today's performances seem to test the limits of the body. As we progress are we giving enough importance to the good teacher's background in anatomy? or kinesiology? This point is recognized and has been discussed at recent congresses of the United States Gymnastic Federation at its Age-Group meetings. The youngest group of USGF-recognized competitors is comprised of children ages 10-11, in the Developmental Division. Fundamental skills and safety are stressed, as are a maximum degree of physical and mental preparation. The emphasis of the specialist in children's dance training—*not* to teach "too much too soon"—has the full support of the country's foremost gymnastic organization.

Ballet is forever basic and is technically essential to every floor exercise and balance beam move. The disciplines of ballet are of critical importance to the developing gymnast, as to any performing dancer. Although years of formal training may not be necessary for the score-oriented gymnast, the automatic body carriage of the trained ballerina is always apparent. In this reference, the philosophy of the teacher determines the degree to which the result is "automatic." If the teacher is concerned with little more than the choreography of a year-end recital, to be sure the student will execute movement onstage to a particular musical background; but if pure technique is treated as an end in itself the student will gradually incorporate grace and fluidity in every movement.

Consideration must be given, however, to the fact that balletic discipline is exactly that—discipline. As such, it is difficult for the younger child to accept, but the teacher has a happy alternative: the Dance Movement Class, introducing modern dance positions, rhythm and locomotor skills. It is here that techniques can be inculcated in such basic activities as walking, running, skipping, leaping and other moves necessary to dance and natural to the young student. The teacher can capitalize on the absence of inhibitions in most youngsters; imagination in class can transform the group into birds, butterflies, flowers, trees, or any other fanciful image—and develop creativity in the process. The class is suddenly alive, enjoyable and successful. The several "cooks" in the group have each been given identical ingredients—and each has created his or her own cake.

At this point we've progressed to a function of modern dance: freedom of movement with technical emphasis on muscle toning, body development and isolation. The student is introduced to dynamics, levels, focus, speed, rhythm and direction changes. Originality is almost unavoidable, and the physical configuration and comfort of the student/gymnast will influence her interpretation of the folk, character, and jazz techniques which will follow. A style emerges which will characterize each subsequent performance.

Floor exercise and balance beam in the United States have incorporated dance movement in the gymnastic world; a form newer to this country is Modern Rhythmical. An individual or group activity, it is entirely dance oriented and always requires hand apparatus such as balls, hoops, wands, Indian clubs, or the like. While compulsory exercises have been defined for competition, no tumbling elements are permitted in Modern Rhythmical. Considered separately as a performing art, it still can be analyzed only as a derivative of other existing styles, predominantly modern or ethnic. Execution tends to be less demanding of the performer, since the attention is often focused on the

Nelli Kim (*International Gymnast* photo)

accessory (hoop, etc.) and faults in movement may be unde-
tected. Its growing importance in sports is noted by the separate
classification of judges' certification recently established in this
country. Even newer things will inevitably be introduced, and
become assimilated into the accepted world of sports. The
gymnast will achieve what is today considered impossible, and
the body of judges will redefine its code of point deductions.

A dancer need not know gymnastics; a gymnast must know
dance; and a competitive gymnast will be judged. Need the
judge be a dancer? No. But he or she should be sufficiently
educated to recognize nicely choreographed combinations
alternating dance moves with tumbling difficulty. The judge
must train him or herself to discount a pleasing background
melody and to concentrate on the gymnast's correctness of
rhythm. The judge must not be overly impressed with upper
body movement, neglecting to observe the execution of the
lower body. An appealing port-de-bras should not prevent the
observant judge from noticing a sickled foot or hyperextended
lower back.

Choreography of competitive events must combine the
subjective creativity of the teacher with the physical abilities of
the performer. The teacher has an obligation to recognize and
capture the strengths of her students; to develop phrases which
display the dancer's attitudes to best advantage; and to learn
from each student as she teaches. The exercise will ultimately
be executed not by the teacher, but by her pupils; accordingly,
in a class of ten, there should be ten visibly different routines,
each one reflecting a successful exchange of information between teacher and pupil.

This demands that the teacher be knowledgeable, first and
foremost, in the several techniques currently used in competitive exercises. She must be thoroughly conversant with the
appropriate terminology; and she must know how to adapt
methodology to her pupils. The general appeal of the 1972
Korbut, contrasted with her 1976 performance, illustrates the
point. Judges had to recognize the comfortable blend of "cute"
jazz technique and gymnastics in 1972, whereas her recent
rendition in forced contemporary did not "fit the gymnast."

A qualified gymnastics judge, of necessity, knows the com-
plexity of elements that comprise compulsory exercises. The

judge is required to demonstrate this knowledge in a series of demanding tests as he or she progresses to National rating or beyond. Defensible scoring, however, requires additional education in dance technique in at least the major forms. Good execution should be rewarded—and it will be, if both the performer and judge recognize it. And so, be the competition in the most remote high school gymnasium, or under the glare of an internationally televised spectacle, credit must accrue to the dance teacher whose knowledge was imparted to both participant and official.

37
The Problems of Judging
Dr. Josef Goehler

Without doubt, judging is one of the biggest (if not the biggest) problem in gymnastics today. There are no objective measuring tools for scoring; every judge has a personal scope for decisions. No matter how hard the judge tries to mete out justice to the gymnast, the psychological "laws" are there: having a personal favorite, seeing the favorite's routine through rose-colored glasses, viewing another gymnast's performance as inferior though it might be equal.

A 9.50 exercise can therefore be judged by three equally competent judges as 9.40, 9.50, and 9.60. This leeway in objective judgment is considered by the FIG in many places in the *Code de Pointage*. The federation has tried for years to word the regulations for scoring in such a way that a good judge can evaluate the true value of a routine precisely.

This has never been easy. Years ago, one judge was supposed to watch for technical perfection, for the number of exercise points and their weight (A, B, and C parts), follow the composition of a routine, the carriage of the gymnast, the originality and risk shown by the gymnast—quite a job! But it could not be decided how to distribute the tasks to two judges. Around the time of the 1936 Olympics in Berlin, the scores of all judges (three at that time) were used for the gymnast's final score.

288

Later it was decided to strike the highest and the lowest of four scores, and to use the average of the two middle scores. For example: with 9.40, 9.50, 9.60, 9.70, and 9.40 and 9.70 are erased, and the 9.50 and 9.60 are averaged for a score of 9.55. Pierre Hentges from Luxembourg and Arthur Gander of Switzerland developed the present system of judging. Their influence was felt in the ethical area, in laying the groundwork for unified opinion (especially on the compulsory exercises), and in the formation of educational courses for prospective judges.

Judges must use different evaluation scales for different competitions, making their task even more difficult. For example: On the first day of team competition (competition 1) penalties are milder than in the finals for the all-around title (competition 2). The judges must be even stricter in the finals for individual titles (competition 3). They must be aware of exactly how many "C" parts are required for the different kinds of competitions.

A further difficulty is that, at large competitions, the judges sit at their tables for many hours grading hundreds of routines and have little time to relax; this is one of the reasons wrong judgments occur—which of course outrages the audience.

Though there is an ombudsman aside from the four judges, he has limited rights and must give substantial reasons for changing a score. Only rarely does positive persuasion succeed. The rest of the time the judges are free in their decisions, if they stay within certain limits, that become higher as the scores climb. Middle scores that range 9.60 and above are not allowed to have a greater discrepancy than a tenth of a point. For example: 9.40, 9.50, 9.60, 9.70 is a valid series of scores; the middle scores (9.50, 9.60) are a tenth of a point apart. If the judges had come up with 9.40, 9.40, 9.70, 9.70, however, the ombudsman would have to step in because the middle scores are too far apart. If the judges do not come to an agreement, the ombudsman's score prevails. Thus, the ideal ombudsman must know all the rules.

A judge who wants to reach the international level must take a series of examinations at regular intervals by the FIG on each continent. The prospective judge does not necessarily have to be a former gymnastics champion, but former gymnasts exper-

ienced at all levels of competition make the best judges. The job
is not only to show up and give scores at competitions, to judge
the degree of difficulty of new exercise parts, and to know the
new compulsory exercises down to each detail; they must have
continuous contact with active gymnasts and study their
training.

The judge must not only have expert knowledge of perfect
technique but also have a sure aesthetic sense—the beauty of the
performance, the rhythm, and the composition.

The gymnast may put in years of training, week after week
after week, but must live with the uncertainty of receiving
unfair reward for his diligence.

Many young gymnasts have given up prematurely because of
unjust scores. How well the active gymnast can judge if his
routines have been over- or under-evaluated is a problem in
itself. Even if the gymnast studies his optional exercises on
videotape, he falls easy prey to the subjective probability of
over-evaluating his routine without being aware of it.

Zoltan Magyar (Mark Shearman photo)

It would be falsely optimistic to believe that a judge never over- or under-scores consciously. But these cases have become fewer and fewer as the FIG becomes more strict. "Black sheep" are being removed more readily than in previous times.

Much refinement is still needed, however. Education of judges around the world must be improved and unified; the composition of juries for each meet must be analyzed and examined better. The final result will be based on morality and on the laws of fairness without which sport cannot exist.

Those who offer the highest accomplishments are the most sensitive about evaluations of their accomplishments. Where stopwatch and measuring tape, goals, or hits do the evaluation, there is no problem; problems come with subjective evaluations based on many criteria that cannot be determined precisely. The four-judge system, by erasing extreme evaluations, may be as good as any to lead to an objective score that reflects the actual accomplishment. It is the declared goal of the FIG to make judging even more exact, more just, more sportsmanlike, an achievement that will give gymnastics new friends all over the world.

38

The Dangers of Subjectivity

Hardy Fink

My purpose here is to point out some aspects of judging that do not necessarily pertain to the rules but of which each judge should be aware. These factors may be psychological, physiological, philosophical, but if they can affect the judge or vice versa an awareness is essential for a complete understanding of judging. Perhaps the judge can take steps to minimize any detrimental effects.

Judge-Gymnast Relationship

From the socio-psychological literature we can deduce that a judge's attitudes about the personal characteristics of a gymnast (race, personality, appearance, etc.) will affect his rating. A judge's expectations of the gymnast gained from previous experience, rumors, announcements during meets, etc. and his knowledge of a certain range of scores along with a pre-set from the gymnast's behavior can affect rating.

Ego involvement with the gymnast may occur if the judge knows the gymnast well. Awareness of the tendency to mark high because of ego involvement may result in overcompensation. A judge would ideally have no knowledge of the gymnast being observed.

Judge's Rating of Himself as a Gymnast

There is a tendency for judges to rate opposite to their self-perceived ability to do a certain exercise. Those who rate themselves high in a certain trait tend to rate others low, and vice versa. This problem may be overcome either by using experienced judges who were themselves only average gymnasts, or by using a group of judges who range widely in gymnastic abilities so that the various effects might cancel.

Human Judgment

Research into this area indicates that a judge cannot be relied on to reproduce the same decision every time, given the same information and also given that he is not very good at processing information. Furthermore, training and experience do not appear to improve the accuracy of judgment.

Central Tendency

There tends almost invariably to be a central tendency of the scores for all the performers in any meet. The better performer is invariably cheated with respect to the poor performers.

The lack of extreme scores can be due to a number of factors:
1. Incorrect knowledge of the rules (lack of competence).
   (a) Failure to know all of the deductions that apply.
   (b) Failure to take into account the degree of error and range of possible deductions for that error.
2. Reluctance to award extreme scores (lack of confidence).
   (a) Fear of appearing ridiculous or of being challenged on that score.
   (b) Conformity pressures due to the feedback mechanism of flashing scores. Feedback tends to increase agreement among judges but in so doing decreases objectivity.

Mistake Perpetuation

A score awarded by a group of judges may be undeniably wrong occasionally, but instead of admitting to the error the judges will adjust the scores of subsequent performers to provide some sort of ranking on that event. Ranking cannot preserve the differences between performers that the scores should reflect, and results in progressively greater errors involving many performers. Let us assume that gymnasts *A, B, C,* and

D do routines worth exactly 6.50, 7.00, 7.50, and 8.00 respectively (see attached summary). For some reason—and this may understandably occur—A's performance is awarded 7.50, which the judges will see through the influential flashing system. B's performance will still be worth 7.00 but since it was obviously about 0.50 better than A's, the judges will tend to give 7.80 (8.00 seeming too high). C can subsequently expect an 8.10 and D an 8.40. The mistake has been deliberately perpetuated but now fails to differentiate adequately among any of the performances. This can have quite an effect in the all-around placings.

During ranking, one gets invariably to the point where there is no more room to adjust because the scores have become too high or too low. Instead of having made one excusable error, the judges have deliberately cheated several times.

MISTAKE PERPETUATION

Due to: Recognition of an error,
          Feedback from flashing,
          Desire to rank athletes.

Result: Perpetuation of an initial error,
          Destruction of true score differences among all subsequent performers,
          Cheating of many performers with respect to each other,
          Probability of loss of correct all-around ranking,
          Destruction of any possibility for upholding an appeal on the initial score,
          Underrating of best performer with respect to other (if upward perpetuation) or underrating of earlier performers with respect to later performers (if mistake was low score).

Gymnast	HIGH SCORE FOR "A" True Score	Mistake on "A" and Perpetuation	LOW SCORE FOR "A" True Score	Mistake on "A" and Compensation
A	6.50	7.50(!)	6.50	5.50(!)
B	7.00	7.80	7.00	6.20
C	7.50	8.10	7.50	6.80
D	8.00	8.40	8.00	7.50
E	8.50	8.70	8.50	8.20
F	9.00	9.10	9.00	8.80
G	9.50	9.50	9.50	9.40

Counting and Noncounting Scores

If four judges evaluate objectively, but do not agree exactly on a score, each judge's score should count exactly 50% of the time, especially over a large sample of scores. Furthermore, each judge's scores should be each of low non-counting, low counting, high counting and high non-counting 25 percent of the time. If the judge's scores agree randomly, these percentages will vary somewhat but the 50-50 trend should still appear.

The deviation should not be great, although the exact percentages may never appear and should not be expected. If large deviations do occur, an investigation may be warranted to discover if a particular judge was concerned only with counting rather than judging objectively or if one or more of the judges was deliberately cheating. Counting or not counting 80-100 percent of the time in meet after meet is certainly suspect. Even if one judge drops out every time (deliberately or not) each of the judges should only have in the range of 66 percent of their scores counting.

If Your Score Drops Out

A judge whose score drops out still has a major effect on the final score. He dictates which scores will be the middle two counting ones. Let us see what the potential effects of dropping out can be. To facilitate understanding and interpretation, I will use the attached chart and assumptions.

J3 SHOWING FAVORITISM

Case	Example	Gymnast	J1	J2	J3	J4	Score	Difference
Case 1	a	A	3.5	3.6	3.7	3.6	3.60	
(below 4.00)		B	3.5	3.6	3.4	3.6	3.55	0.05
	b	A	3.9	2.8	4.0	2.9	3.40	
		B	3.9	1.9	1.8	2.9	2.40	1.00
Case 2	a	A	9.7	9.8	9.9	9.8	9.80	
(above 9.60)		B	9.7	9.8	9.6	9.8	9.75	0.05
	b	A	9.8	9.7	9.9	9.6	9.75	
		B	9.8	9.7	9.5	9.6	9.65	0.10

Assumptions

1. Gymnasts A and B should receive identical scores when judged objectively.
2. Judge No. 3 (J3) favors A and disfavors B; that is, J3 is willing to drop out above for A and below for B.
3. Case 1 assumes a "below 4.00" level for both gymnasts.
4. Case 2 assumes an "above 9.60" level for both gymnasts.
5. In example "a" for both Cases 1 and 2 only J3 drops out.
6. In example "b" for both Cases 1 and 2 the middle two scores are apart to the limits allowed. (Code of Points; p. 11; art. 11 par. 2)
7. Judges 1, 2, and 4 do not all agree on one more, otherwise J3 dropping out can have no effect.

Several observations follow directly from the table.

1. In example "a" of both cases, J3 has assisted A as an individual by 0.025 and with respect to B by 0.05.
2. In Case 1, example "b" J3 has assisted A as an individual by 0.50 and with respect to B by 1.00.
3. In Case 2, example "b", J3 has assisted A as an individual by 0.05 and with respect to B by 0.10.

Some interesting implications can be drawn by extrapolating somewhat. If J3 judges six events in the same manner he cannot avoid keeping gymnast A and B apart in the all-around from 0.30 to 6.00 points depending of course on the caliber of the gymnasts. The consequences of two judges cheating in this way, as may occur in dual meets, are even more extreme. The judges could conceivably force the middle two scores apart to the allowable limits and can assist one gymnast by 0.40 to 4.00 points per routine, again depending on the caliber of the gymnasts. For these extremes to be possible the scores of the other judges are also decisive. These extremes are nevertheless at least theoretically possible and even more so if the allowable middle score spreads are ignored. Looking at a team total (with five counting), one judge could affect a difference between two teams of from 1.50 to 30 points and double that if compulsories are involved. Quite impressive: the power that we have. It is apparent that the actual possible effect of one judge would be intermediate to these extremes—say in the range of 1 to 2 points in the all-around for a good Canadian performer. Can we ever excuse a judge's playing with the scores if even "dropping out" can have such a great effect?

This is the fun part of the book, where you can read about your favorite gymnastics champions. Ludmilla Tourischeva was the reigning queen of gymnastics from 1968-72, to be replaced by the daring, crowd-pleasing Olga Korbut in the 1972 Olympics. During this period also, a young American gymnast named Cathy Rigby made her debut in international competition and for the first time swerved American media and public attention to the sport of gymnastics. In 1976, a 14-year-old Romanian, Nadia Comaneci, ousted Olga from her number one position, stunning the world gymnastics community with the first perfect scores in Olympic history.

On the men's side, Nicolai Andrianov has been the premier men's gymnast for six years. An interview with Peter Kormann reveals the joys and frustrations of an amateur athlete living in an unsubsidized America. Finally, a first-hand portrait of Kurt Thomas explores America's hope for Olympic gold in 1980.

9

THE CHAMPIONS

Ludmilla Tourischeva (Tony Duffy photo)

39

Ludmilla Tourischeva: Looking Inside a Champion

David Reed

A pretty young woman with a calm serious expression walked along the sandy beach at Varna. She seemed to possess the quiet sensitivity you would expect of an artist. Her round stocky legs, muscular arms, unusually broad shoulders, small, firm breasts, and slim waist, however, indicated she was an athlete. She wore her long dark brown hair pulled straight back in a ponytail which made her high cheek bones and large, thoughtful brown eyes enticingly attractive.

A chilly autumn wind started to blow, and she sat down in the warm sand. Her eyes surveyed a picturesque scene of bright oranges, reds, and yellows of the setting sun that was slowly being vanquished before a rolling fogbank. Steamy mists rose like bubbles surfacing from the ocean's depths until they were caught in the blanket of fog which slumbered along, enveloping everything before it—the windswept pink clouds framed in yellow by the setting sun, the wide expanse of azure-blue ocean tinged with spots of green and the inky black breakwater far ahead.

She crossed her limber legs and sighed. Her chest heaved and her nostrils expanded as she breathed in the refreshing, salty ocean air. Transfixed by the vision of nature's harmonious process, she was content to let handfuls of linen-white sand slip playfully between her fingers.

Her thoughts focused briefly on her new hometown, Rostov-on-the-Don, and then she concentrated on the day's gymnastics competition. She and her teammates had just completed their compulsory exercises. Everyone had trained hard—especially her—with the perseverance, seriousness, and skill demanded by the highest technical levels.

Today's performance had been mostly good and sometimes excellent. The scores were generally high, although as usual the scoring among the team members had been quite close. Challenged by a popular young teammate for the individual title, she had performed with the consummate artistry of the defending champion. There was, nevertheless, room for some improvement in her routines. The challenger had performed with enthusiastic charm, the champion with artistic serenity.

Immediately after the competition she and her teammates had relaxed in a sauna bath. Its warmth had been both physically and mentally pleasing. Then they enjoyed a modest dinner.

The challenger loved public attention; the champion loved books. The one thrived on press conferences where she re-

The Champion . . . (Mark Shearman photo)

sponded with equal ease in her native language or in English to the reporters' innumerable questions; the other was content with more personal satisfactions. The challenger sought victory as the champion yearned to perform the "ideal routine."

Lost in a reflective reverie, the calm and composed champion breathed in more of the crisp, salty air. She sat quietly on the beach contemplating the day's events as she waited for her coach to arrive. An intelligent girl and an excellent student at the pedagogical institute, her mood symbolized her aesthetic awareness, great ethical sense, and personal dedication to her beloved sport of gymnastics.

A few hundred meters to her left, the sports arena stood with its tan walls and red tile roof in proud tribute to the athlete's industrious dedication, technical skill, and competitive virtuosity.

She reflected on the quality of the team's routines, which had been planned carefully and precisely by the coaches. Their floor exercises had been excellent, but only she and the challenger had received superlative scores in all the events. The other teams received comparably high scores only in vault.

Although the Soviet team was in the lead, tomorrow's competition for the team title would be fierce and, as expected, her younger teammate would challenge her further for the individual championship. But she remained unperturbed.

The sand still filtered between her fingers. For months she had listened attentively to her coach's well-reasoned advice, polite criticism, and firm encouragement. She had trained diligently with her usual serious and dedicated calmness so she could give the judges (she hoped) the "ideal routine" during the World Championships. She considered such an accomplishment a priceless gift to gymnastics, and therefore an achievement of much more personal value than the exceptionally high scores which she undoubtedly would receive. Her chest heaved and she sighed again, the cool fall wind frolicking with her hair. Tomorrow would be a special day for her, and she looked forward with eagerness to its hopeful promises.

A brief but pleasant conversation began as her coach, an excellent teacher of gymnastics, approached from the arena. He saw his young pupil sitting on the beach, chatting with a family visiting the beach and he knew that she would perform in tomorrow's competition with her usual relaxed confidence, personal dignity, and technical virtuosity. Yes, she would successfully defend her individual title.

The coach reached the group and greeted everyone. They were surprised when he informed them casually that she was the current Olympic and world champion. Embarrassed, she blushed. Then the pretty young woman arose, said good-bye to their children playing with the seashells, thanked the family for its sincere courtesy, and left with her coach.

The therapeutic effects of the sauna's warmth and of her teammates' quiet conversation over dinner lingered—her mind was uninjured and felt strong. Tomorrow her calm competitiveness and determined composure would relax her teammates. washing away their anxieties. Their spirits would renew her own confidence (if that was necessary), encouraging everyone to perform at their highest level.

... and the challenger (Horst Muller photo)

As she and her coach walked away from the foggy beach, the champion again hoped that tomorrow—for the very first time in competition—she would execute the ideal routine. She was anxious, confident, and almost certain. Tonight a movie or a book before retiring—tomorrow simply another day in the life of a young woman, an athlete who was very much an artist.

Majestically dressed in red uniforms with white trim, the defending championship team marched proudly into the gymnastics arena bathed in the lively sounds of a military march. Their parade movements meshed in mechanical union, a result of their team spirit and sense of purpose. It was not a conscious effort, nor did it reflect any previous rehearsals in precision.

With much enthusiasm, the gymnasts warmed up both collectively and individually. The champion's exemplary self-assurance filled their hearts with a determined pride. Then, lost in a world of complete mental concentration, they chalked their hands.

The champion's stomach knotted with the excitement of the occasion and her impending exercises. The feeling was customary and anticipated if not altogether pleasant and one to which she had been long accustomed. Indeed, she would have been more worried if she had not felt the sensation of expectant nervousness. With muscles warm and hands chalked, the stage was set. She appeared relaxed and confident.

Prepared for her team's attack on the gymnastics apparatus, the champion's usual calm soothed her teammates. Their performances were generally very good, the scores were again high. The routines of the spirited, charismatic challenger were excellent; those of the talented, dignified champion simply without blemish. In all the events, the champion's technical merit reigned over the challenger's spontaneous and innovative style.

The challenger's coach had cleverly designed her routines around a physiological phenomenon, her extremely flexible body. He had planned new techniques for her and she had responded by training hard. Her breathtaking routines included backflips on the uneven parallel bars and, uniquely, on the balance beam as well as in her floor exercise. And he had developed a daring new vault for her if executed flawlessly (unfortunately it was not) would have won her the gold medal in that event. But even excellent coaching and proper planning could not compensate for confident dedication combined with serious concentration, two of the champion's most notable merits.

It came as no surprise to the champion's coach that her concentration produced powerful routines on the uneven parallel bars in an extraordinary fashion. Her great extensions (for which she was famous, in that exercise) were unrivaled that evening. Immediately after her dismount, an elated smile blossomed through the perspiration on her cheeks.

Her perseverance earned her another gold medal on the balance beam, an event in which she had improved tremendously the past two years. In vault nothing less than faultless execution by the challenger would have been a sufficient threat to the champion's high, strong vault. She had such a long afterflight that even the most exacting judges were amazed—the third gold medal for the champion that evening. But she remained rather concerned and even a little dismayed. The "ideal routine" had eluded her thus far.

As at the Olympics in 1972, the floor exercise and the Soviet team's best event, was the last scheduled competition. The first teammate performed a powerful routine with strong tumbling but little expression, which prevented her from receiving the highest scores. The second girl presented an extremely choreographed performance that won her high (but not superlative) marks. A third teammate's routine exemplified the influence of the rhythmic, gracefully beautiful native dances of her province. She earned the highest marks thus far. The next teammate's exercise harmonized strong tumbling with pleasing musical expressiveness. Still higher scores were awarded.

As anticipated, the challenger's innovative performance emphasized the natural appeal of her slender, puppet-like physique and her very flexible body. Spirited tumbling, dance-like expressiveness, and extreme but sometimes dangerous, flexibility defined her performance. The judges awarded her a 9.8. The wildly popular star responded to a brief standing ovation with her broad, enthusiastic smile which was universally appealing.

The champion presented herself to the judges with her

usual calm and dignified confidence, masking her fierce competitiveness. As she approached the edge of the floor exercise mat, she momentarily recalled that at home she had circled the dates of the World Championships on the calendar which hung above her desk and with modest simplicity had noted under the circles, "VICTORY!" Lost as before in intense mental concentration, she stood at the edge of the mat waiting with relaxed self-assurance for the music to begin.

The past few years her own floor exercise routine had progressed from a choreography of Russian themes for the previous year's all-Union Championships to the more lively choreography of her performance in the Olympics. She had received the well-deserved score of 9.9 at Munich and thereby won the all-around title. Her current, rather unusual (or at least unconventional) choreography had been fashioned around African rhythms.

The music began and her body suddenly catapulted forward in extraordinarily high and graceful tumbling. The champion's athletic artistry shone! Her performance paid a gracious compliment to gymnastics with power and technical excellence. Superb, beautiful movements and expression were combined in a harmonious, flawless whole that was devastatingly graceful. She presented to gymnastics a virtuoso performance of singular excellence and deceptive power.

In appropriate fashion, the crowd reciprocated her gift. Like a concert hall audience that once or twice in a lifetime is so enchanted with the spell of a Mozart sonata played to perfection that it merely sits quietly, the crowd paid the same homage to the champion's compliment to gymnastics. It sat in rapt, breathless silence. She had attained the ideal, a fact confirmed by the judges' perfect scores.

Congratulated on the victory stand by a prolonged and hearty standing ovation the dignified champion camouflaged her bashfulness. So sensitive was the young woman that her seriousness and confidence were mirrored only in the triumphant way in which she extended both arms high, waving her hands with outstretched fingers to the crowd in appreciation for their enthusiastic and elongated applause. She slowly turned, still waving, in a victorious pirouette. She smiled to the crowd, happy for her achievement and understandably pleased with herself. It was a consummatory experience, an event which symbolized for her all that aesthetic expressiveness, healthy competition, and an ideal gymnastics routine could present.

The champion stood at attention on the victory stand as her national flag was raised high above to the arena's rafters with the melodious chords of her country's national anthem echoing splendidly throughout the sports hall. The gold medal which hung across her chest were worthy of a queen and she regaled in the wonder of this momentous occasion.

Yet she realized that hers was a shared achievement. She was as pleased with the team's victory as they were happy for her individual title. Her country, hometown, family, and friends were as proud of her as she was grateful for the opportunity to represent them. Everyone shared her job, for she had achieved a personal goal by means of her serious dedication, sincere perseverance, calm confidence and patient love for gymnastics. She had given to her beloved sport the precious gift of an ideal performance in competition.

40

Nicolai Andrianov: From Bad Boy to World Champion

Lyn Moran

The name *Andrianov* somehow seems synonymous with the Soviet men's gymnastics team, and it is difficult to remember a time when Nikolai was not part of the Russian scene. Although he is only 26, he has participated for so long in so many internationals one feels that he is the "old man" of the national team. There is no question that Andrianov has been the focal point, the pivot around which the others revolve. His guidance and leadership have produced the current crop of spectacular performers, including Markelov and Tkatchev. When he retires he will have left quite a legacy for his countrymen, and (as they say) quite an act to follow.

Andrianov is a very strong ring man, the one most feared by the Japanese. His 9.90 score in the 1978 World Cup topped all others, including a great layed out double back somi. Although he had a clear lead over foreign competitors, teammate Markelov managed to tie Andrianov in the all around, which would have been unthinkable a year or so before. But the younger Russians have been learning from the old hand: year after year even his famous triple flyaway dismount off the high bar has been emulated by teammates, but unsuccessfully. This move excites Nikolai. He loves to perform it in front of a large audience, like the one in California in November 1977. Although it had only a slight break on landing, "Kolasha" was not happy with it and did the trick again with complete mastery and to resounding applause. In this sense he is every bit a showman, accepting as his due each and every plaudit for a task well performed.

Andrianov is an artist; he works very hard at polishing and making precise each gymnastic skill, while extracting from it the greatest possible risk element. Since there was no competition involved in the series of exhibitions in California, many a performer would have been content merely to take part. Some did just that, performing very poorly. Nikolai, however, has a strong sense of personal obligation and duty to his audience, and it is impossible for him to do a careless routine or one lacking in competitive spirit.

The post-Olympics year of 1977 saw Andrianov staying out of competition for the most part. He did not compete in any of the major tournaments, leaving the European Championships, Moscow News, and Riga Cup meets to his younger teammates. At the ripe age of 26, Nikolai knows his best days as a gymnast are over—especially when he sees the talent of the younger Soviet team members. He saves himself now only for the biggest meets, and for the ever-popular exhibition tours.

Andrianov reached his peak as a world gymnast in the 1976 Olympics with a remarkable 116.650 in the all-around. Nikolai scored over 9.65 on every event, making him by far the most consistent performer, even though consistency has been a continual problem during his career. Always one of the more spectacular gymnasts, he was able to maintain an even set of routines, resulting in steady well-balanced performances.

But he was not always so consistent . . . .

HUMBLE ORIGINS

When Nikolai was a child, his mother worked hard to feed and provide for her four children in a fatherless home. Young Nikolai was anything but a help, often mischievous and in trouble. At school his teachers despaired of how to cope with his wild ways. He did not bother with homework assignments and continually plagued authority figures. Teachers warned Mrs. Andrianov about the boy's future, but it was when things seemed at their worst that lady luck stepped in.

A pal of Nikolai's suggested that they join a gymnastics club. At the age of 11 this seemed less than exciting, but young Andrianov liked the danger involved in the high bar exercises. So they joined, and it was here that Andrianov met the man who would turn out to be the most important influence of his life: Nicolai Tolkachev.

Tolkachev was a coach, but more importantly, he was also a much needed father figure. The two Nicolais soon became

Nicolai Andrianov (Mark Shearman photo)

inseparable. The older man made sure that this wild youngster received the necessary education and that his growth in all areas of life was not neglected.

Over the years Andrianov progressed further and further under the guidance of Tolkachev. When Nicolai was 17, the coach thought he was ready for competition, and entered him in the 1969 Junior *Spartakiad*—a national age-group competition emphasizing not only precision and grace of movement, but also team spirit and comradeship. Although young Nikolai tried hard, he was not among the top finishers.

He decided then and there he would work much harder in in the future . . . .

One year later, Andrianov made it as an alternate with the Soviet national team. Yes, he was outclassed by such greats as Voronin and Klimenko, but that was not to be for long. In 1971, Tolkachev entered him in the European Championships— this time as a performer—and he fared surprisingly well for a gymnast whose trademark was inconsistency. Andrianov scored 9.30–9.45 on his six events, which was pretty good for the bad boy from Vladimir, though nowhere near Klimenko's 9.60. The press suddenly referred to Andrianov as "the coming man in the Soviet Union," and hinted at "better things" for Munich the following year.

Before Munich, however, Nikolai entered the Riga International meet, placing first in vaulting and rings, but scraping into 6th place all around. Once again, he was up for one event and down for another, and Tolkachev despaired.

At the Olympic Trials, Andrianov finally defeated Klimenko, and his chances for success certainly looked brighter. If he could defeat Klimenko, surely the Japanese would be no problem . . .

MUNICH, 1972 AND MARRIAGE, 1973

During the Games in Munich, Nikolai suffered that old "problem." His Pommel Horse routine (8.80) brought him way down; it was just not expected of a world calibre performer. In other events his top mark was 9.6. When it came to the all around he was noticeably better, pulling out all stops for a 9.75 vault. Floor exercise was where Andrianov excelled, and it brought him a gold medal in the individuals. Although he surpassed his Russian teammates in overall scoring, Nikolai was beaten out by Japan's three top men. It seemed he was not yet ready for the world titles his coach so ardently desired.

The year of 1973 was a good one for Nikolai; apart from gymnastics he fell in love with woman gymnast Lyubov Burda. Both entered the University Games Competition in Moscow that year: Lyubov took second all-around (behind someone named Olga Korbut!), while Andrianov won the all-around, pommel horse, and floor exercise titles.

A contender for the European Championships title, he missed by a fraction when perpetual nemesis Klimenko nosed him out. In the finals, the stocky blond defeated Klimenko to take the floor exercise title, as well as vaulting. (He could only manage to tie for second in both rings and parallel bars, and although he was favored to win the High Bar, unpredictable Andrianov fell on his tail instead and thus did not even place!) Nonetheless, Nikolai Andrianov was now known; he had color and ability and for the first time the international media talked of his "future" with the Soviet team.

Nikolai and Lyubov were married soon after the meets. Lyubov encouraged and helped her husband, and in a bold and determined frame of mind Andrianov headed toward Varna for the 1974 World Championships. The Russian was not faced with Klimenko this time, who had been injured in a pommel horse spill.

Instead there was Kasamatsu of Japan, who picked up three gold medals, but Andrianov still won a gold for his rings routine and a silver medal for the all-around.

Nikolai was now among the world's top six gymnasts, and this gave his long-time friend and mentor, Tolkachev, a tremendous thrill. Surely he would soon reach his peak and leave the Japanese men behind.

EUROPEAN CHAMPIONSHIPS 1974 AND WORLD CUP 1975

Nikolai bypassed the Moscow News and Riga Cup meets the following year to prepare for the prestigious 1974 European Championships in Switzerland. He trained hard, knowing he had youth in his favor against the older Klimenko, and besides he would not have to compete against any of the Japanese greats at all.

Here he hoped to prove himself in front of his countrymen and all Europe. Magyar, Detiatin, Gienger—all were highly touted. Magyar was the world's great pommel horse man, so Nikolai knew he would have little chance there. But the floor exercise, vault and bars—ah, there he could show what he could do.

Show he did! Andrianov had little trouble with the all-around, winning by more than a point over Gienger of West Germany. Amazingly he achieved the same score as Magyar on the pommels: 9.70! In the individual events Andrianov tied for the gold in floor, and clearly won the vault and parallel bar events, and placed second in high bar. Andrianov was The Man of the Hour! He was accepted as a true world champion at last, and no one was more delighted than Lyubov Burda, herself a champion of the past.

Just about everyone who is "anyone" shows up at the World Cup, and that 1975 meet was no exception, attracting Tsukahara, Kajiyama, Magyar, Shamugia, and Detiatin. In such classy company only the very best could possibly emerge; to say it was a tussle of giants would be mild; it was the best against the best.

In royal Empire Pool, Wembley, the audience (including Princess Anne) was attired in dress suits and long gowns. In his mind's eye, Nikolai saw himself on the award stand and set out to win the World Cup title. He succeeded. Nikolai edged out Kajiyama in the all-around to win the gold, and in individuals he won the parallel bar title and took silver medals in FX and pommel horse. It was an exciting day for everyone, but most of all for Andrianov who now had a 10-month-old son watching from afar his daddy's "doings" in distant England.

By the 1975 winter international rankings, Nikolai had moved up to occupy first place, followed by two Japanese, Kajiyama and Tsukahara. A taste of things to come for the year ahead, the year of the Olympics in Montreal.

1976 OLYMPICS

During the first six months of 1976, every gymnast in every country was in hectic training for the upcoming Olympic Games, as always the epitome of sports competitions. The top gymnasts were noticeably absent from international competitions, fearing possible injury. Andrianov was no exception. As a result, when the half-yearly 1976 all around rankings were released Nikolai's name was well down the list—in 21st place!

So, when Montreal rolled around, people looked at the oldest team there—Japan's. Every single Japanese team member was ranked before Andrianov by virtue of the first six month's statistics. This then was the way it looked to the public when he appeared in The Forum in Canada: A highly touted Japanese team, and a Russian team of indeterminate history. The media desperately wanted a battle between these two gymnastic giants, so they did their utmost to make it seem that Andrianov

First gymnastics lessons of Andrianov-junior (V. Un Da Sin photo, USSR)

was a man of suppressed talents and hidden brilliance, just waiting to pounce on the unsuspecting men from the Land of the Rising Sun. His own Federation knew what Andrianov was capable of, and also just how he could "blow" the big routines. They were therefore more concerned with how their women would do against Nadia, as this was where the "eyes of the outside world" would be.

After the compulsories, Nikolai led in the all-around with a score of 58.10, although the Russian team was having difficulty. Russian officials and the judges were arguing and the Japanese team—even with injuries—was performing well. The support of the Forum crowd was overwhelmingly with the Japanese. It was revealed that Fujimoto had broken a leg (though it turned out to be a painful knee injury), but he was still in competition for the honor of the team.

Yet Andrianov was magnificent. His 9.80 and 9.85 won him the rings title in the finals, along with vault and all-around. He was second on parallel bars, and won the floor ex title. Lyobov watched with pride. Tolkachev could not believe his eyes. There he was, his bad boy Nikolai, the erratic genius of gymnastics, with no score under 9.65. A truly remarkable display of consistency! After the "hurrahs" had died out, Nikolai Andrianov of the Soviet Union had won a grand total of four gold medals, two silver, and one bronze. Only the most minute of point percentages separated the Japanese from the Russian team, but it was enough to give the Japanese the gold medal for team title. Most observers felt that the overall difficulty performed by the Soviet squad should have resulted in higher scores being awarded. That they were not was thought to be partly because of the sympathy felt for the handicapped Japanese team.

Following his triumph in Montreal, the Soviet Union decided that Andrianov merited a special award, and conferred upon him The Order of Lenin. Before the Olympics the name of Andrianov was known only to gymnasts and gymnastic fans, and the Soviet people. After the Olympics, he was named by sports journalists, without hesitation, as the best Soviet athlete of 1976. The unruly boy of the 1960s is the Man-of-the-Hour in the 70s; a great testament to the world of gymnastics.

41

Cathy Rigby:
The American Whirlwind

Marilou Sturges

To the Swiss she is "The American Whirlwind," to the Germans she is "Cookie," and to her coach she is "Peanut." Her name is Cathy Rigby, the first American woman gymnast to win a medal in international competition. The Swiss have nicknamed Cathy most accurately because she is indeed a whirlwind. On the beam, her favorite and strongest event, her aggressive, risky routine is performed so rapidly and fearlessly it is quite easily forgotten that she is on a beam only four inches wide and four feet above the floor.

Cathy Rigby was born on December 12, 1952, in Los Alamitos, California. She was born two months prematurely with collapsed lungs. Her first five years were spent in and out of hospitals with critical respiratory illnesses. This was only a temporary setback, however; once Cathy's bouts with pneumonia and bronchitis were over, she made up for lost time by becoming an extremely active child. Her natural energy and fearlessness put Cathy on the road to becoming America's top woman gymnast.

Anita and Paul Rigby, Cathy's parents, encouraged all their

five children to take an active interest in sports. Cathy discovered her love for tumbling in elementary school. Her father
enrolled her at the age of ten in a trampoline class where she
was doing backflips the first day. Her tumbling coach suggested
that her parents take Cathy to see Bud Marquette who had
recently formed SCAT—the Southern California Acrobatics
Team. Marquette recognized Cathy's incredible natural ability
and she became an integral member of the team. Cathy's
devotion to gymnastics was a total one from this point on.

YOUNGEST OLYMPIAN (1968)

She developed into one of America's finest gymnasts during
the next five years. Under Marquette's guidance, she gained in
skill and in the calm confidence so vital in gymnastics. She
gained confidence not only in her gymnastic ability but in
herself. At 4'10" and 89 lbs., Cathy was so small and looked so
young for her age that she was often teased by her classmates.
Her natural inclination for tumbling and gymnastics kept her
active and built her self-confidence, natural grace, and charm.
Cathy's small size, her incredible coordination, her courage, and
her willingness to make sacrifices helped to make her, at fifteen,
the youngest member of the 1968 Olympic Team.

"Making the team was one of the most thrilling experiences
of my life," says Cathy. "After that, the Olympics itself was
almost anticlimactic. I just never had dreamed of being in the
Olympics so young." Although Cathy had toured with SCAT,
this was her first major international competition. She placed
fifteenth in all-around scoring, the highest Olympic position
ever achieved by an American gymnast.

An even bigger moment in Cathy's career came in 1970 when
she won a silver medal on the balance beam at the World Games
in Ljubljana, Yugoslavia. To a gymnast, the World Games are
just as important as the Olympics. In 1970 the United States, as
always, had some extremely tough competition, particularly
from the Russians and East Germans.

Her victory represented an incredible American break-
through—not only did she beat Tourischeva, the Russian who
became all-around World Champ, but it was the first medal ever
for the United States in women's gymnastics. Cathy's wire to
her parents upon winning read: "Have won second place on

beam, the silver medal for the U.S. and you."

The next two years of Cathy's life were devoted to gymnastics even more than ever before, for she was preparing for the 1972 Olympics in Munich. Her already rigorous training schedule became even more rigorous, for she was America's number-one hope for an individual gold medal on the balance beam or the bars.

Two very important events occurred in Cathy's life during these two years. She graduated from high school and entered Long Beach State in 1971, but dropped out soon afterward to totally dedicate herself to her Olympic training. Life as a college student and life as America's top gymnast were incompatible. School would be postponed at least temporarily. One thing Cathy would not postpone, however, was her budding friendship with Tommy Mason, the former all-pro running back with the Minnesota Vikings. Though their dates were limited, Cathy and Tommy spent as much time together as their training schedules would permit. They announced their engagement in August, 1972, but they would not see each other again until after the Olympics.

Cathy's specialties were the balance beam and the uneven bars. She dedicated most of her training schedule for the Mun-

Cathy Rigby talking with Olga Korbut (Mark Shearman photo)

ich Olympics to strengthening her performances in vaulting and the floor exercises—events where taller women have an advantage. Cathy and Coach Marquette spent days choosing music that would complement Cathy's vibrant, pixie style. They finally settled on a combination of "Beer Barrel Polka" and "Singing in the Rain," a drastic switch from traditional symphony music used in the free exercise.

By the time the Olympic Trials started, Cathy had increased her daily training from six to nine hours. Then with the Olympics just within reach, she pulled a tendon in her right ankle, eliminating her chances of competing in the Olympic trials, and therefore in Munich. After deliberating, the United States Olympic Gymnastics Committee did something unheard of before: A special vote was taken, permitting Cathy to be one of the six regular members of the Olympic team without completing the trials. All hopes for a medal rested on Cathy's performance.

Though Cathy did not win a medal at the Olympics, she placed tenth overall, the highest place any American gymnast has ever placed in the Olympiad. Cathy Rigby and the American team had shown the world that they were worthy of competing with the best in international competition.

Cathy's decision to retire from gymnastics competition was a difficult one for her. She could try again for a gold medal in the 1976 Olympics if she retained her amateur status. Going professional, on the other hand, would allow her to try acting and to start her own gymnastics school.

Cathy made the difficult decision to retire and has done both. Her television credits include major guest roles on the *Six Million Dollar Man* and *Police Woman*. She put her years of gymnastics training to use when she toured the United States as the star of NBC's Peter Pan. In addition, Cathy serves as a sports commentator for ABC-TV and as the national spokesperson for the frozen food industry.

Most importantly, she has started the Cathy Rigby gymnastics camp in Mission Viejo, California, where girls from the age of two months and up are trained in ballet and gymnastics. In January 1973, Cathy married Tommy Mason in a simple home ceremony. They now live in Newport Beach with their son Buck, born September 24, 1975.

Cathy Rigby is, without a doubt, America's most famous and most loved woman gymnast. As the first American woman to take an important place in international gymnastic competition, she has led the way for many others. America's interest in gymnastics, roused by increased Olympic coverage in 1960, was spurred by Cathy's incredible achievements in international competition. Her vibrant style and calm confidence were a winning combination in the eyes of America and the world.

42

Peter Kormann: An Interview

Dick Criley
Associate Editor, **International Gymnast** *Magazine*

Peter Kormann, third place Floor Exercise at the 1976 Montreal Olympics, was the first American gymnast to win a medal at the Olympic Games since 1932. In 1976 Peter also won the NCAA Division I and Divison II All-Around Championships plus winning the All-Around title in the "Champions All" international competition in England. Peter received the United States Gymnastics Federation's "Male Gymnast of the Year" Award at the 1976 Annual Congress. In 1977 Peter placed 3rd in the All-Around and led his team to a third place team title Nissen Award from the National Association of College Gymnastics coaches at their annual banquet.

Peter was born in Braintree, Massachusetts on June 21, 1955. He is 5'7" and weighs 128 lbs. Peter was a student at Southern Connecticut State College and was coached by Abie Grossfeld.

International Gymnast: What did you do after the Olympics last year? Did you have a chance to relax?

Peter Kormann: The rest of the summer I spent relaxing. I went to the beach quite often. I did Freddy Turoff's summer camp in Pennsylvania. I got back into competition in September with the meet in Spain.

IG: Last year, before the Olympics, you'd had a large number of competitions. That puts a great deal of pressure on you doesn't it?

PK: Physically, but even more mentally, because you have to get "up" for all of them. I had way too many things to do in terms of competition. Just the combination of the NCAAs, the Olympic qualification matches, and the Trials all going on about the same time. I went into very few college dual meets, only those which our college team had to try to win with the best possible team. I had about 40 competitions last year with those qualifying matches, the Pan-American Games, the college Championships, and the Olympics.

IG: Have you ever had a serious injuries, the kind which would keep you out for a while?

PK: Not really. Last year before the Olympic Trials, I sprained my ankle rather severely and didn't do any tumbling until the competition.

IG: How have you avoided injury? Has it been training method or just luck?

PK: I did many other sports when I was younger. I played soccer, ran track & field. A sport like soccer tends to build one up physically; it's very demanding, especially on the legs, knees and ankles. Shoulderwise, I just try to be careful. I do some stretching every day after strength exercises for my flexibility to keep the range of motion. A large range of motion aids one in not injuring the shoulders. Gymnasts who have shoulder problems tend to be a little tight in the shoulders. Eventually that catches up with you.

IG: Do you have a regular training program, like morning training?

PK: I've gone some seasons of the year with morning training. Last year I did it often, but this year I've been neglecting it. I think it helps prepare you for the afternoon workout. It's easy to warm up and you feel like you can get started right away without having to spend an hour getting ready to work out.

IG: Do you lift weights?

PK: I never did any weight training. Abie has a circuit where we do exercises. They're actually exercises you do in your routines. For example, we do a number of stiff-stiff presses, a number of hollowbacks, and other exercises like 440 sprints and a lot of standing jumps. We have a whole circuit he's worked out over the years the exercises he's found have been best. I think any exercise is good if you do it a lot. The idea is to find a routine that you're going to do every day. Then do it every day.

IG: Do you try to get yourself in a special mental attitude before a big meet by meditating or being alone? How do you prepare yourself mentally for the big events?

PK: I just try to think to myself that I've had a lot of competitions, and I've had very few mistakes, really. I try to relax and think about what I have to do to do a good job. With that attitude I can usually do what I want to do. You know, don't fall off the Side Horse and things like that.

IG: How does one develop the capacity to handle the "problems" of the gymnast?

PK: I haven't had to deal with that too much, but I've seen a lot. I think a coach can instill a relaxed atmosphere that allows a gymnast to train as hard as he wants to and set a pattern for looking at competition as a "fun time" as well as an important one to do well. You can train hard, try to do your best, but if you make a mistake, OK, you made a mistake. But you did

Peter Kormann (*International Gymnast* photo)

train hard, and you did try to do your best, and it's not so important what you actually did; it's how hard you tried. You have fun in trying hard to do well, even when you make a mistake; it's fun to make a mistake sometimes. Then when you don't make a mistake, you really feel good. It's important when you make mistakes. It's important when you try to do your best. Some gymnasts put too much emphasis on always trying to do their best and they get carried away with it. I think that can lead to problems. I think a coach can instill a certain atmosphere of Try Hard and Let's See What Happens. He shouldn't add extra pressures to the gymnast but let the gymnast learn how to compete for himself. Don't give him extra things to worry about. Don't say, 'you have to do this for the team,' or 'you've worked so hard now, you don't want to miss in this competition'. Those types of things don't help any and just add extra pressures which no one likes.

IG: Here's a theoretical question. What are the qualities of an ideal coach? Or, let's make it more specific, if you could pick out a bunch of qualities for the ideal coach for you, what would you like to see in a coach?

PK: There are certain qualities that are very important. One would be understanding of the things that you need to learn before you can go on to learn other things. On each event, to me, there are certain aspects of that event that are very important. If you don't learn them, you're going to be in big trouble later on.

For instance, on the floor: you have to learn a good backhandspring, a good round-off, backhandspring, one that is technically sound, so that when you go to do a layout, you can do it with a straight body. You don't have to pike or bend down to make it. There are exercises that go along to make it possible: a good snap-down, a good straight round off, where you push with your arms and turn your body over efficiently without wasting power. On Side Horse, good circles and loops. That means when you go to learn a moore, it's not going to take you a year to learn it and just make it. It means, on rings, how do you teach a good handstand: A good coach should know that you must lock your arms and turn the rings all the way out. You can't have your handstand with your hands the way they'd be on the High Bar; it has to be more like Parallel Bars. That may be a little tidbit, but it's very important. I see many people in this competition with the handstand not technically sound. Each event has the things you should learn before you go on.

I think that is the most important quality in coaching to set that background and that basic information so you can build on it. When you get a little more advanced you have other things you add on, like how to twist, how to do a stutz to handstand every time. If you have a solid background, it's much easier to build on. I had trouble in high school and I still have it now. I never really took the time to learn a lot of things properly; I rushed into many things.

IG: Are you going to get into coaching?

PK: I hope to some day.

IG: There seems to be no plan right now for developing gymnasts for 1980. As a gymnast who hopes to be around for that time, what would you like to see in the way of developmental plans, both on the elite level and on the developmental level?

PK: Starting on the elite level, it doesn't seem feasible to develop a central training spot in this short amount of time. Many of the gymnasts are still in school and are not going to be able to leave school to train there year around. Some have families and they wouldn't want to leave them for any long amount of time. I think the next best thing would be something like they had last year over the Christmas break which was a week of training where 15 top gymnasts trained together for a week at a university. I don't see why that can't be two weeks or maybe three or four or five times a year. That means some sacrifices like being away from school or family for a while, but it's not to the degree where you'll upset your life. You can still be in school and make the training sessions. That helped me tremendously. I know others I've spoken to who were there: it helped them.

Other than the people in the Eastern league, I never saw anyone else do the Olympic compulsory exercises this year until this meet, but I would like to have seen Thomas, Conner or Beach do the compulsory exercises before I had to do them in a meet like this. I think it's good just to get everyone together just to talk over what we're supposed to be doing, what's the best way to go about learning a certain move or whether we should be doing an early drop or a late drop in the compulsory.

That's one thing I think might help the program.

Another thing would be some kind of broken time payments to help the athletes who need financial support. For example, without some type of financial support, say from the Federation. I just can't take a full-time job and still train and do well at either one of them. When I don't feel good, I don't improve. Realistically, I don't think I could train as hard as I could as long as I could unless I had an opportunity to train at maximum while working a minimal amount.

IG: Have you ever seen anything, or talked with gymnasts from other countries that have a system you'd like to see here?

PK: A government subsidy program is almost out of the question in our country now. That may be a future thing, but I don't think so in my generation of gymnastics. When I was in Japan, I stayed in a university there, NiTaiDai, which was the leading college at the time. Kenmotsu, Tsukahara, and others were there. They have jobs in private industries, banks, TV stations. These corporations allot them time from two to six in the afternoon to train. The firm finds it very prestigious for an Olympic athlete to be working for them; it helps them, and for them to give him time off in the day is a very small thing that they can do to help. They know in turn that they are helping their country gain respect internationally. Can you imagine an American athlete working in a bank getting that kind of time off? Every day?

Our country is among the richest in the world and private industry is the reason. I would think that this would be the way to go in terms of athletic support. Why can't a gymnast seek sponsors in industry and, through the USGF, funnel money in? The gymnast can get this in broken time payments. I'm not sure whether this is legal, but I think that payments given by your federation as broken time payments are completely legal in terms of the effect they have on your amateur standing. Our skiers do that now.

IG: What about our lower level? Where are the next generation of gymnasts to come from?

PK: That's a frustrating question for me to answer. I hear so many things about how the eastern bloc countries are developing their younger gymnasts through fantastic age group programs. Like the East Germans. I understand that they pump millions of dollars into developing top gymnasts at early ages. All that energy spent developing those young kids can only help them. I can't see how we can expect to compete with them, ever, unless we get with a program where we're putting money into the age-groups and making an honest effort to train our young gymnasts. It's not enough to give them a set of compulsories and just a couple of meets a year to go into. That's leaving too much up to the individual coach and gymnast. At that age, I think a structured program with training involved should be set up. Not just competitions, actual training facilities.

Why can't the same thing I just mentioned for the elite program be set up on a junior level? They'd meet a few times a year, where he could get his way paid to some training facility with some top coaches that really know the things that will work. They can give the kids the exercises and tell them and their coaches what they should be working on. Then, over a period of a year, you educate the child and the coach both. There won't be an immediate result, but I think that something like that has to be started. I don't know where the money will come from.

I don't even understand how the USGF works financially. Sometimes I wonder why the U.S. doesn't have a tour with its own gymnasts. Why can't the U.S. Olympic team go to Madison Square Garden and put on a exhibition, rather than the Rumanians? Maybe I'm living in a dream world with stars in my eyes, I don't know. But I think that people all over the country would pay to see the Olympic Team. A U.S. tour with American gymnasts if it's publicized and there are people behind it, I can't see why it wouldn't work financially and make money for the Federation so they can start these programs. I don't see any of that being done, but then again, I'm not aware of all the variables.

I think the big thing is to get it down to a concrete, structured program. It's too scattered. I had nothing when I was starting, and most of the East coast is very unstructured for the young kids. They don't know what they should be doing. They train by themselves and there's no one there to say that you should learn this before you learn that. Or, here's how you learn a layout on the floor.

43
Olga!
Lyn Moran

Wilt thou, Olga, take Leonid, to be thy lawful, wedded husband" . . . . not words in just any wedding service, nor for just any person. Words which in fact, denoted the end of an era. In 1978 the sweet-faced little pixie from Grodno, who enchanted the entire world with her performance at Munich, not only announced her retirement from competitive gymnastics, but also her emergence as a mature, married woman. This Peter Pan of gymnastics was to many the epitome of vibrant, impetuous youth. Laughing, crying, pouting, grimacing, teasing—a totally capricious individual, capable of stirring up more powerful emotions than any other single person in gymnastics history.

There was something about Olga Korbut from the very beginning that captured the imagination of the world, sporting or otherwise. She was not the stereotype Russian, for one thing. Most of our friends in the Soviet Union are very much in control of themselves at all times. They come across as a cheerful people, a stoic people, a brave people-but hardly an emotional people. Tears in public? Tantrums? Refusal to conform? No, not the Soviet women....at least not until Olga, that is!

Olga revolutionized gymnastics. More important: she encour-

329

aged participation in the sport such as had never been known before. Almost like spontaneous combustion, interest in the sport grew just as affection for Olga grew. No one asked "Olga, who?" Her name was known to all in a way that had never been matched; not even by the great Charlie Chaplin, Mae West, or Gary Cooper. The answer, of course, was television. Olga was a "child of the tube," just as much as a product of the new Russia. Television can make or break an entertainer. Some gymnasts react poorly to the cameras' all-seeing eye—Olga Korbut thrived on it.

Was there ever a beginning? Can one visualize what it was like "before Olga"? How much did she achieve within her own specialized field of sport? As we will no longer be able to see Korbut perform we should take the time to look back in retrospect, at this veritable "giant" of women's sport.

Ljubljana in 1970 hosted the World Championships. Among the starry competitors were names such as Janz, Tourischeva, Zuchold, Hellman, and Voronina. Writers spoke of the enormous gap left by the absence of the incomparable Caslavska

Olga (Horst Muller photo)

and Kutchinskaya. Pauline Prestidge of Great Britain comment- ed then, "Although these championships will be remembered as the most highly organized of any and certainly the most enjoy- able, there was I feel a dearth of great emotional moments...." Perhaps the most perceptive statement was, "Even the great Ludmilla Tourischeva, the world champion, did not infuse deep feeling to the beholder, despite her great technical ability and skill." Perfection in itself does not always breed adoration. Men are mortal and seek identification with others to complement their hero-worship. People who inspire; those of "great stature" who often lack physical beauty, or wit, are referred to as having "charisma." That day, in Ljubljana, waiting in the wings as a re- serve, was one such person. They did not know that at 4 ft. 11 ins. and 82 lbs, this 15-year old was to be the next great leader in the world of gymnastics.

During 1970, little Olga was not entered in any major inter- national competitions, the "big names" being Tourischeva, Petrik, Burda, Voronina. The legendary Kuchinskaya had re- tired and all over Europe gymnastic lovers bemoaned this loss to the sport. In Ljubljana, Tourischeva's main rivals were the East Germans—Zuchold and Janz. It looked for all the world as though the Soviet Union was going to lose ground to the girls from the German Democratic Republic. Within two years, how- ever, a young teenager from the Soviet town of Grodno would have the entire world at her feet.

Everyone has now heard of Grodno, a one time part of Poland. It was here that Korbut first emerged as a gymnast: in a town comprised of industrial workers in soap, tobacco and candle factories, known to be hard working and independent. Independent can best describe Olga also. She is also strong will- ed, and this certainly had to help her at school for she was very small for her age and was a target of others. As so many, she was determined to excel in sports and thus make up for her tiny stature. She was nine when she sought a place in the local gymnastics school. At this time 35 of the special sports schools had a gymnastics course with gymnastics instruction, and Olga's school in Grodno was one of these. The man who was the Senior coach was Renald Knysh. He looked her over and placed her in the care of Elena Volchetskaya, who had been in the Tokyo Games of 1964, and Tamara Alexayeva. Thus Olga was to be tutored by two coaches who had plenty of international experience, and this is doubtless where she acquired her taste for international competition.

The story of Olga really began at this special school under Knysh's associates. Knysh identified her obstinacy with determination, and in this he was right. She was an indefatigable worker, who took great chances with her routines. Again, this may be compensation for her tiny stature—just as small men become weight lifters and jockeys; both are sports with risk element. She was 15 when she first performed the back flip at the Soviet Championships. During this 1969 meet, Korbut's moves caused criticism among the staid members of the European gymnastics set. They were not enamored with "circus type" acrobatics, viewing the sport of gymnastics as being purely artistic and elegant. In 1970 Olga entered the Nationals again and this time won a gold for her Vault. Larissa Latynina, the great coach, had herself been impressed with Olga and had given her encouragement.

During the next International Championships, Korbut was placed on reserve. The Soviet Gymnastics Federation recognized her talent despite the reserve status and conferred upon her the title "Master of Sport," at age 16. One of Olga's greatest assets has been her extreme flexibility and much of this was due to the extra work Renald Knysh put in on back exercises to improve suppleness of the spine. This was to really pay off later.

Now we are up to Ljubljana again. Around this time Olga Korbut emerged as an outspoken young woman, devoid of perhaps that percentage of tact which we all need in times of stress. Either way, she is said to have "talked herself" into an elaborate rebuff by friends and teammates alike. She had been told that she was too inexperienced in international competition and was to observe and to learn. Instead it is said that she complained of being passed over in favor of teammates who were not as well qualified as herself (this may have been true in the sense that she had the talent, but her teammates did indeed have much more literal experience). This was about the first time that Korbut had publicly criticized her fellow gymnasts and this was seen as a sign of arrogance by many who were all too willing to find fault in this spectacular youngster.

Schoolgirl "Olga", with all the bounce and ego of the young, bruised many feelings during this period of her life, and she was finally warned to "cool it". Hurt and rebuffed, she applied herself more diligently than ever to the sport, determined to show that she was among the world's best, or soon would be. Possibly because of pressure, wounded pride, teenage growing problems, etc., Olga became ill during 1971. Some said it was mainly emotional, and probably this was as much a cause as anything else. She did take part in the Soviet National Competition, placing 4th with Ludmilla Tourischeva, the teammate she had yet to beat. Olga missed most big meets, while Tourischeva cemented her world status by winning the European Championships.

The quiet, shy Renald Knysh did not despair. He was looking at his protege with a view to the next Olympics. Olga Korbut was as yet an unknown name in the sport, but he was as determined as she that this state of affairs would not last for long. In early 1972 Olga was training as she never had before, and during the Riga Cup International, Knysh felt she was close to being ready. In the UPB event Olga did a lay-out back off the high bar to regrasp, and was by far the best gymnast there. But—she did not compete against any of the top names, as Tourischeva, Kim, and the top East German women were missing. Olga won the All Around over teammate Koshel, tied for Floor Ex, won Beam easily, nipped Gerke of the GDR in Vault and narrowly won Unevens. It was, despite the lack of star names, a tremendous boost for Olga and for Knysh. The experience was what mattered most.

Then came the USSR Cup, and for Korbut her biggest triumph thus far. Everyone expected Tourischeva to win with quite a margin over all-comers, but it did not turn out as anticipated. At 4 ft 11, Olga was one of the smallest competitors, and still thought to be no real threat to her older teammate. Ludmilla led through the first two nights, but the Gods did not favor her. She suffered a bad break on Beam and this seemed to make her overly cautious from then on. Meanwhile Olga's routine was a delight, with a front aerial dismount after a back somersault. This brought her a 9.70. For her Floor Ex, Ludmilla pulled out all stops for a 9.80 performance, to Olga's 9.60. It was not enough. Korbut won the All Around title 76.275 to Ludmilla's 76.125. Of Olga, Jan Barosh said, "Her forte seems to be risky moves." And it was this risk element which was to make the little girl from Grodno world famous, in conjunction with a very basic emotion—tears.

A week before Munich, Olga had second thoughts about her music for the Floor Exercise. She had finished secondary school in 1972 and considered herself now a mature person, capable of making her own decisions. Her music was a source of worry now, and she consulted—no she demanded of Renald Knysh and Latynina that she be given new, more suitable FX music. Everyone tried to dissuade her, but Olga remained adamant. Knysh knew Olga well enough to realize that if she were to perform to the Bumble Bee composition, her heart would not be in it. So, he and Larissa set about getting something new to appease their willful protege. After much discussion and contact with composers and choreographers, Knysh came up with the now famous "Java" combination, which delighted his determined gymnast and pleased the other coaches. Olga had to learn her Floor Exercise routine to this new music in less than seven days. With a cast iron will, the 17 year old was able to do it.

Finally came the biggie. Munich 1972. The East German greats, Zuchold and Hellman, Karin Janz, Tourischeva, Rigby, and Saadi—they were all there, mustering up their great skills for this one fantastic curtain call for the watching world. And Olga waited her turn. And the television cameras awaited theirs.

Tingling with anticipation, Korbut hugged her knees and watched the East Germans warming up. Here, she knew, would be a major threat. When it came time for her to perform, she was like a young gazelle. She floated from the Balance Beam, with hands held high and a wide, engaging smile on her features. Her backwards somi had caught everyone unaware, and they now watched the little gymnast with renewed interest. Her Floor Ex was tailor-made for the pixie-like Olga, (although Renee Hendershott writing about it, thought her 9.80 in the AA was definitely overscored). Certainly there was originality and enormous gymnast-spectator relationship, as well as that of the gymnast to the music. Olga's mimicry of insects or animals is second to none and she captured the imagination of all present with her original Floor Exercises.

In competition one, Olga was given a 9.60 in FX to Ludmilla's 9.80 and she again was assessed a 9.60 along with Hellman and Tourischeva, for her Uneven Bars. Olga's Optional FX was better, her tumbling and handsprings performed at a fantastic pace. Her 9.75 was a worthy result. The audience was now working with "little Olga," as they had started to call her, and the empathy shown her was very evident. Korbut was able to project a child-like—no, waif-like, image, and this plus the radiant smile and hand waving when they applauded, enraptured the Munich audience. Even now, the press were still no Korbut addicts, favoring the great Tourischeva and the svelte Karin Janz.

Olga, of course, was feeling her "oats" as the saying goes, and this may have been conducive to who followed. There is no question but that in the early 1970's Olga was indeed a very contrary, headstrong young lady, flourishing on praise and easily influenced by admiring throngs. Whether or not she was over-confident is not important now. But she was in a very good position, with the audience behind her, when she headed for the Uneven Bars. She had planned a flic-flac from the top to bottom bar, just as she had done in earlier rounds, which had brought her a 9.70 score. She mounted on the low bar, stubbing her toe on the matting as she did so. This seemed to throw her off stride, as she misjudged her move and came off of the bars, after having performed part of her difficult exercise quite successfully. She had suffered at least three, if not four, breaks in her routine.

Olga ran immediately over to the pit area where her coach was, and burst into tears. She had been a gymnast long enough to realize that in Olympic competition she would have many deductions for her routine and this would drop her behind Tourischeva and Janz. The judges did what they had to do, without prejudice. They awarded her a 7.50, and Olga's tears continued to flow. The audience whistled and booed, jeered at the judges, who remained unmoved. Meanwhile, Olga's teammates remained in their own area, concentrating on their own routines. Erika Zuchold of East Germany (GDR) walked over and put her arm around Olga and tried to soothe her. After all Korbut had not had that much international experience and the pressures on her were great. The television cameras, sensing something dramatic moved in for a close up—and more close-ups. Olga continued to weep, and the cameras continued to turn.

When she returned to the Olympic Village, Ludmilla tried to persuade her everything would be all right. Her teammates comforted her. The television crews followed her also. On being asked about her terrible mistakes on the UPB, Olga declared openly, "I will not make any more blunders." She was a determined young lady by now, and sought to redeem herself in the eyes of the world.

The following day, pictures of the sobbing Olga decorated many newspapers and so it was that, from comparitive obscurity, this little girl from Grodno suddenly blossomed into an overnight sensation. Curious fans gathered to watch her arrival at the arena and the audience was tense and excited as their new-found "heroine" made her appearance. Many wondered if she would lose her nerve and lack of confidence would make her cut down her high risk moves. They overlooked the courage and determination of the Byelorussian people here; Olga accepted this as just another challenge and she entered the arena with head held high.

The ticket scalpers ran amok when the Finals rolled around; everyone wanted to see Korbut perform, and Olga did not mean to disappoint them. With a wave and a smile she was ready for Vault. She hit her Yami well and stuck the landing, for a final score of 19.175. The other girls did better with their vaults, with Janz and Zuchold nailing down 1st and 2nd slots, and Olga lying 5th. On the Unevens people watched with trepidation as Olga approached. She had muffed things up before. Was she ready? Scoring was high, with Ludmilla at 9.80, along with Zuchold. Olga's routine—from stand, grab LB, glide, Kip, grab HB, straddle over LB, kip to HB, stand on HB, layout back to regrasp HB, wrap around LB, eagle regrasp on HB, drop to LB, front hip circle, to handstand, straddle back, up to HB, handstand on LB, bouncing off with a ½ turn to stand on LB, forward sole circle on HB, pushoff HB to back layout over LB.

The judges conferred, and decided on a 9.80 score, which was certainly enough. The Soviet delegation did not think so, and once again little Olga was the center of heated controversy as the Russians frantically tried to get her score raised. Gander refused. The audience saw what had happened and joined the Russians in a chorus of boos and yells against the judging. This outburst continued right through the routine of the next performer, the lovely Angelika Hellman, who tried to make the audience quiet, but to no avail. She did very well, but faltered on her dismount and took several steps. There is no question that hers would have been a superior routine but for the audience behavior, as she was still awarded a creditable 9.65, although so upset that she too let the tears flow. The tears of the East German went unnoticed by the press, however, unlike the elf from Grodno who had won everyone's heart. But, it was Karen Janz who again took top honors with a superb 9.90 routine.

Then came the moment everyone was waiting for—the Balance Beam. Olga waved, and grinned, and the crowd responded. She hopped on, into a wide splits, press, turn, legs swinging to stand. Back walkover, body wave, ½ turn, cartwheel, pose, body wave, quick jumps, stag leap, back walkover, back layout dive through chest roll, through straddle seat, back roll, back walkover, to straddle, whip back up to stand (slight break here), into stag handstand, step, step forward, turn, forward walkover, arm waves, pose, turn, split leap, sideway wiggles, back somi to front off for dismount. The crowd went wild! They cheered thunderously. She had previously managed both a 9.75 and a 9.80 for Beam, so surely she would equal this mark? She raised her arms happily and ran to her seat. Everyone waited. She had had several bobbles and a small break so a 9.85 would be a good score. The judges conferred, and feeling generous gave her a 9.90. Olga had done it! She would now win the Gold Medal for Beam.

Olga was overjoyed and showed it! She lavished her smiles and her waves all around, and the crowd lapped it up. The tears were long gone and she was once again the laughing, happy child they wanted her to be. The press and television had taken her to heart and concentrated on her every move. They could sense the charisma she imparted to others and in this could very well be a story. Olga was NEWS!!

Another event was to come, that of Floor Exercise, pitting the mature Tourischeva against the slender Saadi, Karin Janz and Angelika Hellman. It was a veritable battle of giants. This was a good event for the Russian, Lazakovitch also, so Olga would have her work cut out. Hellman got a rather low 9.60, followed by Lazakovitch who performed very well for a 9.80. Then the dainty Karin Janz and a well deserved 9.80 also. Ludmilla was next, and went into it ahead of Olga by .075. Another great routine by Ludmilla brought her a 9.80—a trifle low maybe. Olga was in the best spot, the last one up. Her routine comprised a high arch dive roll, little girlish wiggles, handspring, front somi, step out into RO, FF, delayed back, dance steps, side split leap, scale, more steps, RO, FF, layout back dive to chest roll (considered by the writers too short and crunched up) aerial walkover, to chest stand, leg scissors, RO, FF, low layout to final pose. At the finish she sprung happily off the FX mat, knowing it had been a good routine for her. The audience sensed it also. The judges had made their decision. Up went the score. A 9.90. Olga had won another Gold Medal!

While Olga only placed 7th All Around, she had won a team medal, the Balance Beam and Floor Ex golds and a silver for her Uneven Bars. A great performance for this 17 year old, and a tremendous reward for her coaches and their faith in her. She was, by now, the darling of the Olympic Games, and was amassing millions of fans all over the world.

44

Nadia Comaneci: Perfection at Montreal

Bob Wischnia

The first competition at the 21st renewal of the modern Olympic Games at Montreal in 1976 was gymnastics. It was to be the premiere, showcased event; during the first four days of the Olympics, the first lady of the Games was crowned: Nadia Comaneci.

Fourteen year-old Nadia came to Montreal from her native Rumania with some international experience (she was the 1975 European champion), but to the vast majority of the countless millions watching gymnastics on world-wide television, she was a complete unknown. As the compulsory exercises began on July 18, 1976 (an historic day in gymnastics), most of the attention was focused on the Russians Olga Korbut, Ludmilla Tourischeva and Nelli Kim.

Scalpers were doing a brisk business on St. Catherine Street outside the Forum. Sixteen-dollar tickets were going for $100, even $150 each. The 16,000 spectators expected a spectacular performance as they settled into their seats, but no one was prepared for the unprecedented drama that was about to unfold.

The Russians began the compulsory exercises for the team event on the uneven parallel bars and came away with good marks. It was clear from the beginning that Kim, Korbut and Tourescheva were close to their best form; it would take an extraordinary gymnast to unseat them. The Rumanians, meanwhile, were working slowly on the balance beam. Many gymnasts dislike starting a competition on the beam because it places such a premium on skill and balance.

The Russians finished on the bars, then were obliged to sit and watch as Nadia Comaneci began the first of her historic routines. The Russians, led by their coach and ex-great gymnast Larissa Latynina, sat down in a row and stared at the tiny girl readying herself for the beam. The crowd, too, sensed the significance of these opening moments of the competition.

An army of cameramen picked up on the vibrations in the Forum and closed in on the beam, disturbing the silence with their motordriven cameras. As Nadia began, she could have easily been flustered by the disturbing noises but she never hesitated for a moment.

She went through her compulsory routine without apparent error. On her headstand, she lifted her legs overhead so gradually and slowly it appeared she wouldn't have the momentum to reach the position. But she did it so smoothly and with such precision, the crowd began to realize this was a little girl with something special.

She finished to tumultuous applause, and the Russian team turned away, collected their bags, and moved to the next apparatus because it was obvious that the adulation Nadia was receiving was an embarrassment. Her mark of 9.90 proved from the onset that her European championship form of a year earlier hadn't been a fluke. When the Russians followed the Rumanians on the beam, Olga Korbut came away with a solid 9.80 because of a minor fault.

Later that afternoon, Nadia showed that she was perfection personified. On the uneven bars, she scored the first 10 in the history of the Olympics—a feat heretofore thought impossible.

From then on, she was the principle focus of attention. From then on, each time Nadia competed the television cameras searched for Olga and her teammates' reactions to the tine

Rumanian's performances. From then on, Nadia was the star.

Russian depth won out in the women's team competition, and they took home the gold while the Rumanians, the youngest team in Olympics history, took second place.

As they had the day before, the Rumanians began the competition with the beam. Teodora Ungureanu, Nadia's closest

Nadia Comaneci (*International Gymnast* photo)

friend, was the second to the last to compete and responded with an excellent 9.90 to put some pressure on Nadia.

A surging murmur was audible throughout the Forum as Nadia walked up to the beam. The girl with something special performed something special. The crowd responded with thunderous applause. To everyone's amazement and confusion, one judge scored Nadia with a 1.00. The sophisticated electronic computers had not been programmed for a routine such as Nadia's. Instead of showing the perfect 10.0, the scoreboard spewed out a 1.00 which stunned everyone until they realized that the scoreboard was trying to say what everyone already knew: Nadia was perfect again.

From those scintillating moments that raised goosebumps on millions, the lithe schoolgirl from the industrial city of Onestia proved her supremacy again and again. She followed her precedent-shattering perfecto with six more perfect marks of 10.0 and three gold medals. Her style defined a new gymnastic concept. Routines were named for her, songs were dedicated to her, television specials were produced about her, and Nadia Comaneci graced the cover of nearly every news and sports magazine in the world. Sports commentators quickly discovered that Comaneci was pronounced "Comaneech."

Nadia took all the hoopla with typical aplomb. She said that she wasn't nervous at all nor was she surprised by her accomplishments. "Yes, I was very happy to score the first perfect score in Olympic history," she was quoted as saying, "but I have already scored 19 perfect scores before the Olympics so I wasn't very excited."

She was probably the only one who wasn't.

At the all-around competition the next day, 18,000 spectators crowded into the Forum *expecting* to see a perfect mark or two. It had the aura of a Western shootout: Russians vs. Rumanians. And to these two countries, the pride and gymnastic knowledge of years of training were on the line. Olga Korbut had, by this time, long since relinquished center stage to Nadia.

When the Rumanians entered the Forum, they were met with the most enthusiastic of all the welcomes. Everyone wanted to see a perfect 10 for themselves, in person, to say, "Yes, I saw one for myself."

After Nadia did her vault, the scoreboard read 9.85. A very good mark but Olga's performance on the uneven parallel bars was rewarded with a 9.90. The fickle audience heaped its affection on Olga, constantly chanting her name again and again.

Then the drama increased. Nadia's uneven bars performance and Olga's turn on the beam were scheduled for the same moment. But as Nadia started her spine-tingling routine, everything else came to a stop. She perfectly executed three new moves, did a faultless handstand on the high bar and capped it all off with her now-famous Salto Comaneci dismount.

The crowd, and other gymnasts, were stunned after her perfect landing. Another 10.0 could be the only score possible and Comaneci was so rewarded. Olga watched from the other end of the arena and her spectacular balance beam routine—with her incredible curl position, sitting on her chest and bringing her body full circle over her head—led many to believe that she, too, might earn a 10.0, but the scoreboard showed a 9.50. The crowd booed and Olga buried her face in a towel. Olga's coach asked for an explanation of the scoring and was told that she had been penalized for exceeding the time limit.

When it was Nadia's turn on the balance beam, the judges gave her another perfecto. If it hadn't been earlier, it was now clear that Olga's reign was officially over. Although Olga did manage a fifth place in the all-around, Nadia's brilliant performance was overwhelming and she won the Olympic gold.

Nadia accepted the gold with her usual seriousness, but she broke into a grin after it was placed around her head and held up her arms to acknowledge the hysterical crowd. Russia's Nelli Kim, who had also scored a perfect 10.0 and won the silver medal, embraced Nadia as did Tourischeva who finished third.

When the Rumanian national anthem had crowned the first Rumanian Olympic gymnastics champion, Nadia picked up her bag—and her doll—and nonchalantly left the arena to become a national heroine and a world-wide celebrity.

45

Kurt Thomas

Cathy Henkel

Kurt Thomas has been called many things, ranging from the "Shaun Cassidy of the gymnastics set" to the "greatest gymnast the United States has ever produced." He has been the subject of countless newspaper articles and has been featured in such magazines as *People* and *Sports Illustrated*. The publicity honcho at his college even tried to book him on the Johnny Carson Show.

"The producer told him 'No thanks,' " laughs Kurt. But this is one young star who doesn't need the talk-show host. He lets his body do the talking—to the tune of five titles in less than three years of international competition, a spot on the U.S. Olympic team when he was just 19, and a billing as the best by the time he was 21.

Not bad for a kid who got his start in what was then considered America's gymnastics wasteland. *Was,* that is, until Kurt Thomas and his high school coach fought to awaken interest in Miami. "Kurt opened the door for gymnastics in Florida," says Don Gutzler, the physical-education teacher at Miami Central High who introduced gymnastics to the skinny teenager who

Kurt Thomas (*International Gymnast* photo)

lived with his mother and his kid sister across the street from the school.

Miami Central is an education factory. It extends seven blocks in length from 95th to 103rd Street, is three blocks wide, adjacent to what some call the Miami ghetto. Kurt was in the racial minority—only about 15 percent of the 2500 students were white—but things like that never really bothered him much. He found an identity in gymnastics when he was 14, an age that would be considered late in life by the Russians and the Japanese.

The only other sport he had attempted was wrestling.

"They needed a 98-pounder on the wrestling team," recalls Kurt. "I didn't have to do much because most of the other schools didn't have a guy at 98. All I had to do was show up and my team got the points automatically."

Then, in his freshman year, he entered Gutzler's physical education class.

"The coach introduced gymnastics to us the first day of class," Kurt said. "I had seen it for the first time a week before at a junior college. It just seemed interesting."

Coach Gutzler was new to the sport as well. School officials had opposed his idea of starting a gymnastics team, but the feisty coach prevailed, and Kurt tried out for the school's first team. "I didn't have much of a problem making the team," he said, "mainly because not too many guys tried out. Coach Gutzler asked me what events I wanted to work and I told him tumbling and p-bars. I guess he saw some ability in me because he told me he wanted me to work all the events. I was kind of excited that he had taken an interest in me right from the start."

Gutzler recalls the tryouts in much the same way, although he admits he didn't hear sirens when he first saw Kurt work out. "I was new to gymnastics, too," said the coach. "I really didn't know what to expect. But it wasn't long before it was obvious that Kurt had a future in gymnastics. What I liked from the beginning was his intense enthusiasm."

He was the only freshman to qualify for the city championships that first year (there were no state-wide championships then). And the Miami Central Rockets, at preseason rated 14th in a 14-team league, didn't lose a meet all year. How Kurt did it, how the Rockets did it, is still considered a downright "miracle" by their coach. "The training conditions were horrible," Gutzler says. "We had to set up the equipment each afternoon in the middle of the gym while it seemed like 200 kids were trying to play basketball around us. We didn't even have crash pads for dismounts. We just had this one thin, three-by-six-foot foam mat that we had to move from event to event."

By the end of Kurt's sophomore year, Gutzler realized he was above the average cut. "I told him I could guarantee a scholarship," says the coach. Again the Rockets went undefeated—they lost only two meets in the four years Kurt was in the program—and at the end of the season, Kurt won the Greater Miami Athletic League all-around title, the first sophomore to do so. He would break all existing prep records by the time he was a senior, taking the GMAL crown three years in a row. Next, Gutzler encouraged him to enter the AAU junior nationals. He did and finished fourth as a sophomore. As a junior, he won it outright . . .

Indiana State

His senior year was a time to think of college. He and Gutzler wrote to several schools, but didn't get a nibble. Florida didn't have much of a reputation in gymnastics," says Gutzler. "They must have thought that all those Southern boys just laid around the beach or something. They all turned him down."

Bruce Davis, a Miami man who had seen Kurt work out at Muriel Grossfeld's gymnastics club, contacted an old friend, Roger Counsil, who was coaching a successful team at Indiana State University. "You oughta take a look at him," he told Counsil.

Counsil took a chance and sent him an airline ticket. Kurt left the Miami airport on a flight to Terre Haute a few days later, trying to figure out how to pronounce it along the way. "I didn't know anything about Indiana really," says Kurt in retrospect, "but then there weren't very many other coaches who were interested in me."

Once in Terre Haute, Kurt met the coach and the team and went to a meet. He was impressed with the school, the team's spirit, and especially with Counsil.

"I wanted him to go to a place where he could keep going strong and where he wouldn't get lost in the shuffle," said Gutzler. "And I wanted him to find a coach who genuinely cared about him as a person as well as a gymnast. Counsil seemed like that kind of guy."

Gutzler had developed into a father figure to Kurt, especially since Kurt's own father had been killed in an automobile crash when he was very young. Gutzler decided to back Counsil when he offered a full scholarship. Kurt didn't bother to look any further; he had changed from a Rocket to a Sycamore before he could learn to pronounce "Terre Haute."

"I had heard a little about Kurt," said Counsil, an easy-going sort. "He wasn't highly touted, though. But he had excellent basics, and he didn't have any bad habits. He's the kind of gymnast who makes his coach look good when it's really because he learns so fast and performs so well."

"I'm a coachable gymnast," Kurt explains. "I didn't have any basic problems with technique and I didn't really have any weak areas that stood out."

He stayed pretty much in the background his first year at ISU, but it wasn't long before people began to repeat his name. He received All-American honors at the 1976 NCAA championships. By the end of that year, he got his first taste of international competition.

He was just 19 when he made the team for the Pan-American Games.

"The Pan-American Games really set me off," Kurt recalls enthusiastically. He had finished third in the all-around and was the top American competitor. "It was my first spot on an international team and it was exciting. It had always been a goal of mine to be an Olympian but I really never thought it was possible. After I made the Pan-American Games, it became real. I thought then that I was as good as anybody in the United States. I'd say it before then, of course, but I knew in my mind that it wasn't true. Then it became true. I had a chance to become an Olympian."

"I joke about it now," laughs Counsil, "but all the kids I recruit say 'Coach, I want to be an Olympian.' I hear it from

most of them and I heard it from Kurt. I had no reason to think when I was recruiting Kurt that he had any special chance for the Olympics. But he proceeded to do just as he said he would."

1976 OLYMPICS, MONTREAL

Kurt had made the team along with Wayne Young, Peter

Kurt Thomas (Lorraine Rorke photo)

Kormann, Mike Carter, and Bart Conner. Kurt was the highest ranked American after the first two days of competition. But on the third and last day, he dropped behind Young and Kormann, finishing 21st overall.

The 1976 Olympics, though thrilling and the attainment of a long-term goal, was really just a launching pad for Kurt. He piled up five international titles in the next two years: the Romanian Invitational for both 1977 and '78; the Barcelona Invitational in Spain in October, 1977; the U.S.–Japan dual meet in Eugene, Oregon, in February, 1978; and the Champions-All Meet in London in April of 1978. He was the 1977 NCAA national all-around champion as well as gold medalist on the parallel bars; he was second at the American Cup in Madison what he says was his most flawless performance ever—he won each of the six events and the all-around. He also placed ninth at the World University Games and was in the top five in Japan's famed Chunichi Cup both times he entered.

The list goes on. This is the record that identifies him as the best gymnast America has ever produced.

"Well, my record so far has proved that I'm the best," he says when asked about the "best" tag. "But I just don't know. I feel like there are guys just as good as me. It's just a matter of who hits at the right time."

Kurt would learn very quickly that, in the politics of international competition, the best gymnast may not always be named Number 1 by the judges. He watched young Kathy Johnson take fifth place at the Romanian Invitational in 1978 after she had obviously given the best performance in the meet. At the end of the men's competition, Kurt and his coach added the marks.

"We figured we had won by three-tenths of a point but they never announced the winner during the competition," he said. "The next day, I heard that I had won, but only by five-hundredths of a point."

Judging seems to be the eternal stumbling block in the international scene, while in most other sports, the scoring is much more clearcut—a basket is worth two points, a touchdown scores six, etc. But in gymnastics, the subjective attitudes of the various judges can complicate the outcome.

"I'm getting used to the judging, but it will never be acceptable," says Kurt. "You just have to try to perform flawlessly so there's no room for deductions. If you make a mistake worth one-tenth to four-tenths off, they may take off four-tenths for you, then take off one-tenth for another guy who has made the same mistake. You just have to forget about the judging and the politics and do your best, hoping that some day the scoring system will improve."

Kurt became celebrated in the gymnastics world while winning more and more meets, of course, but a new group of fans cropped up. An NBC commentator, watching him after a meet, spotted a dazed teen-age girl hand him a fan letter. He was tagged with the Shaun Cassidy comparison when the commentator colorfully reported what was going on. And, after the American Cup, Kurt began receiving fanmail from quite a few teen-age girls, mostly 12 and 13, who had developed a "crush" on the youthful looking gymnast. Kurt's new wife decided to take pen in hand and answer each one.

Kurt met Beth Osting at a sorority party at the college. They were instantly attracted to each other and were married a year-and-a-half later on New Year's Eve. He redshirted from collegiate competition that same year.

"I redshirted to catch up in school," he explains. "My international and collegiate competition limited the number of hours I could spend with my studies. I decided to sit out of collegiate competition and devote that time to school. But I didn't slack off from gymnastics altogether—I still competed about once a month. I guess getting married was part of it too. But I would still have married Beth even if I hadn't redshirted."

Beth was a neophyte to gymnastics when she met Kurt. She quickly picked it up, though, and learned coaching techniques and how to do a few tumbling tricks herself. The two of them spend part of the summers on the gymnastics camp circuit, working with the younger kids in developmental programs.

"I can't believe these kids!" says Kurt. "They are really great. Programs like the USGF has are really going to help the United States become a real power in gymnastics. Before, we'd just slap a team together and compete. Now we're starting to prepare gymnasts at younger ages."

Even at the age of 22, Kurt was asked when he would retire.

"I don't know what to say," he would reply. "I never really

think about it. I'll be 28 by the 1984 Olympics and I want to be on the American team, of course. When it's time to leave, I guess I'll know."

He has worked toward a college degree in health and safety education, and will someday teach gymnastics. "You have to have something to fall back on," he says philosophically. Until then, he's got some new goals to meet. One is to beat all the specialists at their own game.

"I want to be the best floor-ex man, the best rings man, the best side horse man . . . and it's hard. It's hard to beat a college specialist when he has worked four years in one event. By setting my goals higher than the specialist, it motivates me. I can improve by working with specialists."

The pommel horse began as his best event and still is, Kurt claims. He has even invented a special scissor combination move: the Thomas Flair. The Russians and Japanese have paid him the highest compliment by copying the move in their own routines.

Gymnastics moves so quickly; it's anything but a static sport. New moves, new difficulties not even dreamed of a few years ago become commonplace. Counsil says Kurt's biggest virtue is the continuing desire to improve. "The problem with American gymnasts in the past has been that they got complacent too soon. They became resigned to be the best in the United States but never the best in the world. Kurt's different. He's never satisfied. He always wants to improve, increase the difficulty. He's still after the big guys."

"When you're satisfied," says Kurt, "you sit back like a fat cat and people start walking all over you. Gymnastics is changing constantly and you have to change with it. You can never stay the same or you'll be lost."

Kurt Thomas is one gymnast who will never sit back and enjoy his reign. He's too busy trying to become better than he was the day before, better than any American has ever been before, better than anyone has ever been before.

He just may do it someday.

Despite the sport's problems in a few areas, the future for gymnastics appears bright indeed. Gene Wettstone, an American gymnastics institution, writes of the pressing need for a code of ethics for international men's gymnastics judges. Gymnastics Art and Soul *postulates that in modern competition artistic elements are being sacrificed for precision, and that youth is being overemphasized.* Visions of Tomorrow *closes the book with a lyrical tribute to the gymnastics of the present and an imaginary tour through the "New Gymnastics" of the future.*

10

THE FUTURE

(Tony Duffy photo)

46
Olympic and
International Problems
Gene Wettstone

I t's never too early to look ahead toward the next world and Olympic Games. So, as we close the books on Montreal, it is already time to think about [1980].

The 1976 USA Men's Olympic Gymnastic Team experience was perhaps the most frustrating ever encountered. Never was so little accomplished for so much effort and money. It is difficult to understand this after the well organized developmental program with literally hundreds of gymnasts all over the country involved in Olympic preparations, with excellent financial support for development and team preparations by the United States Olympic Committee, and with excellent cooperation from the USOGC, the United States Gymnastic Federation (USGF), and coaches throughout the country. The gymnasts were the most talented ever assembled and demonstrated complete dedication and discipline throughout the year. The third place finish in Floor Exercise, a marvelous accomplishment by Peter Kormann, could be considered a miracle after 44 years without a medal. Although the 7th place team standing was consistent with past games, the 1976 Team deserved better. The compulsory exercise judging of the American men was more stringent in relation to gymnasts from the other countries. Consequently, the USA filed a protest with the Technical Committee of the Federation International Gymnastics.

Unfortunately, no one has of yet found a way to score gymnastics with a stop watch or in some other objective manner. No one has found a solution to minimize politicking, collaborating and cheating. Alexander Lylo, acting chairman of the TC/FIG/M from Czechoslovakia speaking to the Olympic judges following the compulsory and optional team competitions said, "I have been satisfied with the organization of the Games and with the performances of the gymnasts, but I have not been satisfied with the judging." His remarks were then followed by those of judge Marcel Adatte of Switzerland who read a statement on behalf of his nation: "The problem of judging is a serious one and speaking for my country, we can no longer tolerate the actions we have witnessed at these Games. Judges are collaborating with each other and deciding not only on scores, but also on the distribution of medals. I also regret to say that some members of this technical committee sitting before us are guilty of the same offenses". Mr. Lylo's response to this statement was, "This is not the time for such discussions. We have come here to work and prepare the judges for the competition tonight."

It is my conviction that steps must now be taken to improve judging and minimize the nationalistic fervor of nations which have such an obsession for winning medals that judges representing these nations have perverted the whole Olympic ideal.

Now is the time to begin. It is up to the International Gymnastic Federation and the International Olympic Committee to foresee problems that will arise at the 1980 games in Moscow and to move quickly to forestall them.

Two major steps must be taken if we are to expect gymnastics to continue in the true spirit of the Olympic Movement: (1) Establish fairer representation of Technical Committee Members from all continents of the world where gymnastics is promoted; (2) Remedy the judging situation by establishing a strong Code of Ethics for Judges.

The TC is a key group of gymnastic experts who assign judges, make rules and develop regulations for world and international gymnastics. Members act as superior judges at all international matches and decide what is best for the sport from the standpoint of rules and regulations. Without voice of representation on this committee a nation in the North American continent cannot adequately take issue on policies or offer corrections to many of the irregularities. The compulsory exercises are designed by this group without considering whether they are current or practical for the rest of the world.

One needs only to look at the accompanying map of the world to see that the distribution of technical committee membership is anything but representative of the world and certainly does not represent the thinking of other parts of the world. An issue must be made of this fact to the International Gymnastic Federation, or if necessary, to the International Olympic Committee (IOC) requesting that other continents such as signified by the five Olympic Rings be included in this now rather closely knit group of experts.

Of the seven TC members presently serving world gymnastics, four are from eastern European nations: Alexander Lylo, chairman from Czechoslovakia, Karl Heinz Zschocke of East Germany, Boris Schaklin of the Soviet Union and Sandor Urvary of Hungary. Three members are from "western" nations: Akitomo Kaneko of Japan, Enrique Gonzalez of Spain and Tuomo Jalantie of Finland. The committee members from Spain and Finland did not have qualified teams from their nations at the Games. It must be said in fairness to these technical committee men that they do serve and work very hard without pay.

The former technical chairman, Mr. Ivan Ivancevic of Yugoslavia, resigned last May for reasons unknown to many. In a recent voting for an additional TC member to replace Mr. Ivancevic of Yugoslavia, the USA put up the name of Frank Cumiskey, three-time Olympian and one of the world's most respected technicians. To our embarrassment, he was defeated and Mr. Urvary of Hungary was added to the committee. This shows still another person from essentially the same area of the world.

A strong case for the USA representation on the TC can be

made. In a very brief manner it is fair to say that the USA has been represented as a team in World and Olympic competitions for over 50 years; has contributed financial support to the FIG above that of any nation in the world; has promoted the sport here and abroad in a more vigorous manner than any other country; has probably the strongest coaches and judges organizations anywhere. The USA has never had the privilege to seat one single technical expert on this exclusive rules-making committee. It is doubtful whether there is another national gymnastic Organization more active and more productive than the United States Gymnastic Federation (USGF).

If something isn't done immediately, the western hemisphere nations and nations from other parts of the world without representation on the TC face potential disaster in Moscow. One possible solution to this problem is to expose the unequal balance of world technical voice to Lord Killanin and the IOC membership. If the IOC had the power to reduce the FIG Olympic Gymnastic Program to 12 teams instead of the un-limited number of former years, then it seems possible that they would also be concerned about improving the future of the Games by insisting on a better and more equitable distribution of TC representation.

Another question that needs to be explored is one which involves the selection of judges to Olympic and World Games without a rigid Code of Ethics for Judges. At this moment there is no Code of Ethics. Any judge named by the Gymnastic Federation of a country is accepted by the FIG/TC, if he has passed the necessary international judge's course. It doesn't really matter if the judge is not the most competent or whether he is biased or whether he happens to be the coach of the team or the national coach of the nation. There are no penalties from cheating, collaborating with other judges from other nations, or exchanging favors.

Eastern European countries and officials have been known to hold special meetings to assure judges of bias judging and to restrain from liberal judging of Japanese and American gymnasts. One such meeting was revealed in Varna, Bulgaria in 1974, just prior to the World Games. A strong code of ethics must be established that has penalties attached. Gymnasts have conduct and performance rules and penalties; judges do not.

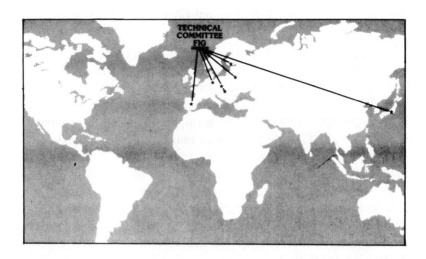

An investigation of the causes of bias, collaborations and irregular judging with remedial steps to minimize this, is now in order. A Canadian national coach said, "The United States and Japan, and one or two other countries are the only ones who do not politic with other countries. Unless the USA begins to press for favors in return for other favors, it will never obtain the top positions which it merits." The tide of nationalism and collaborations will only subside if nations mature and political rivalries and conflicts give way to genuine global cooperation. Until this takes place the FIG and the TC must take steps to curb the injustices which occurred.

It is imperative to the dignity and growth of the sport of gymnastics and for our international program that judges be well educated in the details of the sport, thoroughly prepared for each assignment, and as unbiased as humanly possible.

The proposed code of ethics below is only a beginning. It needs further refinement but a firm code must be established with penalties from immediate suspension if scandalous scores are in question. This may also require the return of the open scoring system. Gymnastics is still the only Olympic sport which tolerates a closed system of scoring. Not to this date does any one coach or Federation know what scores were awarded by which judges; only the Men's Technical Committee has access to such information.

A Code of Ethics for International Gymnastics Judges for Men

1. Judges selected for international competition should be chosen from judges organizations and not just from the rank and file of coaches or officials from the gymnastic federation.

2. Judges selected to judge international competitions should not be the head coach of the team, or the national coach or coaches, or the Chef de Mission, or manager of the team. Judges should be bonafide judges with an international card and whose main profession is the sport is judging and not coaching.

3. Any judge or coach who collaborates with other judges and coaches from other teams should be penalized by being dismissed from his assignment.

4. Judges who feel they are prejudiced for or against any competing team should voluntarily eliminate themselves from such duties.

5. Gifts, favors or privileges to judges which can be interpreted as attempts to influence their judgment in favor of a national team must result in penalty.

6. Judges must avoid coaching or even appearing at workouts prior to international meets.

7. Judges must stay aloof of their national team or any team. They should not travel, lodge or mingle intimately with coaches or teams.

8. Judges' organizations must name from their ranks only those judges who are exceptionally high in integrity and superior in technical knowledge rather than those who tend to favor one's national team in order to gain acceptance from the gymnasts or national body.

9. Judges should not accept before or after-meet social invitations unless the same invitations were extended to all other judges.

10. Judges must refrain from giving the appearance of any particular friendship with other coaches or teams on the competition site.

11. Judges who are so involved in the outcome of their national team that they frequently watch the performances of their national gymnasts on one event while in the process of judging another event must be warned and then eliminated from such duty if they persist.

47

Gymnastics Art and Soul

Hal Straus

With few exceptions, the American women-gymnastics community has resigned itself to the worldwide "trend to totdom." It is now generally accepted that, as far as competition is concerned, a woman gymnast "peaks" at age fourteen to eighteen and is "over the hill" by the time she is old enough to vote.

The reasons (or rationalizations) for the trend have been varied: (1) the need to stay competitive with the East European-Russian axis, which seems to have instigated the trend with its Kindergarten Korps and scores 9.9s with them; (2) the physical transition that takes place in the late stages of teenhood and supposedly interferes with the coordination and precision necessary for top-level performance; (3) the simple economic dictates of earning a living as an adult and the inability of competitive gymnastics to provide that living.

Yet, it will be theorized here that there are more deep-seated reasons for the trend and that these reasons must direct the sport of gymnastics to question seriously the idea of the fourteen-year-old *maitresse d'arte*. Touching only the surface at this point, gymnastics is the sport of grace, courage, and ingenuity—

qualities, few would argue, that come only with maturity and experience; in short, living.

Instead, with the predominance of the Comanecis and Korbuts over the past decade or so, the Sport of Grace has been changing into the Sport of Precision. Now precision has always been a major component of gymnastic performance, as it has been with all sports—and arts. A ballet, piano solo, or film would not be considered genuine art without certain technically precise movements. All art motifs demand the quality almost a priori for the artist to accomplish such basic tasks as gaining the confidence of the audience, crafting a world different and more interesting than the present, i.e., generally creating the "suspension of disbelief" or "illusion of reality" so crucial to the success of the artwork.

But precision is obviously not the only quality necessary for great performance in the arts, nor is it the most important. No performance of *Swan Lake*, for example, would be great without grace and dignity no matter how flawless the *pirouettes* and *tours jetes*; no performance of Beethoven's Fifth would be triumphant without inspiration no matter how perfect the tonality. The arts are subtle blends that operate on many levels, too rich in emotional and intellectual content, personal experience, and yes magic—to be judged on the basis of technical precision.

I am not suggesting that these qualities I have deemed so important to artistic performance are being ignored on the gymnastics floor by either gymnasts or judges. Certainly I am not implying that gymnastics is purely an art like dance or music; gymnastics is *more than an art*; it is a mysterious mixture of art and athletics that makes it unique and potentially such a strong bridge between the two that it could evolve into a powerful cultural force in America.

What I am suggesting is that, over the past decade, precision has gradually been given an alarmingly high priority in gymnastics competition. Routines that lack many basic artistic qualities are rewarded, as long as they are done flawlessly; routines containing them are penalized if done without precision.

I am also inferring that girls of fifteen rarely have the physi-

cal grace or emotional maturity to achieve the kinds of performance in which the best gymnastics can culminate.

But the accent-on-youth syndrome is not the cause of the
precision problem, but merely the innocent reflection of its
hidden intricacies.

What then exactly is the precision problem?

First, gymnastics is not pure sport any more than it is pure
art. As a meld, the "artisport" is different in nature from other
team or individual sports. In other competitive sports the team
or player is awarded "points" for accomplishing an *objectively*
recognizable "goal" at the end of performance: crossing a goal
line; putting a ball into a basket or hole, hitting it over a fence,
etc. *How* it is done is of secondary importance to the final score
and thus the results of the competition. A football, soccer, or
basketball team does not win if it does not score, no matter
how stylish its team members.

Gymnastics has no such objective goal. Gymnastics is as
much concerned with the "how" as it is with the "how much";
the intrinsic nature of the artisport is steeped in style, as much
(or more) connected with means as with ends.

Gymnastics people acknowledge this publicly, speaking often
in the media of the "subjective nature" of the sport. Yet public
acknowledgment and action are two different things. While the
vocal chords talk of "subjective nature," the mind (whether
consciously or subconsciously) is trying to mold the artisport
into a traditional, western team sport. The attempt is fostered
by the present system of judging that dissects a performance
into categories (execution, difficulty, risk, etc.) and parts
(movements), subjectively subtracts points for objectively
imprecise movements, thus structuring judging of the event to
give emphasis to the parts rather than to the whole.

This kind of system is essentially imitative of the traditional-
sport concept of awarding points for goals, baskets, etc. Moreover, the greatest emphases are given to execution and difficulty
(the technical-precision elements); the stylistic elements (combination, risk, virtuosity, originality) are deemphasized relative
to the technical elements.

The other side of the coin would be to view the routine in its
entirety (a "gestaltist" view, if you will), in the same way a

ballet or concert is experienced as *composition* rather than as a *breakdown* of individual movements or notes. With this perspective, concentration would be on intangibly aesthetic style elements such as grace, structure of routine, mood, virtuosity, originality, etc. Precision, another element in the overall picture, would be deweighted to a more balanced footing with other facets presently suffering second billing. A gymnast who does not achieve proper position on a split could make up for the deficiency easily with superior harmony of composition, for example, and would be no more guilty of destroying her routine than a virtuoso pianist who hits one C-sharp instead of a C-natural in a concerto that might include 1000 notes—assuming, of course, that both the gymnast and virtuoso have created a certain harmony of composition, mood, structure, dignity, grace: the magic that makes an artist an artist rather than a technician.

The issue then amounts to balancing the art and the sport in gymnastics, a balance that now seems shifted to the sport side of the scale. This has not occurred accidentally. In America, gymnastics has been struggling for status, recognition, and popular acceptance; and so gymnastics' courting of the sport world is entirely understandable. One segment on ABC's Wide World of Sports will do more toward solving financial problems (equipment, lack of subsidies, insurance) than six years on educational television and a rave review from the Queen of England. Organized sport is where the money is: There are few 50,000-seat stadiums (or $50,000 salaries) for prima ballerinas.

When perceived in this framework, it is easy to understand the swerve to precision, because gymnastics is merely following the lead of major American sports whose aims have also been popular acceptance and the economic prosperity that inevitably follow. Major organized sports are corporate conglomerates composed of team-companies. For the company to survive it must turn a profit; to turn a profit it must win, and winning presumably only comes through "science." (Football has become so technically complex, for example, teams' playbooks resemble engine-wiring diagrams more than plays, the players themselves more machine cogs than athlete-artists.) "Science-envy" in organized sports is a mutant of society's reliance on science as the panacea for its many problems, the blind belief that only through technology can the future of the twentieth century be ensured.

As an artisport, gymnastics need not fall into this trap. The artisport's distinctive dual nature must be preserved by adopting judging methods and criteria that will do justice to both sides. (One suggestion might be to use two groups of judges, one for composition and one for execution, as in modern rhythmic gymnastics.) Although newly adopted scoring criteria will be critical in determining the future of gymnastics because of the competitive aspects, the active participants, the gymnasts and coaches, must also strive to elevate the artistic component. Harmony of movement, continuity and structure of routine, even giving the routine an *intellectual* basis (i.e., the routine as an expression of an *idea*) are some avenues for exploration.

By discoursing on the necessity of maturity and experience in competitive women's gymnastics, I am not suggesting that training should not begin early in childhood, just that it need not be aborted in puberty. And the point has not been to criticize elements inherent in gymnastics itself but rather to illuminate the fact that a too limited perspective of its potential could change a sport of sophisticated beauty into children's drill exercises, potential artists into Swiss watches.

The world has enough watches; it has too few artists.

48
Visions of Tomorrow

Daniel Millman

In its future evolution, the form of gymnastics will help determine its artistic development. Let's take an overview of gymnastics today and tomorrow for a glimpse of what may be in store:

When movement is intensified, refined, lightened, energized and freed of assumed limitations, it becomes gymnastics, which requires (and therefore develops) suppleness, balance, strength, coordination, stamina, timing, as well as increased mental and emotional capacity.

Practiced well, gymnastics is an ideal psychophysical laboratory for studying, getting to know, and really making friends with oneself and with others. It is an intense arena of body-mind training; the way of the peaceful warrior, where latent weaknesses surface and hidden strengths are revealed.

One of the finest side-benefits of gymnastics training is the confidence that comes with gaining mastery over the most complex and beautiful human-sculpting art form ever devised. As we accomplish movements of which we didn't believe ourselves capable, we can reach a psychological state that renders the word "can't" insignificant in our daily lives. We form the habit of transcending our limited self-images and beliefs.

Today, gymnastics is a sport that allows people to test themselves in a "moment of truth" in the competitive arena. To see gymnastics *only* as a sport, however, is to limit its ultimate potential. One of the fastest-growing forms of gymnastics practiced in Europe, just catching on in the United States, is *acrosport,* an exciting gymnastic sport which doesn't use apparatus, but instead consists of tumbling, pair (trio and quad) handbalancing; with elements of dance, strength, suppleness, and unbelievable aerial maneuvers! Closely associated with acrosport is the U.S. Trampoline Federation, with competitions and performances on trampoline, synchronized trampoline (two people, mirroring one another's routines), space-ball, double Mini-Tramp, and tumbling, a visual treat for any audience.

Modern rhythmic gymnastics is more closely associated with dance—a nonacrobatic form of gymnastics that shows graceful relationship between performer and small hand apparatus such as ball, hoop, or ribbon, one of the most beautiful movement arts.

In the future, we will undoubtedly see other developments on the basic gymnastics theme. For example, we'll probably have more use of music. (Russian men are already incorporating music into their floor exercise routines.) We'll see flashier costumes and greater use of lighting effects. The apparatus will continue to change. For example, here is a vision of what might be called the New Gymnastics, based on principles of overall health and performance appeal:

Event 1: Floor-exercise/Beam: (men and women): Two-minute time limit, spring floor, with beam along the side of the area. Performers work to music, and must make at least two passes along the beam.

Event 2: Trampoline: Ten-bounce routine; form, height, control, and style, as well as showmanship, rated most important. Difficulty elements: 3 required. . .but not to escalate beyond perfect form and control.

Event 3: Double bars: Like men's horizontal bar, but performers (men and women) fly from one bar to the next 2-3 times during a routine.

The New Gymnastics could surely include more teamwork, pairs practice, and synchronized work.

Visions of tomorrow are enjoyable, but *now* is the time to recognize gymnastics as a great performance art. . .(to which we happen to assign scores). The gymnasts of today are gifted with lithe, lively bodies and daring minds. Their qualities are admirable, but they must be shown the way of feeling (not reactive emotions) if they are to become artists. In their competitive conditioning, in their haste to be better than Mary Spice or Johnny Handsome, the children must not lose the fundamental wonder of turning over and seeing the sky upside down. That is the magic of gymnastics.

People love to watch gymnastics. It gives an audience pleasure to see even an average gymnast enjoy himself while upside down. It makes the old feel younger in their identification with this somersaulting, swinging fun. It inspires the young, who want to emulate these modern aerial magicians.

I remind my students, "You are performers, not machines. Enjoy it! Revel in it! Stop worrying. Feel the gratitude of your audience, and return the feeling. Put all jealous ghosts of your childhood that cry 'showoff' into the dark closets of unfeelingness where they belong. Sweep your own insecurities under the rug of your mind; never be afraid to enjoy that unreasonably happy feeling."

In the stress of competition, it's so easy to forget that, above all, gymnastics is an extraordinary human celebration. It's dancing through the air. You can feel like thunder and lightning for a few moments. You can enjoy your developing talents and those of your friends. No one wants to be a gymnast in an empty room; so share your talents. Enjoy your audience as much as they enjoy you. They do not want to see you preoccupied with the few mistakes you make—of course you'll make errors! They want to see you burst with happiness at the movements you perform well!

Can you remember what it was like to be a child without the least trace of self-consciousness or self-criticism? You are a budding artist only as long as you can remember.

We all have personal peaks to scale; great mountains lie before us in the journey of our lives. We can climb as high or as far as we choose.

Gymnastics can be the Everest of our dreams, and its peaks gleaming in the sunlight await us. Let's remove the blinders, ready our gear, and hold to the image of a flaming sunset seen from the climb. However modest the heights, they will still be higher than where we once stood.

Yet what significance is gymnastics artistry if the time spent outside the gymnasium is casual, shallow, or full of haste? The ultimate promise of gymnastics-art is that it forms a doorway to the art of living. When you can do gymnastics well, with feeling, you can do anything well. You will have developed all the raw materials to become a master of life. The concentration, clarity and courage reawakened in training and competition will give you a presence that allows you to begin training in the Life Art.

When you can feel the pleasure of walking, opening a door, sitting down gracefully and well, along with every other ordinary movement of daily life, you will know the real power of gymnastics; the power to bring art to daily life.

We must all begin somewhere. For many people, this beginning is still a hidden seed. Others have begun the practice of another art form. For us, the art is found in the kip, the salto, the smooth swing, and lively dance opening the magical way.

Art or not, gymnastics is a mirror of your life, showing you where you are and what you need to grow. Every movement you make is like a snowflake; no other movement in your entire life will be exactly the same. Appreciate each movement's individuality! Accept it for what it is and go on. Each move you make has a unique life of its own, like a separate person, and deserves feeling-acknowledgment. One attempt at a new trick may be a silly clown, deserving hearty laughter. Another may contain the character of a courageous warrior, deserving respect. Then, hardly expecting it, the next movement may contain all the quality and feeling of art: the perfect "snowflake."

On your most mediocre training day, a young child might enter the gymnasium door, catch sight of your crooked cartwheel, then run out to tell her mother, excited, inspired by what you look on with disdain. Adopt the child's perspective and let go of self-pity, frustration, anger, haste.

Achievement is fine but is a terrible master if it is your only obsessive goal. You can't take your skills with you forever. Now is the time to celebrate. Someday you'll have only the shadows of memories. Achievement will naturally lead to achievement.

All these bodies miraculously here in time and space are only on loan. They will soon be gone. Remember this and you cannot fail to become an artist. This life is your one chance to create a little beauty by exhibiting through your finest feelings. Now, while you're young, use the air as your canvas, your body as a brush. Treat your "brush" with kindness so it will create beauty through time for yourself and for others.

Just be happy to practice your art. Stop looking for reasons to be happy. Just feel it, and let that radiance shine through the expression of your movements.

Through feeling-happiness, your presence becomes a gift to others. Every day can be Christmas in the gym. You walk in and share yourself; you give, and are given to, in a whirl of energy. That whirl of energy, filled with feeling, spiced with laughter, is the first stirrings of life as an art. It is the true spirit of gymnastics, of magic—filled with thunder, with lightning, with grace.

For Further Exploration

Books

Bowers, Carolyn O.; Fie, Jackie; Kjeldsen, Kitty; and Schmid, Andrea B. *Judging and Coaching Women's Gymnastics.* Palo Alto, California: Mayfield Publishing Co., 1972.

Carter, E.R. *Gymnastics for Girls and Women.* Englewood Cliffs, N.J.: Prentice Hall, Inc., 1969.

Drury, Blanche and Schmid, Andrea B. *Gymnastics for Women.* Palo Alto, Calif.: Mayfield Publishing Co., 1977.

Loken, Newton and Willoughby, Robert J. *Complete Book of Gymnastics.* Englewood Cliffs, N.J.: Prentice-Hall, Inc., 1959.

Salmela, John H. *The Advanced Study of Gymnastics.* Springfield, Ill.: Charles C. Thomas, 1976.

Taylor, Bryce; Bajin, Boris; and Zivic, Tom. *Olympic Gymnastics for Men and Women.* Englewood Cliffs, N.J.: Prentice-Hall, Inc., 1972.

Pamphlets

The United States Gymnastics Federation publishes the following:

Code of Points for Women; Measurements and Dimensions, Rules and Policies for Women's Competitions, National Compulsory Routines for Girls.

Write to: USGF, P.O. Box 12713, Tucson, Arizona 85711.

Periodicals

International Gymnast magazine, Sundby Publications, 410 Broadway, Santa Monica, Ca 94040.

FIG Quarterly Bulletin, International Gymnastics Federation (write to USGF, P.O. Box 12713, Tucson, Arizona 85711).

Contributors

Maria Bakos was advisor and dance coach for the 1972 and 1976 U.S. Olympic gymnastics teams. She also served as choreographer of the U.S. Olympic floor exercise compulsory for 1972 and will be choreographer of the national floor exercise compulsories in 1980. Her record albums "On Beam" and "Warm-up Fever" (Statler Records) accompany the dance exercises in her article.

Valerie Braithwaite has written for *Gymnastics World* magazine.

James R. Brown is assistant professor of gymnastics at Indiana University.

Dr. Linda Carpenter is an associate professor at Brooklyn College of the City University of New York.

Noreen Connell holds a degree in dance from the Boston Conservatory. She is currently serving as Massachusetts state chairman for the USGF Women's Committee, and is a national official and judge for gymnastics competitions.

Dick Criley is an associate editor of *International Gynmnast* magazine.

Jack Einheber is a Ph D candidate in physical education at the University of California (Berkeley).

Jackie Fie was a member of the U.S. Olympic team in 1956. As a brevet judge, she has judged at the Olympic Games in 1968, 1972, and 1976. In 1976, she was elected to the FIG Women's Technical Committee for a four-year term.

Hardy Fink holds a master's degree in biomechanics and is the technical chairman of the Canadian Gymnastic Federation. He is also the editor of *The Gymnastic Technician* and an international judge.

Janice and **William Freeman** have worked to develop beginning gymnastics programs in several local communities. Janice has taught gymnastics to girls of every age group from kindergarten through college.

Sho Fuhishima coaches the University of California (Berkeley) gymnastics team, a perennial NCAA powerhouse in gymnastics.

Dr. Josef Goehler, former editor of *Olympische Turnkunst,* is currently international editor of *International Gymnast* magazine.

Helena Greathouse is a member of the USGF Modern Rhythmic Gymnastics Committee. She has written on rhythmic gymnastics for *Gymnasts of America* and is author of *Introductory Lessons in Competitive Rhythmic Gymnastics.* She is a master coach of rhythmic gymnastics at Portland Gymnastics Center, Tigard, Oregon,

Sandra Hammond trained in ballet at Julliard School of Music, the Metropolitian Opera Ballet School, and the New York City School of Ballet repertory. She teaches at the University of Arizona.

Cathy Henkel is a sportswriter for the *Eugene Register-Guard* in Oregon. She has written often on gymnastics competition.

Dr. Joe Massino is chief psychologist for the Newton public school system in Massachusetts. He has written extensively on the psychological aspects of gymnastics for *International Gymnast* magazine.

Daniel Millman, coach of the women's gymnastics team at University of California (Berkeley), has written many articles on gymnastics for *International Gymnast.* In 1964, he was world trampoline champion; he captained UC Berkeley's NCAA championship gymnastics team in 1968.

Linda Metheny, a member of three U.S. Olympic gymnastics teams, was U.S. all-around champion six years. She runs the Oregon Academy of Gymnastics in Eugene with Dick Mulvihill, former gymnastics Olympian.

Lyn Moran was the first woman international sportswriter, handling publicity for the first touring Soviet sports team, the USSR ice hockey team in 1959-60. She is now associate editor and staff writer for *International Gymnast* magazine.

Judy Niesslein of Eugene, Oregon, has written articles for *Gymnastics World* and *International Gymnast* magazines.

Charles Pond's University of Illinois gymnastics teams won eleven Big Ten conference championships and four NCAA titles. He was associate Olympic coach in 1956 and a member of the

U.S. Olympic Committee for the 1960, 1964, and 1972 games. He is the inventor of many gymnastics safety and training devices, including the Pond Training Belt.

Fritz Reiter is the coach of the Gymnastics Olympica club team in Van Nuys, California.

William Roetzheim was a member of the 1948 and 1952 U.S. Olympic teams. He is on the USGF executive committee, the Olympic committee, and is a National Judges Association technical director. He holds national and international judges cards and judged at the Olympic Games in 1976.

Dr. John Salmela, President of the Canadian Intercollegiate Gymnastics Committee (1975-77), is editor of *The Advanced Study of Gymnastics*. He is research chairman of the Canadian Gymnastics Federation and a professor of the University of Montreal.

Marilou Sturges is a freelance writer and photographer. She lives in Berkeley, California.

Sandy Thielz is a women's national elite judge and has written for *Gymnastics World* magazine.

Don Tonry is author of *Gymnastics Illustrated* and *Sports Illustrated Olympic Gymnastics for Women*. He was a member of the 1960 U.S. Olympic Team, and holds a FIG certification for judging. He currently is the coach of the Yale University gymnastics team.

Anita Verschoth has written often on gymnastics for *Sports Illustrated* and other national magazines.

Ernestine Russell Weaver has been coach of the Clarion State College gymnastics team for six years. Her 1977 team achieved its second straight AIAW National Collegiate Championship. She was a member of the 1956 and 1960 Olympic teams, and was an assistant coach of the 1976 U.S. Olympic team. She was recently named coach of the 1978 U.S. women's team for the World Games. She is author of *Gymnastics for Girls and Women*.

Gene Wettstone has served on the U.S. Olympic committee for twenty-four years. His Penn State gymnastics teams won nine NCAA titles and sent thirteen gymnasts to the Olympics. He was U.S. Olympic coach in 1948 and 1956, and Olympic judge in 1952 and 1968.

Holly Wilson is the trainer of the Indiana State University women's gymnastics team. She also served as trainer for the 1970 World Games Trials and the 1972 Olympic Trials.

Bob Wischnia has been a staff writer for *Arizona* magazine and West-coast writer for *Sport* magazine. He is currently assistant editor of *Runner's World* magazine   and senior editor of *Marathoner* magazine.

Leslie Wolfsberger holds numerous titles and records. For the last two years she has been a member of the U.S. National gymnastics team and in 1976 was a member of the U.S. Olympic team.

Dick Wolfe coaches the Cal-State Fullerton men's gymnastic team which went to the NCAA championships in 1978.

Walter Zwickel is America's only gymnastics tailor. He was named official tailor for the USGF in 1975 and official outfitter for the 1976 Israeli Olympic team.

Cover photos: Olga Korbut on beam, Nadia Comaneci floor exercise (Rich Clarkson); Nicolai Andrianov and Kurt Thomas on rings *(International Gymnast)*

Index

A

Accommodative resistance, 97
Adductors, 80
Ancient gymnastics, 20-22
Andrianov, Nicolai, 4, 14, 309-316
Arm movement, 170-175
Art of gymnastics, 37-44, 363-367

B

Back flexibility, 81
Ballet
  allegro, 149
  for balance beam, 177-178
  for floor exercise, 176-177
  judging, in competition, 284
  turns, 154
Bare, Frank, 4, 6, 10
Beam
  judging, 275-277, 281
  scoring, 255

staying on, 134-137
training, 50
Belt mechanic systems, 219-222
Braglia, Alberto, 12
Bukh, Niels, 27

C

Cardano, Girolamo, 22
Caslavska, Vera, 18
Choreography of routines, 286
Coaching
  beginning, 195-196
  psychological factors in, 197-199
  techniques, 200-204
Comaneci, Nadia, 3-4, 8, 19, 43, 132-133, 339-343
Competition, conducting, 246-248
Cumiskey, Frank, 13

Books of Related Interest

Acrobatics Book by Jack Wiley

An illustrated guide to performing balancing and tumbling stunts; routines for men's pairs, women's pairs, mixed pairs, women's trios, men's fours. 220 pages, soft cover, $3.95.

Better Gymnastics: How to Spot the Performer by William T. Boone

Hundreds of step-by-step photos provide an invaluable coach's aid for developing spotting techniques. 300 pages, soft cover, $6.95.

Complete Weight Training Book by Bill Reynolds

Over 70 individualized weight training exercise programs for many different sports, including gymnastics. 222 pages, soft cover, $4.95.

The Complete Diet Guide for Runners and Other Athletes, by the Editors of *Runner's World* magazine.

Principles and practices of proper nutrition: menus, recipes, weight control programs. 232 pages, soft cover, $4.95.

Runner's World Yoga Book by Jean Couch

Achieving optimum physical and psychological flexibility with this completely illustrated book of yoga exercise programs. 200 pages, spiral, $7.95.

World Publications

Box 366
Mountain View, CA 94042